# DEVON AND CORNWALL RECORD SOCIETY

New Series, Vol. 33

For my parents

**Saylors**

## Townsfall

| Names | Ages |
|---|---|
| Arthur Staplhill | 20 |
| John Smyth | 22 |
| Robert Ellener | 25 |
| Peter Wakeham | 18 |
| Ch:ter Currye | 24 |
| Philip Strilye | 19 |
| Serenus Tucker | 20 |
| Peter Prentice | 18 |
| William Packhell | 20 |

**Marmers at home**

## Dart-mouth

| Names | Ages |
|---|---|
| Gilbert Wreyford | 40 |
| Thomas Browne | 35 |
| Will: Eliott | 36 |
| Peter Bassard | 35 |
| Peter Tyrrye | 38 |
| James Goodridg | 52 |
| Gregory Taply | 28 |
| Henry Mill | 34 |
| Richard Mayne | 30 |
| Peter Luscomb | 52 |
| Will: Sherrom | 42 |
| Will: Leach | 31 |
| Arthur Richard | 42 |
| Vincent Winchester | 25 |
| John Holigroud | 25 |
| Thomas Hodge | 54 |
| John Comer | 32 |
| Alexander Cuttrill | 49 |
| Edward Follett | 45 |
| Robert Squarye | 45 |
| Ed: Winchester | 52 |
| John Blackaller | 55 |
| John Newman | 28 |
| Will: Simons | 45 |
| Edmund Follett | 36 |

**Marmers**

## Dart-mouth.

| Names | Ages |
|---|---|
| James Foscue | 52 |
| Rich: Waterdom | 33 |
| Robert Sparke | 45 |
| Will: Constable | 50 |
| John Bennett | 37 |
| Ch:ter Tapley | 32 |
| Nich: Escott | 48 |
| John Lucomb | 45 |

**Saylors at home**

| Names | Ages |
|---|---|
| Joseph Bowden | 40 |
| Willia Labye | 40 |
| Thomas Giles | 30 |
| John Hill | 55 |
| Peter Hill | 20 |
| Robert Hill | 22 |
| Thomas Almxton | 35 |
| William Moore | 20 |
| James Roberts | 20 |
| Philip Boys | 40 |
| Daniel Boyts | 25 |
| Ch:ter Duck | 28 |
| Robert Cally | 35 |
| Willia Jefferye | 35 |
| John Cash | 36 |
| John Corney | 35 |
| Richard Coscu | 36 |
| Thomas Dick | 35 |
| Charles Good | 45 |
| John Salter | 30 |
| Thomas Lozer | 25 |
| John Chop | 36 |
| James Farr | 30 |
| Walter Tucker | 40 |
| Samuel Wills | 30 |
| Will: Foster | 23 |
| Owen Foard | 24 |
| Edmond Dayys | 40 |
| John Dayys | 25 |
| Richard Dayys | 20 |
| Richard Hill | 23 |
| James Prowt | 35 |
| Edward Wright | 36 |

Frontispiece: From the Duke of Buckingham's Survey of South Devon, 1619. Photograph, slightly reduced, by courtesy of the Master and Fellows of Magdalene College, Cambridge.

DEVON & CORNWALL RECORD SOCIETY

New Series, Vol. 33

# EARLY-STUART MARINERS AND SHIPPING
## The Maritime Surveys of Devon and Cornwall, 1619-35

Edited with an Introduction by

## TODD GRAY

Institute of Cornish Studies
University of Exeter

1990

ISBN 0 901853 33 X

*Printed for the Society by*
BPCC Wheatons Ltd,
Hennock Road, Exeter, England

# CONTENTS

# LIST OF TABLES

# LIST OF MAPS

# INTRODUCTION

Of all the early-modern record sources available to the historian occupational censuses, that is lists of names of those who were employed in particular trades or crafts, are particularly rare and thus highly valued. This is especially true of the maritime professions whose members were also largely at the lower end of the social scale and thus traditionally featured least in early-modern record sources. Lists of ships are relatively more available and can at least be compiled from port customs books but this cannot be done for the mariners, sailors and fishermen, the men who were working at sea. This volume comprises the early-Stuart maritime surveys of Devon and Cornwall, together with some ancillary records, and although they are not complete the two counties remain among the best documented in the country. These reports are the only 'maritime censuses' extant between those of the 1580s and those of comparatively modern times.[1] Some of the figures have previously been drawn upon[2] but none of the surveys has hitherto been published in full, and the earliest and most informative has only recently come to light.

## THE SURVEYS

In the late 1620s England was again at war with Spain and then France and the government charged its Vice-Admirals with providing surveys of the maritime resources of all parishes within their particular jurisdictions. The reports which were returned varied in the amount of detail.[3] The principal survey of the South West known until now has been that compiled by Sir James Bagg of Saltram, Vice-Admiral of south Cornwall from 1622 to 1641 and of south Devon from 1628 to 1637. It lists the parishes in the five ancient hundreds of south

[1] For the surveys of the 1570s and 1580s for Devon see M.M. Oppenheim, *The Maritime History of Devon* (Exeter, 1968), 38-40; Joyce Youings, 'Raleigh's Country and the Sea', *Proceedings of the British Academy*, LXXV, 1990, forthcoming; Ronald Pollitt, 'Devon and the French and Spanish Wars' in M. Duffy, S. Fisher, B. Greenhill, D.J. Starkey, J. Youings (eds), *The New Maritime History of Devon*, forthcoming and for Cornwall see A.L. Rowse, *Tudor Cornwall* (1941), 70.

[2] Oppenheim, *Maritime History of Devon*, 61-2 and William Page (ed.), *Victoria County History of Cornwall* (1906), I, 495.

[3] For national totals see Public Record Office (hereafter PRO), SP16/155/31, 283/120 and below, Appendices G and H. For Dorset, SP16/138/11; Isle of Wight, SP16/33/3, 132/20; Hampshire, SP16/132/34, 32/72; Kent, SP16/132/19, 34/109-11, SP14/142/52, 142/39, 140/64-9 and Hastings, SP16/142/24-5; London, SP16/135/38, 135/4; Norfolk, SP16/34/31; Lincoln, SP16/33/129, 138/60-1; Northumberland, SP16/34/42; Chester, SP16/33/120 and Lancaster with Liverpool, SP16/36/1; North Wales, SP16/35/12, 31/56; Bristol, SP16/39/50, 138/4.

Cornwall, in three hundreds in south-west Devon as well as in only four hundreds in the north of the county.[4] Although undated it was most probably compiled in 1626 (see below, p. xii). There are also two surveys of north Cornwall which were undertaken, apparently after considerable difficulties, by Francis Basset of Tehidy, Vice-Admiral of that coast from 1623 to 1642; the first report was made between 31 July and 10 August 1626 and Basset completed the second between 12 January and 3 February 1629.[5] All these are in the State Papers in the Public Record Office.

But there also survives for the south coast of Devon an earlier survey of 1619 which provides more comprehensive information on the size and extent of its maritime resources and which has remained unknown to the county's historians. As its heading shows, this report was requested by the Duke of Buckingham, Lord High Admiral of England, of Sir Edward Seymour, Vice-Admiral of Devon, and of Sir William Courtenay, Jaspar Swyft an Admiralty official and Gabriel Dennys a local gentleman. It was signed by Courtenay and Swyft. It appears to be unique to Devon, and for that date, and could have been undertaken in connection with the planning for the naval expedition which was proposed that year and left Plymouth for Algiers in 1621.[6] The survey itself was dated 28 February 1618/19. A generation later it was 'borrowed' by Samuel Pepys when he was at the Navy Board and has remained with his private papers which are now housed in the Pepys Library at Magdalene College, Cambridge. It is far more detailed than the later surveys, recording, in the case of ships, their home-ports, tonnage, ordnance, age, owners and sometimes even particulars of current voyages. It also lists all mariners 'belonging to all the ports, harbours and sea-towns within the Vice-Admiralty of the south part of Devon' as well as their ages and occupations (see Frontispiece).[7]

The surveys of the late 1620s were collected together and the numbers of men and ships collated by officials of the Navy Board in 1629 and again in 1635. However, clerical errors resulted in different totals: for example, the 27 seamen of Braunton in north Devon who were recorded in 1626 were overlooked in these two later reports and this accounts for some of the discrepancies in the totals given of Devon seamen. Similar errors were made when adding up the Cornish figures: for example, there were 208 fishermen listed in Powder Hundred in 1626, including 41 seinemen, and these were mistaken for sailors, presumably by the clerks in London. Again, the result was

[4] PRO, SP16/34/98-108; R.G. Marsden, 'The Vice-Admirals of the Coast', *English Historical Review* 23 (1908), 741; Andrew Thrush, 'The Bottomless Bagg? Sir James Bagg and the Navy, 1623-8' in Duffy *et al, New Maritime History of Devon*, forthcoming.

[5] PRO, SP16/33/69, 135/5; Marsden, 'Vice-Admirals', 739 and see Royal Institution of Cornwall, Truro, HB/17/4.

[6] Oppenheim, *Maritime History of Devon*, 53-4; Todd Gray, 'Turkish Piracy and Early Stuart Devon', *Devonshire Association Transactions*, 121 (1989), 162.

[7] Pepys Library, Magdalene College, Cambridge, PL2122.

different totals of sailors and fishermen in the 1626 survey and these later tallies of 1629 and 1635 (see below, Appendices G and H). The shortcomings of these collations serve to reaffirm the importance of the original reports on which they were based as well as the importance of the 1619 survey of south Devon which the Navy Board surprisingly did not use. Taken all together the surveys printed in this volume comprehend the whole of the coasts of Devon and Cornwall except the parishes in north Devon west of the river Taw.

## THE COMPILERS

The government's interest in the country's potential maritime resources stemmed from the great need to augment the meagre forces of the Royal Navy by impressing mariners and ships. On 20 June 1626 the Council of War at Whitehall requested that the Lord High Admiral order 'a general muster' from his Vice-Admirals:

> of all such mariners, sailors and seafaring men as are within their jurisdiction and to return true certificates to his Grace of their numbers, names, ages and dwelling places.

The Council also asked for:

> the numbers, strengths and burthen of all ships and barques belonging to each port and haven, as well of those that are there at this present as of those that are abroad.[8]

Curiously although Sir James Bagg was singled out to advise the sub-committee of the Council as to 'where the best store of shipping and mariners was to be found'[9] the report which he sent for Devon was remarkably incomplete. Less than half of the coastal area of the county was covered and the reports indicate inadequacies in those that were made: the return for Plympton hundred noted that 'the rest [were] not brought in'. Further, a comparison with the survey of the south Devon coast in 1619 suggests that the 1626 reports were only of seamen then at home. The difference in the number of men recorded is considerable (only 567 in 1626 as compared to 3,653 in 1619) even allowing for the effects of plague and war, both of which severely affected the county from 1625 to 1630.[10] The inadequacies of the reports may have been due to political considerations and constraints: the office of Vice-Admiral of south Devon was held by Sir John Eliot, a rival of Bagg's, from 8 December 1622 until the summer of 1626 when proceedings were begun against him by the Admiralty. On 4 August a commission of inquiry was issued, on 25 October the council requested that Eliot be suspended as Vice-Admiral and during October 1627 the commissioners met in Plymouth and

[8] PRO, SP16/28, p.12.
[9] PRO, SP16/28, p.11.
[10] Paul Slack, *The Impact of Plague in Tudor and Stuart England* (1985), 83-99, 113-19.

Totnes to hear testimonies about Eliot.[11] It was during the month of August
1626 that the survey has been thought to have been made: that the survey was
taken that year, and not later, is given further credence by the listing of a
number of shipowners, such as Robert Trelawny senior of Plymouth and Sir
Robert Chichester of Raleigh in Pilton, who died in the following year.[12] At this
time Eliot was imprisoned in London. Eliot never had the office officially
taken away from him but the assassination of Buckingham in August 1628
terminated his appointment. During these last few years of the 1620s it is most
likely that Bagg and Sir John Drake of Ash in the east Devon parish of Musbury
temporarily acted as Vice-Admirals, as Bagg apparently had on 25 September
1623; both are cited in various documents as Vice-Admirals of the county.[13] It
is possible that Bagg could have been requested to survey only the south-west
portion of the Devon coast and that Drake was to have undertaken the
remaining coastline. The Dartmouth return, which bears Bagg's signature, is
in marked contrast to the highly organised structure of the rest of his reports.
If Drake did undertake a survey of the rest of Devon it does not appear to have
reached the Navy Board. The partitioning of the county into separate Admiralty divisions was not without precedent: the Earl of Bath held north Devon
as a separate Vice-Admiralty at the beginning of the seventeenth century.[14]
The general uncertainty of the Devon Vice-Admiralty in 1626 was expressed
in a letter from the Earl's son written in November. In it he asked for the North
Devon Vice-Admiralty and wrote that the Devon Vice-Admiralty was 'void as
is reported'.[15] Curiously, it was James Bagg's own father who, in 1595, had
been responsible for impressing mariners on the same coast from Plymouth to
the west side of Dartmouth.[16] But Bagg should have been familiar with the
exercise in 1626 as he had already had experience in impressing mariners there
in the previous year.[17] In contrast to the Devon reports, his survey of his own
Vice-Admiralty of south Cornwall appears to be complete although unfortunately there is not an additional report of that coast with which to compare it.

On 27 November 1601 the Lord High Admiral set the boundaries between
the two Cornish Vice-Admiralties when Haniball Vivian and William Roscar-
rock were appointed Vice-Admirals. The jurisdiction of the southern Vice-

---

[11] Harold Hulme, 'Sir John Eliot and the Vice-Admiralty of Devon', *Camden Miscellany*
XVII (Camden Society, 3rd series, 64, 1940), x-xii.

[12] Oppenheim, *Maritime History of Devon*, 61-2. The survey is undated but the Public
Record Office has suggested August as the most likely date. Trelawny died in
December 1627: J.P. Baxter (ed.), *The Trelawny Papers* (Portland, Maine, 1884),
xix. Chichester died on 24 April 1627: J.L. Vivian, *The Visitations of the County of
Devon* (1895), 174.

[13] Hulme, 'John Eliot', viii; Marsden, 'Vice-Admirals', 739-41.

[14] Marsden, 'Vice-Admirals', 740-1. See Appendix G for an indication that Bagg
shared the duties of Vice-Admiral of Devon with Drake.

[15] PRO, SP16/40/22.

[16] *Acts of the Privy Council, 1595-6*, 274-5.

[17] *Acts of the Privy Council, 1624-5*, 498-9 and see next paragraph.

Admiralty lay from the river Tamar westward to Land's End then inland across the county to St Madron, Kenegie (near Penzance), Ludgvan, St Erth, Camborne 'and thence in a direct line to a bridge called Horsebridge' in the parish of Stoke Climsland. The north Vice-Admiralty began at Land's End to the Brisons (small islands off the parish of St Just-in-Penwith) and then along the length of the north coast to the Devon border and then back inland to Horse Bridge (see Map 3).[18]

The government obviously had longstanding difficulties with impressing men and ships in the South West for Royal service: on 2 April 1628 Sir John Drake wrote to Edward Nicholas that 'to press men is in vain for they will not go'.[19] On 2 April 1625 Bagg had complained that the muster of up to 600 mariners and seamen at Exeter had been interrupted by Sir John Eliot. Eliot claimed that he had sent the men home because he understood that the death of James I, and the accession of Charles I, negated the impressment orders.[20] In April 1628 Bagg also wrote to the county's JPs asking for their help with delinquent sailors.[21] During that month the mayor of Saltash was reported to have treated the impressment order with contempt. He was said to have encouraged the seamen in avoiding the press by first publicly reading the impressment warrant in his own home and then openly declaring in the street that he did not know where to find any seamen.[22] The navy also had trouble with the mayor of Dartmouth. Captain John Pennington wrote on 9 April 1627:

> I presently sent my Lieutenant and master away to Dartmouth to get me what men they could... they returned from Dartmouth but brought me never a man, not withstanding I had formerly sent warrants to Sir John Drake, Vice-Admiral of Devon, as also to the Mayor of Dartmouth for the pressing [of] 160 men for us, but their answer is they can find none. But I know there be men and good men, which do absent themselves and [are] winked at.[23]

Pennington wrote to the Lord High Admiral in February 1626 that he had bargained with the mayor of Plymouth that if a sufficient number of men were brought into the Guildhall for the press there would be no further 'recruitment' in the town. However, whereas Pennington had expected 300 to 400 men the constables of the wards brought in '10 or 11 old men not fit for service'. He suspected that the remainder of Plymouth's mariners were concealed.[24] Bagg

---

[18] PRO, HCA49/106/Packet A.

[19] PRO, SP16/102/47. On 1 May 1628 the Commissioners for Martial Law in Plymouth wrote of their great difficulty in obtaining mariners, 'partly from the late mortality and not least from their shameful and ungrateful desertion of the King's service': PRO, SP16/103/1.

[20] *Historical Manuscripts Commission Twelfth Report* (1888), Appendix 1, 12, 190.

[21] Devon Record Office, DQS OB 1/6, 1625-33, 160, 161, 163.

[22] PRO, SP16/101/50, 100/40. See also ibid., 100/47.

[23] PRO, SP16/60/15.

[24] PRO, SP16/20/25.

also complained of the lack of assistance given to him by the mayors of Dartmouth and Plymouth; he suggested in a letter to the Duke of Buckingham that to 'have him [the mayor of Plymouth] by the heels will give example to others'.[25] The government's intended use of the surveys is unmistakable: the press-masters would have had clearly listed before them all the seamen's names with their home locality, their ages and occupations.

Likewise there were problems with impressing ships: in 1627 when Bagg was trying to organize the hire of some transport ships he warned Edward Nicholas, Secretary to the Lord High Admiral, that:

> you may not be carried away with the opinion that the owners of these ships will willingly contract and so employ themselves but it is nothing else but warrant and command that must draw them to it.[26]

Therefore the surveys were supposed to list all the information regarding ships that the government might require.

The surveys are arranged by parishes or other 'locations' and in Sir James Bagg's survey these are grouped according to the ancient hundreds in each of the two counties. Each survey is written in a single hand throughout, indicating that fair copies were compiled from the parish details. The surveys either bear the signatures of the local compilers or were accompanied by signed letters (below, p. 53), thereby indicating that they were prepared locally. There is some evidence within Bagg's survey (below, p. 67) that it was the parish constables who collected the information for the Vice-Admirals: the return for East Looe has the names of three constables at its foot. This was not without precedent for in the previous press of the spring of 1625 the constables had been ordered to first summon all of the seamen resident within their parishes and then record their details onto a roll or book which was then to be sent to the Navy Board.[27] The Vice-Admirals would also have had their own officials in some of the ports such as the man Bagg employed as a deputy Vice-Admiral who was living at Penryn in 1627.[28]

## INTERPRETING THE SURVEYS

The maritime surveys are almost top heavy with detail, providing information about over 6,000 men and more than 600 vessels in Devon and Cornwall. It is possible however to assume a completeness in the documents which may not even have been the intention. For instance, as is clear from their headings, the reports did not purport to list all the men engaged in seafaring occupations or all ships based in the vice-admiralties. They would not necessarily have recorded the great number of men who were employed only occasionally in the

[25] PRO, SP16/109/66.

[26] PRO, SP16/80/77: see Appendix D. Likewise he wrote in August 'neither will the master, owner nor mariners without command entertain this journey': Appendix C.

[27] *Acts of the Privy Council, 1623-5*, 499.

[28] PRO, SP16/58/72.

seasonal overseas fisheries, or even in the inshore pilchard and herring fisheries. Also, the government was not interested in very small vessels, those of five tons or so, engaged in short-distance coastal trade or in the inshore fisheries. Those responsible for the surveys were simply not asking questions which would have resulted in a comprehensive list of all men and ships in the maritime trades.

The apparent precision with which the mariners' ages were noted is also misleading. The two reports for the north Cornish coast most ably demonstrate this: although there is a clear two and a half year interval between the two surveys, rarely do the ages of the men who appear in both reports reflect this. Sometimes the men got younger. It could have been that those who made the survey merely reported the men's approximate ages. Indeed in the Devon parish of South Huish in 1626 of the 19 sailors recorded there, 14 were listed as being 'between the ages of 20 and 40 years of age' and the remainder as 'between 40 and 60 years of age'. It could also have been that the men themselves did not know their ages or possibly even gave inaccurate ages to discourage a potential press-master.

The surveys identified men by a great number of occupational terms, their 'qualities' as they were termed in Bagg's report, and their 'profession' in Basset's survey of 1629. Besides shipowners, the Duke of Buckingham's report of 1619 used eleven terms, namely mariner, master, master's mate, sailor, fisherman, seineman,[29] cooper, surgeon, bargeman, sounder and shipwright. The 1626 surveys also specified in some cases those who were apprentices or servants, and used another thirteen categories: pilot, boatswain, sailor-apprentice, sailor-servant, fisherman-servant, trumpeter, bargeman-fisherman, gunner, sailor-fisherman, fisherman-sailor, sailor for coal, seafaring men and also included one 'captain-mariner'. The terminology can be misleading as well as confusing. Terms such as 'pilot', 'boatswain' and 'trumpeter' all referred to recognized skills. Other terms also had precise meanings: 'master' referred to the captain of a merchant vessel, a 'master's mate' was the master's chief officer, a 'sailor' was a member of a ship's company below the rank of officer who was professionally engaged in the sailing of the vessel and 'seamen' refers to men of all ranks concerned with the sea. However, the term 'mariner' had two separate definitions: in one sense it referred to any man employed on board a ship, in the same sense as the term 'seaman', but it also applied to the most senior class of seamen, sometimes indicating masters of ships who entered into voyages on their own account.[30]

The apparent precision with which these men were described in the surveys also masks their varied work experience for many men had dual-employment. For example, Thomas Eve of St Just in Penwith may have been representative of the many men who mixed fishing with some husbandry: his probate inventory of 1607 showed that he owned one quarter of a fishing boat as well

---

[29] Sir James Bagg's survey also used the more familiar term 'seiner'.
[30] F.C. Rhodes, 'Mariner; Sailor; Seamen', *Mariner's Mirror*, 51 (1965), 79.

as three goats and a kid.[31] More striking is the example of Geoffrey Wheller, a yeoman of Chivelstone near Salcombe in south Devon, who owned at his death in 1598 a quarter of a seine net along with 12 lambs, 13 ewes, a ram, a mare, four pigs, one acre of peas, two acres of barley and an acre of wheat.[32] Also, many of those men described simply as sailors would have regularly served aboard the Newfoundland and New England fishing fleets. In some cases the surveyors clearly gave very loose occupational definitions. This is clearly seen by comparing the two surveys for north Cornwall: in 1626 all the seamen of St Columb Minor were listed as fishermen whereas in 1629 these same men were recorded as sailors.

Finally, another comparison between the two north Cornish surveys highlights the risks of drawing too precise conclusions from one single documentary source. In February 1629 a total of ten barques were recorded on that coast, three each of St Ives and Padstow and four of Boscastle. In contrast two and a half years earlier Basset had reported to the Lord High Admiral that on the north coast:

> there is not any ship either in or belonging to any of those ports only three small barks no way capable of any ordnance, the biggest not being above twenty tuns.[33]

The marked increase in the number of ships may have been due to the capture of prize-ships but the relevant point is that very different impressions of the character of the north Cornish shipping could be obtained from consulting only one of the surveys. Interestingly, Basset's statement was itself at odds with the report he had enclosed with his letter which actually listed not only two barques of 28 tons but another of 40 tons. All three were Padstow ships. There are also striking differences in shipowning between the two surveys which also makes this point: in 1626 two of the three Padstow ships were owned by Morgan Phillips and the third by Peter Quinte, but three years later neither of these men appear as shipowners. In this case however the reports were not necessarily inconsistent as there was a reason for Phillips' omission from the later survey: he 'and some of his company' were drowned off the Welsh coast within four months of the first survey.[34]

## MARINERS, SAILORS AND FISHERMEN

The seamen of the two counties, which included men with such unusual Christian names as Nephthaly, Amareth, Serenist, Tippet, Harkenval, Mel-

---

[31] Cornwall Record Office, AP/E31/1,2.

[32] Devon Record Office, 48/13/2/3/2, ff.117-19.

[33] See below p. 53. It is interesting to note that in this letter 'forty' has been crossed out.

[34] Cornwall Record Office, Padstow Parish Register. They drowned on 6 December 1626. The dangers of this coast are highlighted by another entry in the register which noted that on 11 December 1626 six Padstow men were drowned going over the Bar at Barnstaple. They were buried in Northam churchyard.

chisideck and Roman, were spread along the length of the north and south coasts, with by far the greatest number recorded in both counties in the south.[35] In south Devon in 1619 some of the men resided as far inland as Dartmoor (see map 1). The survey listed 3,653 seamen residing in a total of 102 localities (or 'places of abode' as Sir James Bagg later termed them), mostly parishes. Table 1 shows the considerable differences between the areas in the proportion of seamen. As the text shows, some parishes had very small numbers of seamen while others, like Plymouth (278 seamen) and Dartmouth (446), each with its immediate neighbours, as would be expected had a much greater share of the total. What emerges most clearly is the great concentration of seamen in the area to the east of Dartmouth: not only just across the river Dart at Kingswear (93 seamen) and Brixham (153) but in such Torbay parishes as Paignton (100) and St Marychurch (144). With 42 per cent of the total this was clearly the centre of south Devon's mariner population. Other notable parishes included several in the South Hams such as Malborough (112), Blackawton (76) and Stokenham (115) as well as several along the rivers Teign and the Exe such as Stokeinteignhead (115), Dawlish (133) and Kenton (104) which had considerably more than those recorded at Topsham (41), the port of Exeter. The only places in east Devon with significant numbers of seamen were Sidmouth (103) and Beer and Seaton (80).

## Table 1

### SOUTH DEVON MARINERS, 1619

| Area | Number | Per cent |
|------|--------|----------|
| Plymouth | 604 | 17 |
| Salcombe | 427 | 12 |
| Dartmouth and Torbay | 1,538 | 42 |
| Teign estuary | 489 | 13 |
| Exe estuary | 306 | 8 |
| East Devon | 289 | 8 |
| **Total** | 3,653 | 100 |

Sir James Bagg's survey of *c.* 1626 recorded 407 mariners in south-west Devon and only 165 in parts of north Devon.

However, while as already indicated, the 1626 survey of south-west Devon recorded fewer mariners overall than previously, in some parishes there were actually increases. For example, while in 1619 there were only two sailors recorded in the parish of Diptford, which lies 16 miles inland from Dartmouth, seven years later there were not only two sailors recorded as resident there but two fishermen and a mariner as well. Bargemen were recorded along the rivers Tamar and Tavy as well as in Totnes. Surprisingly there were none listed along

[35] Other uncommon names included Pancras, Juell and Dowell.

the river Exe but this was almost certainly due to the 1619 survey omitting the recording of 'watermen' in the Exe valley.

The report for south Cornwall shows that the greatest concentration of seamen there was near Plymouth. Millbrook, with the rest of Maker, had the single greatest number: 76 sailors, 15 mariners, ten fishermen, six shipwrights, five gunners, eight pilots, two coopers, six sailors and servants and one trumpeter. These 129 seamen formed a considerable portion of the 1,340 men listed in the survey (see Table 2). The greatest diversity of maritime occupations within Cornwall was to be found in this area, obviously a result of its proximity to Plymouth. Other places within East Hundred which also had significant numbers of seamen included Saltash (85 seamen), Antony (55) and Sheviock (41). Likewise other havens of importance further along the south Cornish coast were East Looe (88), Fowey and Polruan (108) and finally, the Mount's Bay communities of Mousehole, Newlyn, Penzance and Marazion which together had 144 seamen. Fishermen were recorded along the entire length of the south Cornish coast, particularly large numbers being listed in East Looe and St Keverne while Gorran had no less than 26 seinemen among its 55 fishermen.

## Table 2

### CORNISH MARINERS, *c.* 1626

| Area | Number | Per cent |
|---|---|---|
| Penwith Hundred | 176 | 11 |
| Powder Hundred | 343 | 22 |
| Kerrier Hundred | 167 | 10 |
| West Hundred | 200 | 13 |
| East Hundred | 454 | 28 |
| North coast | 254 | 16 |
| **Total** | 1,594 | 100 |

The two surveys for the north coast of Cornwall show far fewer seamen resident there than on the south coast. In 1626 there were only 254 recorded in 11 parishes and three years later there were 241 in the seven parishes which were then surveyed (see Map 3). The two principal places of importance, as represented by the two reports, were St Ives and Padstow. Curiously, only in the earlier survey were there bargemen recorded, 29 on the river Camel at Wadebridge in the parishes of Egloshayle and St Breock.

Just as the north coast of Cornwall had fewer seamen than there were in the south so it is unlikely that there were ever as many in the whole of north Devon as there were on the south coast. Sir James Bagg's survey noted that the inland hundred of South Molton had only two sailors and that the hundred of Black Torrington 'does not extend to the sea, neither are there any seamen within this hundred'. Later, in the 1640s, it was said that even the coastal parishes of Parkham and Welcombe in north Devon were barren of any seafaring men. This is in striking contrast to the south coast where in 1619 all the coastal parishes had resident seamen. However, the coasts of these north-west Devon parishes comprised high cliffs and of Parkham it was said that 'neither bark nor boat can safely come within our parish, neither able to travel to the said sea with any horse or other carriage what soever'.[36] Yet Bagg's survey clearly under-estimated the number of resident mariners in north Devon: the inclusion of Bideford and particularly of Appledore in the parish of Northam would have considerably enhanced the recorded number of seamen although the overall number is unlikely to have reached half that of the south coast (see Map 2).

The unequal proportion of mariners between the two counties is marked. In 1582 there were said to be 1,810 seamen in Cornwall and 1,914 in Devon[37] while some 40 years later the early-Stuart surveys indicate that the number of Cornish seamen had fallen to 1,594 while those in Devon had increased to over 3,818 (see Tables 1 and 2).

## SHIPPING

The surveys show that there was, in some cases at least, a great lack of imagination in the naming of ships: it was not uncommon to find several ships of one particular name within the same port. For example, in 1619 there were three ships called the *Hopewell* of Dartmouth and in 1626 there were six ships called the *John* in Dartmouth and Torbay. Personal names were very popular: there was a *John*, a *William*, a *Grace* and a *Mary* in many of the ports in the two counties. This obviously reflected the naming of ships after the owners or their families such as the *Holligrove* of Dartmouth which was owned by John Holligrove, a merchant of that town. Doubtless this was a common practice. The *Blessing*, the *Prosperous* and the *Providence* were also particularly popular names. There were still some biblical names such as the *Adam and Eve*, the *John Baptist*, the *Ark* and even the *Jesus*. Some men evidently preferred to use only such pious names for their ships, as for example Alexander Shapley of Kingswear, a merchant who owned the *Gift of God*, the *God's Blessing* and the *Benediction*. But these ship's names were not nearly as common as those taken from animals or plants: botanical names were particularly popular such as the *Primrose*, the *Rosemary*, the *May Garland* and the *Laurel*, as were native birds such as the *Wren*, the *Swallow*, the *Nightingale* and the *Robin Redbreast*. Names were also drawn from myths or fables such as the *Mermaid*, the *Phoenix*, the *Unicorn*, the *Hercules* and the *Medusa* while other exotic names included the *Lion*'s Claw, the *Antilope* and the *Pelican*. Finally, shipowners, particularly those of Dartmouth, often chose names to fit their mercantile vocations: there was the *True Dealing* of Saltash, the *Merchant Bonaventure* of Penryn, the *Exchange* of Plymouth and the *Sweepstake* of

---

[36] PRO, SP16/538/20, 25-6. Of Welcombe it was said that it 'hath no relation to the sea, but only some parts thereof a cliff bordering to the mean sea; whereof is neither bark nor boat belonging nor can come in without peril of life. Neither have they any seamen within their parish nor any man that hath any dealings in sea affairs.'

[37] PRO, SP12/156/45.

Dartmouth, while there was a ship called the *Fortune* not only in Padstow and Penryn but in Plymouth and Dartmouth as well. There is no apparent reason for some ships' given names. Perhaps it is somewhat curious for Ignatius Jurdain, an MP and mayor of Exeter well known for his radical religious views,[38] to have owned part of the Topsham ship the *Virgin* but it seems less appropriate for Sir Edward Seymour's ship to be called the *Samaritan*, a vessel which repeatedly went privateering in the 1620s against the French and Spanish.[39] The gentry appear occasionally as owning ships. Not only such men as the aforementioned Robert Chichester and Edward Seymour but also Francis Trelawny of Plymouth, Sir Arthur Champernowne of Dartington and Raleigh Gilbert of Greenway on the river Dart were listed as being shipowners. There are two Plymouth ships, the *Ark* and the *George*, which were listed in 1629 as being owned by Lord Baltimore, not a local man, but these may have been the two ships of the same names which in 1626 were accredited to Sir James Bagg. Women feature only slightly more frequently than gentlemen as either partial or single owners, but in East Looe there were at least three widows among the boat owners there.

A major difficulty in identifying individual ships from one survey to another is the misleading use of tonnage or burden. These terms had separate definitions: 'tons burden' measured the actual holding capacity of a ship and 'tons and tonnage' was a measurement calculated from the outside dimensions of a ship and generally was one third greater than 'tons burden'.[40] Thus for any given ship the two definitions could result in greatly different figures. But even more significant was the lack of precision in listing ships' particulars. This could explain the differences in tonnage between the 1626 and 1629 listings of Plymouth and Dartmouth shipping. In the later survey the figures for tonnage are consistently greater. In the report of 1619 the Torbay ships were recorded twice with different tonnages. Of the nine ships concerned only one, the *Providence*, was listed with the same tonnage while the rest varied by between five to twenty tons.[41]

---

[38] W.B. Stephens, *Seventeenth-Century Exeter* (Exeter, 1958), 13, 15; Wallace T. MacCaffrey, *Exeter, 1540-1640* (Cambridge, Mass., 1958), 273.

[39] PRO, HCA25/211, 25/224, 1 April 1626; 25/5, 25/7, 7 February 1627/8; 25/212, 13 December 1628; John Appleby, 'Devon Privateering from early times to 1688', in Duffy *et al*, *New Maritime History of Devon*, forthcoming.

[40] Ralph Davis, *The Rise of English Shipping in the Seventeenth and Eighteenth Centuries* (1962), 7; William Salisbury, 'Early Tonnage Measurement in England', *Mariner's Mirror*, 52 (1966), 41-51 and also 'Rules for Ships Built for, and Hired by, the Navy', 173-80 in the same volume.

[41] In the first list they appear as Torbay ships and in the second as being of Tormohun and Cockington. Another anomaly in the shipping lists concerns that of the *Patience* of the Exe estuary. There is one listing for the *Patience* of Exmouth (of 40 tons, 14 years of age, no ordnance, at Newfoundland and owned by four men) and another for the *Old Patience* of Lympstone (with the same tonnage, age, ordnance and owners). It was recorded as 'from home'.

Although the tonnage figures must then be treated with some caution and cannot be counted upon to provide exact figures, an impression can be obtained of the main locations of ships. Table 3 shows that in south Devon ships were spread along the entire length of the coast but that the greatest number, not only in terms of the total number of ships but also of tonnage, was located in and around Dartmouth. Plymouth was second in rank in Devon but this does not take into account the shipping on the western side of the Tamar. An addition of the tonnage of the ships of Millbrook, in the county of Devon but in the Vice-Admiralty of South Cornwall, places Plymouth and her satellite havens as the leading port in the South West. The shipping of the Exe was of lesser importance as would appear to have been that of Devon's north coast, although the inclusion of ships from the river Torridge would undoubtedly have considerably enhanced the totals.

### Table 3
#### SOUTH DEVON SHIPPING, 1619*

| Area | Number | Percentage | Tonnage | Percentage |
|---|---|---|---|---|
| Plymouth | 57 | 23 | 3,052 | 31 |
| Salcombe | 20 | 8 | 670 | 7 |
| Dartmouth and Torbay | 93 | 38 | 3,916 | 39 |
| Teignmouth | 7 | 2 | 247 | 2 |
| Exe estuary | 53 | 22 | 1,887 | 19 |
| Beer & Seaton | 17 | 7 | 176 | 2 |
| **Total** | 247 | 100 | 9,948 | 100 |

* Plymouth includes Stonehouse and Oreston. Salcombe most probably includes shipping from the parishes on the Kingsbridge estuary: An average has been taken of the seven ships which were recorded there as being between 40 and 50 tons. Dartmouth includes Dittisham, Kingswear, Churston Ferrers, Cockington and Tormohun. Teignmouth denotes the shipping recorded from West Teignmouth. Exe includes Dawlish, Kenton, Powderham, Topsham, Lympstone and Exmouth. Beer & Seaton includes 12 fishing boats which were listed as being between five and ten tons. An average has been taken.

A comparison between the totals of the two counties shows the advantage Devon had in shipping (see Table 4). Not only did the Cornish ships tend to be smaller but the county had less than half as many ships as Devon, with the result that Devon had almost four times as much in tonnage. There were 80 ships with a total tonnage of 2,945 tons on the south coast of Cornwall and the greatest number was located in the eastern part of the county which, like its number of mariners, reflected the considerable involvement with Plymouth. Over 1,800 tons was in East Hundred and of the remainder there were in East Looe 448 tons, in Fowey 209 tons and in Penryn 350 tons.

The surveys provide the names of several hundred ship and boat owners. There was some correlation, at least in Dartmouth, between the number of shares in a ship and its size. A comparison between the 1619 report and a Dartmouth Corporation report of about the same time (Appendix A) indicates that tonnage approximated to two and a half times the number of shares. However, it is by no means certain whether a greater number of individuals corresponded with larger vessels and a higher number of shares. For instance, while five men owned the 180 ton *Providence* of Barnstaple[42] the smaller 150 ton *Pelican*, also of that town, was owned by six men (below, p. 94). It is in fact not clear whether all the owners were listed. Certainly in the case of Salcombe they were not: the 1619 list recorded 18 owners amongst its 21 ships, while the 1626 survey recorded 38 individuals who owned between them 27 ships and in certain cases reveals secondary partners for the same ships previously recorded as having one owner apiece. It may be that in this case only the principal owners were recorded. The Cornish lists show a mixture of single and multiple ownership. Multiple ownership was clearly predominant along the Exe estuary but much less so in Dartmouth. Only in that port is there sufficient evidence to indicate whether single ownership was standard: neither the Corporation's survey, the Duke of Buckingham's of 1619, Sir James Bagg's of 1626 or that of 1629 indicate a great level of multiple ownership. The first survey recorded three cases of multiple ownership and five with 'partners'. Further, a list of Dartmouth ships which paid fees for docking there from 1618 to 1619 (Appendix B) also recorded few instances of multiple ownership.[43]

The surveys are also invaluable in showing the principal areas of shipbuilding activity. The greater number of shipwrights was clearly in Devon, where the industry was concentrated, on the south coast at least, in three main areas: Dartmouth (60), Plymouth (33) and, surprisingly, Otterton (26). It is doubtful whether many great ships were built in Devon and Cornwall: although there are some references to large vessels being built locally, such as the 120 ton *Merchant Royal* which was built in Dartmouth in 1626 and the 140 ton *Resolution* of Exeter which was constructed at Otterton also at that time,[44] these are rare. It is most likely that the shipwrights were primarily engaged in building small boats and in repair work.

The surveys show a great diversity in the locations and types of mariners and ships throughout the maritime communities of Devon and Cornwall. While the 1629 and 1634 naval assessments clearly underestimated the country's maritime resources (Appendices G and H) they nevertheless indicate a high national rating for the two counties. This no doubt reflects the region's traditional interests in coastal and European trade as well as its increasing dominance in the Newfoundland fishery and its growing expansion overseas to New England, Virginia and even the Amazon.[45] Both Richard Carew in

[42] Gillian T. Cell, *English Enterprise in Newfoundland, 1577-1660* (Toronto, 1969), 7; PRO, HCA13/59, ff.758-9.
[43] Devon Record Office, DD 61947, 25-6.
[44] Oppenheim, *Maritime History of Devon*, 59; PRO, SP16/16, ff.43, 8.
[45] Mike Duffy *et al, New Maritime History of Devon*, passim; Joyce Lorimer, *English and Irish Settlement on the River Amazon, 1550-1646* (Hakluyt Soc., 2nd series, CLXXI, 1989), 43-4, 188-9 and see below, p. 25.

## Table 4

### DEVON AND CORNISH SHIPPING, *c.* 1626

| Port | Number | Tonnage |
|---|---|---|
| SOUTH DEVON | | |
| Plymouth | 56 | 3,120 |
| Stonehouse | 9 | 500 |
| Salcombe | 27 | 915 |
| Dartmouth and Torbay | 92 | 5,590 |
| **Total** | 184 | 10,125 |
| | | |
| NORTH DEVON | | |
| Ilfracombe | 3 | 60 |
| Berrynarbor | 1 | 20 |
| Pilton | 2 | 43 |
| Barnstaple | 10 | 789 |
| Braunton | 2 | 30 |
| **Total** | 18 | 942 |
| | | |
| SOUTH CORNWALL | | |
| Penryn | 3 | 350 |
| East Looe | 26 | 234 * |
| | 7 | 214 |
| West Looe | 1 | 30 |
| Polruan | 2 | - |
| Fowey | 8 | 209 |
| Mevagissey | 1 | 18 |
| Truro | 1 | 30 |
| Falmouth | 1 | 20 |
| Saltash | 6 | 400 |
| Antony | 5 | 300 |
| Sheviock | 1 | 50 |
| Millbrook | 17 | 1,050 |
| Botus Fleming | 1 | 40 |
| **Total** | 80 | 2,945 |
| | | |
| NORTH CORNWALL** | | |
| Padstow | 3 | 96 |
| | | |
| **Devon total** | 202 | 11,067 |
| **Cornwall total** | 83 | 3,041 |

\* These fishing boats were estimated as being between eight and ten tons.

\*\* The 1629 survey listed three Padstow barques, three St Ives barques and four of Boscastle.

about 1600 and Thomas Westcote in 1630[46] enthused about the prosperous
state of shipping, fishing and mariners in the two counties. Yet, did the general
prosperity of the South West in the decade or so before the Civil War tempt
mariners into the region from other parts of the country? Did the region partly
meet the needs of its growing maritime trades, particularly in the larger towns
such as Plymouth and Dartmouth, by employing outside men such as the 'ship
loads' of poor Irishmen whom Carew wrote were arriving daily in Cornwall?[47]
Or would it have been as Sir James Bagg wrote in 1627 (Appendix C): that
'men use not to carry coals to Newcastle'? Just how many of these mariners,
sailors and fishermen recorded in the surveys were actually raised in their
'place of abode'? It is from local historians that further work will come in
discovering how many of these apparently Devon and Cornish men were in
fact native born.

## NOTES ON EDITING

The surveys have been printed in chronological order but certain liberties have
been taken with the arrangement of their contents, not only to economize in
space but also to aid the reader. Nothing of substance has been omitted and the
order of the places surveyed has been retained, but personal names have been
rearranged in alphabetical order of surnames and grouped under occupations.
Christian names have for the most part been modernised, but those not in
current use have been given in their original spelling. All surnames have been
printed as in the texts. Ships' names have not been modernised. Place-names
have in all cases been given their modern form but all variant spellings are
given in square brackets as also are all editorial insertions.

## ACKNOWLEDGEMENTS

The editor and the Council of the Devon and Cornwall Record Society wish to
thank the Master and Fellows of Magdalene College, Cambridge, the Control-
ler of Her Majesty's Stationery Office (in respect of Crown copyright material
in the Public Record Office), the Mayor and Corporation of Dartmouth and the
Devon Record Office for permission to publish these records.
    The editor is particularly grateful to Professor Joyce Youings for her
invaluable help and advice, and also to Mr Andrew Thrush who first alerted
him to the existence of the Duke of Buckingham's Survey. Among other individuals to whom he is indebted are Mrs Margery Rowe and Ms Christine North
and their staff in the two county record offices, especially Mr Robert Jago of
Truro, Miss Angela Broome of the Royal Institution of Cornwall, for their
help, Ruth Luffman and the staff in the University of Exeter's Data Preparation
Unit for their assistance in entering the 1619 survey into an earlier data base,

---

[46] Francis Lord de Dunstanville (ed), *Carew's Survey of Cornwall* (1811), 91; Thomas
    Westcote, *A View of Devonshire in 1630* (1811), 67.
[47] Dunstanville, *Carew's Survey of Cornwall*, 184-5.

Dr Roger Kain for the use of his parish maps, Mr Oliver Padel and finally, Mr Paul Ferrie for his hospitality in London which made visits to the Public Record Office possible.

Grampound                                                    Todd Gray
August, 1990

The Council of the Society wishes to record its appreciation of the skill with which Mr Mike Dobson of Project Pallas, University of Exeter, computer-typeset the editor's word-processed text and Mr Rodney Fry of the department of Geography prepared the maps.

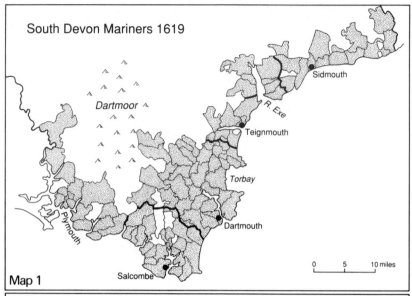

South Devon Mariners 1619

Dartmoor

R. Exe

Sidmouth

Teignmouth

Torbay

Plymouth

Dartmouth

Salcombe

0    5    10 miles

Map 1

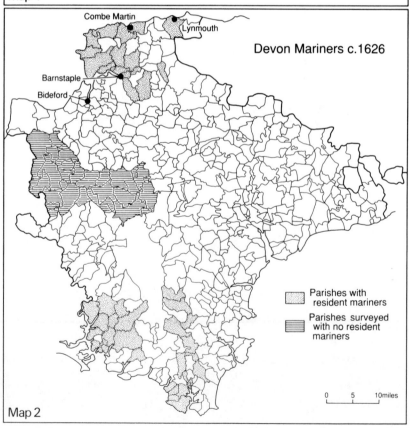

Combe Martin

Lynmouth

Devon Mariners c.1626

Barnstaple

Bideford

Parishes with
resident mariners

Parishes surveyed
with no resident
mariners

0    5    10miles

Map 2

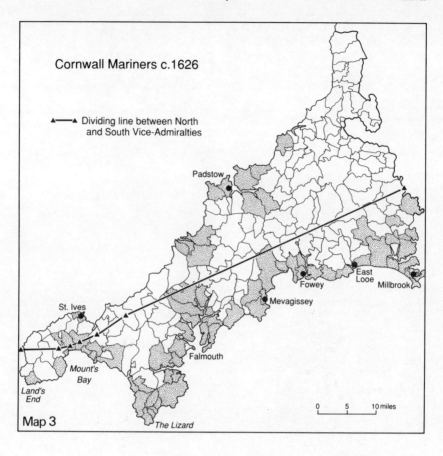

Cornwall Mariners c.1626

▲——▲ Dividing line between North
and South Vice-Admiralties

Padstow

St. Ives

East
Looe
Fowey    Millbrook

Mevagissey

Falmouth

Mount's
Bay

Land's
End

0    5    10 miles

Map 3

The Lizard

# SOUTH DEVON, 1619

THE DUKE OF BUCKINGHAM'S SURVEY OF MARINERS AND SHIPS, 1619
Pepys Library, Magdalene College, Cambridge, PL 2122

A Book of all the shipping with their ages, names, burthens & ordnance, as also of all Mariners, Sailors and Fishermen with their names, ages, & places severally, aswell of them that are abroad as at home, belonging to all the Ports, Harbours, & Seatowns within the Vice-Admiralty of the South Part of Devon: according to an order from the right the Honourable Lord Marquis of Buckingham, Lord High Admiral of England, one of his Majesty's Most Honourable Privy Council unto Sir Edward Seymour, Knight & Baronet, Sir William Courtenay, knight, Jaspar Swyft, judge of the Admiralty of Devon, & Gabriel Dennys, esquire, his Lordship's servant, bearing date February the 28 1618 [1619].

## Plymouth

| | Age |
|---|---|
| MARINERS AT HOME | |
| Henry Adler | 40 |
| Robert Baker | 50 |
| Robert Bennett | 30 |
| John Bickford | 50 |
| Owner Bickford | 28 |
| George Bowlen | 40 |
| Richard Brasye | 40 |
| George Burrage | 40 |
| John Carkeele | 43 |
| William Carkeele | 45 |
| James Carter | 40 |
| Thomas Carvile | 50 |
| Vincent Collins | 40 |
| John Colliver | 40 |
| James Cooke | 43 |
| Ellis Cornish | 36 |
| John Cotton | 46 |
| George Dynes | 45 |
| William Englishe | 25 |
| Thomas Follenger | 46 |
| Silvester Hawkins | 45 |
| Walter Heale | 40 |
| Thomas Hitchins | 40 |
| John Lambert | 50 |
| Edmond Lynnis | 36 |

| | |
|---|---|
| Bartholomew Parrett | 55 |
| Owen Pomeroye | 38 |
| John Pyke | 50 |
| John Rawlins | 36 |
| Robert Sharpe | 55 |
| John Smart sen. | 60 |
| Gregory Triggs | 66 |
| George Waymouth | 48 |
| John Winter | 53 |

| | |
|---|---|
| SAILORS AT HOME | |
| Henry Abraham | 30 |
| Robert Adams | 38 |
| George Allen | 29 |
| Henry Andrew | 40 |
| Henry Ascott | 32 |
| David Austen | 35 |
| Richard Bale | 22 |
| John Barber | 35 |
| Richard Barker | 42 |
| John Barons | 40 |
| Oliver Batchelour | 40 |
| John Bedford | 28 |
| Thomas Bedlamm | 50 |
| Thomas Blaze | 30 |
| Nicholas Blunt | 35 |
| Henry Braye | 48 |
| Richard Bremcombe | 40 |

1

**Plymouth cont'd**

| | | | | |
|---|---|---|---|---|
| George Burgess | 40 | William Kinge | 34 |
| Ralfe Burye | 60 | William Kittley | 26 |
| Thomas Buttler | 30 | Edward Lake | 30 |
| Nicholas Cadwell | 26 | Benjamin Lange | 40 |
| Baldwyn Carkeele | 35 | Thomas Lavers | 23 |
| John Clarke | 34 | John Laye | 30 |
| Robert Colender | 30 | Jerome Lendon | 40 |
| Thomas Collyns | 30 | Richard Littleterr | 44 |
| Peter Colyns | 30 | Ellis Lorye | 25 |
| Christopher Common | 30 | Roger Lovell | 30 |
| Thomas Coursey | 33 | Francis Matthew | 26 |
| James Court | 65 | Sampson Northren | 40 |
| Ferdinand Cripson | 53 | Pascoe Olyver | 35 |
| John Crooke | 36 | John Patrick | 43 |
| Thomas Curveth | 30 | John Penibridg | 40 |
| John Dagg | 50 | John Penrose | 30 |
| William Damerell | 50 | Lewis Philips | 40 |
| Thomas Damon | 30 | Lewis Poape | 25 |
| William Davye | 45 | Thomas Pollys | 33 |
| Thomas Davyes | 53 | Henry Polye | 50 |
| George Dicks | 40 | William Prance | 40 |
| John Dyamond | 25 | Roger Rewe | 30 |
| John Edmunds | 32 | Samuel Rivett | 38 |
| George Eliott | 28 | Robert Sampson | 28 |
| John Engoe | 26 | Nicholas Sander | 32 |
| William French | 24 | John Sanders | 40 |
| Joseph Fryer | 30 | John Smart jun. | 25 |
| Nicholas Gale | 38 | Nicholas Squyre | 38 |
| John Gibbs | 35 | Richard Stentaford | 38 |
| Richard Gibbs | 30 | Hugh Stokema[n] | 33 |
| Henry Gospher | 28 | Thomas Summ | 42 |
| John Growden | 24 | Peter Tabrell | 50 |
| Anthony Guourdon | 28 | John Talant | 36 |
| Roger Halye | 24 | John Tatt | 30 |
| Henry Hawford | 40 | David Tayler | 36 |
| Edward Helgrove | 19 | William Taylour | 35 |
| James Henilaw | 45 | Philip Tincombe | 36 |
| Martin Hill | 36 | John Turner | 38 |
| Thomas Holland | 50 | Edward Tyther | 50 |
| William Hore | 20 | Justinian Ude | 25 |
| Edmond Howe | 31 | Thomas Usecombe | 35 |
| Walter Jago | 35 | John Walter | 37 |
| Owen Jefferye | 30 | Nathaniel Walters | 26 |
| Jacob Johnsonn | 36 | John Welch | 36 |
| Peter J[o]slinge | 40 | Bennett Wills | 38 |
| Henry Jynkin | 35 | William Woods | 59 |
| John Kinge | 45 | William Wrethye | 30 |
| Nathaniel Kinge | 38 | Richard Wright | 33 |
| | | Zachary Yarde | 50 |

SHIPWRIGHTS AT HOME

| | |
|---|---|
| Peter Appleton | 62 |
| William Barefoot | 50 |
| John Barrows | 40 |
| William Burrows | 40 |
| Austen Chipson | 40 |
| Peter Coller | 70 |
| George Crout | 24 |
| Christopher Dicks | 28 |
| Ambrose Diggons | 40 |
| William Foord | 40 |
| Sampson Jope | 26 |
| Mathew Josling | 30 |
| Walter Josling | 37 |
| Henry Rexford | 60 |
| John Richards | 24 |
| Alexander Rule | 35 |
| Walter Slooman | 46 |
| James Taylour | 40 |
| Thomas Tollye | 50 |
| Simon Walters | 35 |
| Francis Warren | 40 |
| George Welsh | 40 |
| John Welsh | 50 |

MARINERS ABSENT

| | |
|---|---|
| William Auton | 36 |
| William Bengha[m] | 38 |
| Stephen Bray | 35 |
| Henry Burgess | 40 |
| Robert Cornish | 55 |
| Thomas Frinke | 34 |
| John Hecks | 35 |
| Richard Hunt | 47 |
| Humphrey Ingleton | 45 |
| John Jope | 50 |
| Richard Lane | 42 |
| Philip Matthew | 50 |
| William Morgan | 50 |
| Richard Rundell | 45 |

SAILORS ABSENT

| | |
|---|---|
| William Alsopp | 34 |
| William Anderson | 40 |
| Adrian Anthony | 40 |
| Richard Arthur | 47 |
| John Atkins | 40 |
| John Bacher | 40 |
| James Baker | 27 |

| | |
|---|---|
| Edward Ballamye | 42 |
| William Barons | 40 |
| George Batchfell | 40 |
| Thomas Baymen | 50 |
| Thomas Bedlam | 30 |
| Richard Blackaller | 26 |
| Richard Blackdown | 34 |
| Henry Bowden | 34 |
| John Braye | 40 |
| Henry Bremcomb | 30 |
| Tristram Brown | 36 |
| Gerrard Burley | 40 |
| Richard Burleye | 50 |
| George Chilson | 36 |
| John Clyfte | 35 |
| William Colewell | 30 |
| John Collins | 46 |
| Robert Collyn | 38 |
| George Collyns | 45 |
| Thomas Dabell | 50 |
| Robert Dier | 27 |
| Edward Dill | 45 |
| James Dove | 32 |
| Arthur Drake | 45 |
| John Dunridge | 26 |
| John Edgcombe | 35 |
| Robert Edwards | 35 |
| Henry Flick | 42 |
| Jacob Foster | 24 |
| Thomas Gill | 26 |
| Roger Gredg | 40 |
| James Hawkin | 23 |
| Christopher Henrye | 24 |
| John Hills | 55 |
| Richard Hogg | 50 |
| John Horwood | 50 |
| Christopher Jacob | 36 |
| John James | 28 |
| William Kerswell | 42 |
| Henry Lange | 46 |
| William Legg | 38 |
| William Love | 60 |
| Bernard Lucas | 43 |
| Richard Marchant | 37 |
| Edward Mariner | 35 |
| Ferdinando Marks | 36 |
| John Marm | 30 |
| William Martin | 40 |
| William Mohune | 40 |

## Plymouth cont'd

| | |
|---|---|
| Robert Molton | 25 |
| James Nettinge | 47 |
| Hugh Nichols | 60 |
| John Onyon | 40 |
| William Palmer | 40 |
| Richard Pell | 50 |
| Henry Perrye | 28 |
| Henry Peryam | 40 |
| Michael Peterson | 44 |
| Thomas Polstagg | 36 |
| Edward Polston | 36 |
| Joseph Potts | 34 |
| John Rawe | 28 |
| Stephen Rawlin | 44 |
| James Rew | 42 |
| Richard Rogers | 24 |
| John Rogerton | 54 |
| John Rolande | 40 |
| William Rouse | 33 |
| James Sampson | 30 |
| Peirce Sanders | 40 |
| George Shirwell | 35 |
| Andrew Simm | 43 |
| John Spencer | 26 |
| Aria' Stanninge | 25 |
| Charles Sumers | 40 |
| Robert Tancock | 30 |
| Mathew Teate | 45 |
| Richard Tuckerman | 35 |
| Francis Vaughan | 53 |
| Robert Walter | 40 |
| James Wattea | 24 |
| John Whiddon | 24 |
| Herman Williams | 27 |
| William Williams | 44 |
| John Wills | 26 |
| Roger Winter | 30 |

## Stonehouse
### [*Stonehouse in Plymouth parish*[1]]

MARINERS

| | |
|---|---|
| John Braye, in Portugal | 40 |
| John Elwell | 50 |
| John Joslinge | 45 |
| Richard Sparwell | 57 |
| Thomas Webber | 56 |

| | |
|---|---|
| William Woode | 40 |

SAILORS AT HOME

| | |
|---|---|
| Peter Adams | 36 |
| Clement Bayliff | 37 |
| Richard Beyle | 24 |
| Richard Bogar | 26 |
| William Burt | 36 |
| John Cornish | 23 |
| Robert Deeble | 30 |
| Walter Dill | 23 |
| Simon Halye | 40 |
| John Hame | 60 |
| Nicholas Hawkin | 25 |
| Thomas Hawkin | 25 |
| Patrick Honicomb | 40 |
| Richard Huswife | 16 |
| Charles Hutchins | 18 |
| Thomas Jefferey | 35 |
| John Jeffery sen. | 50 |
| John Jeffery jun. | 16 |
| William Johns | 24 |
| Leonard Large | 20 |
| William Martin | 40 |
| Gregory Maunder | 40 |
| James Merifeild | 22 |
| Robert Michell | 36 |
| William Oliver | 30 |
| Thomas Parnfrye | 26 |
| Edward Philips sen. | 37 |
| John Potter | 38 |
| John Simon | 20 |
| Thomas Simons | 22 |
| Griffin Stephens | 16 |
| William Turner | 32 |
| Simon Whiddon | 45 |
| Pascho Yeamer | 30 |

SAILORS ABSENT

| | |
|---|---|
| Giles Daniell | 31 |
| Hugh Foster | 30 |
| John Huswife | 30 |
| Peter Huswife | 30 |
| Edward Jefferye | 22 |
| Roger Kingma[n] | 26 |
| Thomas Nicolls | 40 |
| Edward Philips jun. | 22 |
| Edward Rush | 30 |
| Henry Sladinge | 24 |

[1] Presumably to distinguish East Stonehouse from West Stonehouse in Maker.

| | | | |
|---|---|---|---|
| Robert Streek | 35 | Philip Kingman | 56 |
| Digory Vigarye | 24 | Robert Kitt | 20 |
| John Webber | 28 | John Martin | 29 |
| Walter White | 40 | Thomas Moyle | 28 |
| | | Anthony Osborn | 40 |
| FISHERMEN | | Thomas Parnell | 40 |
| Richard Adam | 28 | Gregory Pentyer | 30 |
| Robert Braye | 28 | John Popp | 40 |
| William Burley | 60 | Peter Rogers | 36 |
| Gabriel Chubb | 30 | Peter Searle | 33 |
| William Chubb | 40 | John Stephens | 24 |
| William Cornish | 26 | Philip Stephens | 30 |
| John Davyes | 48 | Thomas Webb | 23 |
| John Fairweather | 28 | Peter Williams | 30 |
| Henry Ferrys | 23 | Anthony Wootto[n] | 40 |
| Pascho Gellye | 16 | | |
| John Goss | 19 | | |
| Peter Hawke | 22 | | |
| Thomas Hayle | 16 | | |
| William Hayle | 17 | | |
| Robert Hooper | 20 | | |
| Griffin Hornbrook | 40 | | |
| Philip Hutchins | 50 | | |
| John Joye | 36 | | |
| John Kingman | 22 | | |

## Weston Peverell[2]
### [*West-towne*]

| | |
|---|---|
| MARINERS | |
| Vincent Collin | 40 |
| John Courber | 26 |
| William Parmiter | 36 |
| Tristram Reed | 38 |

## Plymouth the Shipping

| Names | Tons | Ages years | Ordnance | Absent at |
|---|---|---|---|---|
| The | | | | |
| *Hercules* | 200 | 10 | 7 | Virginia |
| *Judith* | 80 | 7 | 3 | Newfoundland |
| *Pelicann* | 50 | 5 | 0 | Newfoundland |
| *Dolphyn* | 60 | 17 | 3 | |
| *David* | 100 | 24 | 0 | |
| *Elizabeth* | 50 | 20 | 0 | |
| *Adventure* | 30 | 5 | 0 | |
| *God-speede* | 50 | 9 | 0 | |
| *James* | 25 | 10 | 0 | |
| *Wrenn* | 55 | 3 | 0 | |
| *William & John* | 70 | 21 | 0 | |
| *Sampson* | 70 | 3 | 3 | |
| *Esperaunce* | 70 | 9 | 3 | |
| *Richard* | 40 | 8 | 0 | |
| *Robin-red-breast* | 60 | 16 | 0 | |
| *Blessinge* | 40 | 13 | 0 | |
| *Phoenix* | 60 | 21 | 0 | |

[2] In the parish of Pennycross.

**Plymouth shipping cont'd**

| Names | Tons | Ages years | Ordnance | Absent at |
|---|---|---|---|---|
| Blessing of God | 60 | 21 | 0 | |
| Jonathan | 120 | 12 | 10 | |
| Success | 40 | 13 | 0 | |
| Endeavour | 35 | 15 | 0 | London |
| Consent | 100 | 4 | 5 | |
| John | 40 | 10 | 0 | |
| Chudleigh | 120 | 16 | 5 | |
| Elizabeth | 50 | 16 | 0 | |
| Sunn | 70 | 5 | 2 | |
| Great Amitye | 80 | 12 | 5 | |
| Ann-mayde | 30 | 16 | 0 | |
| Jane | 28 | 15 | 0 | |
| Marigolde | 30 | 5 | 0 | |
| Liverett | 38 | 5 | 0 | Alicante [Allicant] |
| Greyhound | 30 | 7 | 0 | Cádiz [Cales] |
| Charles | 60 | 15 | 2 | |
| Returne | 50 | 30 | 2 | |
| Elizabeth Holman | 100 | 11 | 6 | |
| Guyft | 60 | 10 | 0 | Naples |
| Chance | 50 | 30 | 0 | |
| Andrewe | 70 | 20 | 0 | |
| Good-speede | 40 | 10 | 0 | |
| Simon | 70 | 6 | 4 | |
| William & Jane | 28 | 15 | 0 | |
| Grace | 35 | 16 | 0 | |
| William | 30 | 8 | 0 | At La Rochelle [Rochell] |
| True-dealing | 35 | 26 | 0 | |
| Little-David | 18 | 14 | 0 | At Bilbao [Bilbow] |
| Priscilla | 60 | 16 | 3 | |
| Desire | 25 | 14 | 0 | |

## Stonehouse Shipping

The

| Names | Tons | Ages years | Ordnance | Absent at |
|---|---|---|---|---|
| Blessinge | 50 | 1 | 0 | Dartmouth |
| Dove | 40 | 4 | 0 | |
| Ann-content | 20 | 1 | 0 | Morlaix [Mooles] in Britt[any] |
| John | 25 | 2 | 0 | Lisbon [Lisborne] |

## Oreston [Orestone] Shipping At

The

| Names | Tons | Ages years | Ordnance | Absent at |
|---|---|---|---|---|
| Tho[mas] & Margaret | 40 | 4 | 0 | Portugal [Portingall] |
| James | 40 | 11 | 0 | |
| Elanor | 35 | 6 | 0 | Virginia [Virginea] |
| Bartholomew | 30 | 3 | 0 | Bilbao [Bilbow] |
| Blessing | 25 | 20 | 0 | Aveiro [Avero] |
| Tryall | 35 | 1 | 0 | Ireland |

# Plymstock

| MARINERS AT HOME | Age |
|---|---|
| George Bronsco[m]be | 40 |
| William Hackett | 30 |
| John Lange | 55 |
| John Peeke | 50 |
| Nicholas Pegg | 45 |
| John Pimm | 30 |
| Henry Teate | 50 |

| MARINERS ABROAD | |
|---|---|
| William Ashlye | 30 |
| Thomas Browne | 34 |
| Tristram Gowde[n] | 50 |
| Thomas Teate | 46 |
| John Treggs | 35 |

| SAILORS AT HOME | |
|---|---|
| Henry Barnacott | 23 |
| Robert Bays | 23 |
| John Bennett | 20 |
| Mathew Candish | 20 |
| Thomas Craft | 26 |
| John Eastome | 30 |
| Henry Edgcombe | 28 |
| Edward Eston | 30 |
| William Hariford | 34 |
| William Lancastle | 28 |
| Manuel Lavers | 26 |
| Adam Longe | 20 |
| John Longe | 20 |
| Philip Moore | 23 |
| Richard Moore | 26 |
| Richard Paschoe | 20 |
| John Row | 33 |
| Richard Standon | 34 |
| Thomas Standon | 30 |
| Ellis Standye | 20 |
| Christopher Warren | 24 |
| Nicholas Wazen | 18 |
| Christopher Witheridge | 20 |

| SAILORS ABROAD | |
|---|---|
| Thomas Bickton | 41 |
| William Blackaler | 30 |
| Thomas Brickham | 20 |
| Robert Cotton | 34 |
| William Derram | 30 |
| Philip Drake | 30 |
| John Edgcombe | 28 |

| | |
|---|---|
| Thomas Gatherye | 24 |
| William Lange | 28 |
| James Longe | 30 |
| Philip Longe | 24 |
| Allanor Newton | 20 |
| Nicholas Penny | 30 |
| Nathaniel Pim | 30 |
| Philip Post | 20 |
| Richard Pyke | 20 |
| Nicholas Sarr | 30 |
| John Skewytt | 30 |
| William Somminge | 40 |
| Henry Tatt | 36 |
| Richard Teate | 20 |

| SHIPWRIGHTS | |
|---|---|
| Edward Gibson | 40 |
| Hugh Knell | 56 |
| Robert Knell | 34 |
| John Marchant | 54 |
| John Quick | 20 |
| Philip Quick | 40 |
| Robert Ranke | 40 |
| Thomas Richards | 26 |
| John Street | 26 |
| Philip Sweete | 34 |

# Plympton St Mary
## [Plympton St Marye]

| MARINERS & SAILORS | |
|---|---|
| George Adams | 26 |
| Walter Adams | 35 |
| Josias Cooke | 28 |
| John Daniel | 35 |
| John Foster | 40 |
| John Shepherd | 45 |
| Robert Shepherd | 30 |
| Thomas Tale | 35 |

# Plympton St Maurice
## [Plympton Morrysh]

| MARINERS & SAILORS | |
|---|---|
| Jerome Auton | 46 |
| Walter Baskyn | 34 |
| Thomas Came | 16 |
| Thomas Isott | 24 |
| Roger Martin | 40 |
| Thomas Neeson | 46 |

**Plympton St Maurice cont'd**

| | |
|---|---|
| Henry Pomroy | 46 |
| William Primm | 40 |
| John Watts | 37 |
| William Watts | 40 |
| Christopher Webber | 28 |
| Stephen Willinge | 26 |

| | |
|---|---|
| Luke Pope | 30 |
| Henry Townsend | 20 |
| Jeffry Webber | 50 |
| John Webber | 25 |
| Andrew Williams | 40 |
| Henry Winter | 25 |
| John Yallonde | 20 |

## Yealmpton
### [*Yalmton*]
MARINERS & SAILORS

| | |
|---|---|
| Andrew Alger | 30 |
| Nicholas Baker | 36 |
| Nicholas Haniford | 30 |
| Thomas Reynolds | 40 |
| John Suttaford | 30 |

## Wembury
### [*Wemburye*]
MARINERS & SAILORS

| | |
|---|---|
| John Andrew jun. | 30 |
| Edmond Galsworthy | 25 |
| Josias Galsworthy | 20 |
| Mathew Gyst | 24 |
| Thomas Heringe | 24 |
| John Hill | 20 |
| Leonard Knight | 28 |
| Nathaniel Palmer | 30 |
| John Peryne | 28 |
| Edmund Rider | 30 |
| Andrew Rule | 36 |
| Henry Wiginton | 20 |

## Revelstoke
### [*Revelstock*]
MARINERS & SAILORS

| | |
|---|---|
| William Blackaler | 30 |
| Zachary Blackaler | 40 |
| Thomas Drewe | 50 |
| Thomas Foorde | 30 |
| Edward Hardye | 40 |
| Thomas Killye | 40 |
| Andrew Matthew | 45 |
| William Michell | 20 |
| William Peperell | 26 |
| Richard Pollexphen | 40 |

## Stoke Damerel
### [*Stokedamerell*]
MARINERS & SAILORS   [ages not given]

Leonard Knight
William Leight
Francis Mose
John Rickford
John Row
Simon Row
John Vose

## Egg Buckland
### [*Eckbuckland*]
MARINERS & SAILORS

William Averye
John Beele
James Campe
John Campe
Grynfield Smyth

## Tamerton Foliot
### [*Tamertonn foliett*]
BARGEMEN THERE

Philip Beele
George Brush
Michael Foxe
Mark Gu[m]scott
Richard Harrys
John Jesopp
Pasco Jesopp
Christopher Nichols
David Peirce
George Peirce
John Persye
Nicholas Polsland
Christopher Polslande
Andrew Rider
William Skinner

Roger Vowden
William Warde

MARINERS & SAILORS
Edward Badge
Thomas Walter

# Bere Ferrers
## [*Beere Ferrys*]
MARINERS
John Hitchins
Lawrence Stephens
George Stidston

BARGEMEN
William Batters
Nicholas Baylye
Henry Cawse
Robert Cawse
Tobias Driller
Thomas Dryller
Richard Heale
George Hill
Nicholas Hitchins
Thomas Miller
Robert Stokma[n]
Henry Williams
John Williams

# Tavistock
## [*Tavy-stock*]
SAILORS & BARGEMEN
Thomas Burgess
Thomas Burgess
Daniel Collinn
Tobias Collinn
George Gross
Daniel Hawkin
Sampson Hunnicomb
Thomas James
Tristram Jope
Henry Woolacott

# Newton Ferrers
## [*Newton ferrys*]
MARINERS & SAILORS & FISHERMEN
Andrew Briddick, sailor     26

| | |
|---|---|
| John Crympe | 31 |
| John Hanniford | 46 |
| William Hanniford | 25 |
| Nicholas Hannyford | 30 |
| Andrew Hodg | 32 |
| John Penwill | 30 |
| Walter Penwill | 58 |
| William Penwill | 30 |
| Edward Pitton | 36 |
| John Taylour, mariner | 46 |
| Christopher Witheridg | 58 |

FISHERMEN & SAILORS

| | |
|---|---|
| Henry Collin | 58 |
| Anthony Cooke | 36 |
| George Farr | 40 |
| John Fletcher | 30 |
| William Fletcher | 23 |
| Christopher Hatch | 19 |
| John Hatch | 50 |
| George Hinxton | 33 |
| John Hinxton | 20 |
| Jeffrey Lover | 58 |
| Nicholas Lyle | 23 |
| Vincent Maior | 25 |
| Walter Matthew | 34 |
| Thomas Moyses | 32 |
| Clement Pinwell | 22 |
| John Rogers | 22 |
| Peter Sesley | 26 |
| Philip Windsor | 26 |

SAILORS

| | |
|---|---|
| Andrew Baker | 23 |
| John Baker | 23 |
| Nicholas Baker | 22 |
| Simeon Webb | 26 |

# Ugborough
MARINERS & SAILORS

| | |
|---|---|
| Ralfe Cowne | 20 |
| Henry Parsons | 34 |
| Anthony Taker | 25 |

# Modbury
## [*Modburye*]
MARINERS & SAILORS

| | |
|---|---|
| Robert Cleare | 35 |
| Hercules Whitinge | 26 |

## Modbury cont'd

| | |
|---|---|
| John Whitinge | 30 |

## Bigbury
### [Bygburye]

MARINERS & SAILORS

| | |
|---|---|
| Robert Burwood | 35 |
| Richard Cowkeer | 28 |
| Bennet Gross | 24 |
| William Hannifer | 28 |
| Richard Hatch | 40 |
| John Marwood | 24 |
| John Peirce | 22 |
| John Pless | 33 |
| William Sanders | 18 |
| Adam Shepheard | 28 |
| John Shepheard | 33 |
| John Willinge | 20 |
| William Yearell | 20 |
| Nicholas Yellinge | 22 |

FISHERMEN

| | |
|---|---|
| Richard Coyte | 45 |
| Nicholas Rundell | 38 |
| John Steere | 26 |
| John Stone | 70 |

## Ringmore
### [Rinmore]

SHIPWRIGHTS

| | |
|---|---|
| John Hatch | 40 |
| Nicholas Heade | 26 |
| James Huppiell | 30 |
| John Huppiell | 60 |

SAILORS

| | |
|---|---|
| John Cawkeer | 20 |
| Thomas Rundell | 28 |
| Anthony Shepherd | 78 |

## Kingston

SAILORS

| | |
|---|---|
| Osmound Casell | 20 |
| John Courtys | 20 |
| John Cranche | 40 |
| John Crust | 30 |
| John Taunter | 50 |
| Thomas Voysye | 18 |

## Aveton Giffard
### [Auton-gifforde]

MARINERS & SAILORS

| | |
|---|---|
| Walter Drew | 32 |
| Bartholmew Grint | 19 |
| Thomas Leach | 40 |
| Thomas Slowlye | 23 |
| Thomas Stankham | 30 |

## Holbeton
### [Holberton]

MARINERS & SAILORS

| | |
|---|---|
| Ambrose Bawde[n] | 26 |
| Bartholomew Cawker | 20 |
| Robert Cawker | 20 |
| Charles Cottley | 20 |
| William Grey | 25 |
| John Grigge | 43 |
| Thomas Grimslade | 25 |
| Thomas Hayes | 30 |
| Arthur Ley | 21 |
| John Papplestone | 20 |
| Edward Pepperell | 18 |
| Arthur Shepherd | 22 |
| John Steven | 20 |
| Robert Treeby | 30 |

FISHERMEN

| | |
|---|---|
| Thomas Cawkeer | 29 |
| William Courtys | 30 |
| Edward Croft | 30 |
| Thomas Croft | 60 |
| Robert Curtys | 63 |
| John Rogers | 40 |
| Anthony Sheapheard | 55 |
| Richard Sheapherd | 60 |
| William Sheapherd | 18 |

## Malborough
### [Malboroughe]

MARINERS

| | |
|---|---|
| Richard Cookwoorthy | 50 |
| William Cranch | 40 |
| Richard Craunch | 50 |
| Humphrey Rundle | 40 |
| John Towlye | 48 |

SAILORS

| | | | |
|---|---|---|---|
| Richard Adam | 30 | Andrew Lye | 30 |
| Robert Ball | 40 | Thomas Martin | 30 |
| William Ball | 30 | William Martin | 36 |
| Peter Bennet | 30 | William Martin | 18 |
| Roger Blanke | 26 | George Martinn | 30 |
| Peter Brock | 25 | Philip Nichols | 30 |
| John Came | 20 | William Nichols | 30 |
| Dennis Chopp | 16 | John Odemar | 28 |
| John Chubb jun. | 18 | Nicholas Parker | 20 |
| Philip Cookworthy | 60 | William Peirce | 20 |
| Thomas Cookworthy | 25 | Andrew Perne | 50 |
| Thomas Cornish | 40 | George Perrett | 18 |
| Andrew Cranch | 30 | George Perrett | 30 |
| William Cranche | 18 | John Perrett | 20 |
| John Craunch | 25 | Roger Peter | 24 |
| Owen Craunch | 30 | Thomas Peter sen. | 50 |
| Owen Craunch | 40 | Thomas Peter jun. | 18 |
| Robert Cross | 40 | John Pollard | 42 |
| William Cross | 30 | Michael Poolinge | 25 |
| John Crowfoote | 20 | William Poolinge | 30 |
| James Dapshey | 29 | Richard Pound | 18 |
| William Dapshey | 38 | John Quarme | 20 |
| Richard Dew | 18 | Thomas Quarme | 22 |
| Roger Earle | 18 | William Quynt | 20 |
| Andrew Evans | 50 | John Randall | 40 |
| Richard Evans | 24 | Thomas Randall | 40 |
| Thomas Everye | 40 | Thomas Randall | 30 |
| John Fayrewether | 40 | William Reede | 35 |
| William Fayrewether | 24 | Peter Rider | 36 |
| Robert Francis | 41 | James Robins | 20 |
| William Francis | 25 | William Sander | 50 |
| John Gibb | 40 | John Saverye | 20 |
| Roger Gill | 30 | John Snelling | 48 |
| Owen Goss | 30 | John Stone | 30 |
| William Goss | 25 | Peter Stone | 30 |
| Roger Goulding | 50 | James Sullock | 30 |
| Jaspar Hardye | 30 | William Sullock | 25 |
| John Hareward | 50 | John Sulluck | 40 |
| Henry Hill | 41 | William Suttman | 40 |
| Richard Hill | 25 | Roger Tabb | 40 |
| John Hodg | 40 | Robert Torring | 21 |
| Richard Lock | 50 | Robert Townsend | 20 |
| Peter Locke | 18 | John Trebillert | 20 |
| Richard Lovell sen. | 60 | Nathaniel Vibbert | 20 |
| Richard Lovell | 20 | Roger Vincent | 50 |
| Gilbert Luccomb | 25 | Andrew Williams | 20 |
| John Luccomb | 25 | Henry Williams | 46 |
| John Luccombe | 30 | Gabriel Woodmesse[n] | 20 |
| | | William Woodmessen | 30 |

**Marlborough cont'd**

| | |
|---|---|
| Roger Woolcomb | 40 |
| Thomas Yablsey | 30 |
| John Yebsleye | 30 |

SHIPWRIGHTS

| | |
|---|---|
| Teige Adam [sic] | 41 |
| Thomas Edwards | 34 |
| Nicholas Harward | 40 |
| William Michell | 30 |
| John Peeke | 40 |

COOPERS FOR SEA

| | |
|---|---|
| James Craunch | 30 |
| William Yoeman | 31 |

## South Milton
## [*South-milton*]

SAILORS

| | |
|---|---|
| William Blackmore | 40 |
| William Fayweather | 32 |
| Philip Luccrafte | 19 |
| John Reeve | 37 |

## West Alvington
## [*West-Alvingtonn*]

SAILORS

| | |
|---|---|
| John Hill | 40 |
| Edward Lovell | 26 |
| Hugh Randall | 50 |

## Shipping at Salcombe in Malborough

| | Burthen | Ordnance |
|---|---|---|
| The *Tryall* | 130 | [blank] |
| Six ships | between 40 & 50 | 0 |
| Seven barks at home | of 20 | 0 |
| Five barks at sea | of 20 | 0 |
| One bark at sea | of 30 | [blank] |

## South Huish
## [*South-huish*]

SAILORS & FISHERMEN

| | |
|---|---|
| John Ball | 40 |
| Owen Clarke | 45 |
| John Cookworthy | 35 |
| William Cookworthy | 50 |
| Jaspar Cranch | 30 |
| John Crapping | 25 |
| Andrew Curtys | 45 |
| James Fayrwether | 40 |
| Robert Hinxton | 30 |
| Andrew Hynde | 40 |
| William Kue | 50 |
| Richard Lidston | 30 |
| Robert Lovell | 50 |
| John Luccombe | 30 |
| John Lydston | 45 |
| Robert Maddock | 50 |
| Richard Randall | 31 |
| Roger Randall | 20 |
| Richard Wheeler | 27 |

| | |
|---|---|
| David Windsor | 55 |
| Stephen Yabsley | 50 |
| Thomas Yabsley | 20 |

## Thurlestone
## [*Thurlstone*]

FISHERMEN

| | |
|---|---|
| John Beere | 46 |
| Andrew Blackhaller | 40 |
| John Bridgman | 41 |
| Robert Came | 19 |
| Richard Evans | 37 |
| John Filditche | 30 |
| Nicholas Harvye | 30 |
| Richard Hill | 57 |
| Peter Lovell | 50 |
| John Lydston | 45 |
| Robert Lydston | 57 |
| Thomas Lydston | 32 |
| William Lydston | 49 |
| Robert Lydstone | 24 |

| | |
|---|---|
| John Pratton | 40 |
| Samuel Randall | 31 |
| John Shephard | 58 |
| Richard Steere | 20 |
| Thomas Torring | 40 |
| Henry Torringe | 50 |
| John Torringe | 25 |
| Richard Torringe | 50 |
| David Yoeman | 56 |
| Thomas Yoemann | 25 |

### Kingsbridge
*[Kings-bridge]*
SAILORS

| | |
|---|---|
| Thomas Archer | 28 |
| William French | 50 |
| John Glanfeild | 40 |
| John Hexte | 22 |
| Jonas Hill | 33 |
| Thomas Hill | 35 |
| John Jott | 48 |
| John Warde | 32 |

### East Allington
*[East-alvington]*
SAILORS

| | |
|---|---|
| Arthur Batch | 30 |
| John Bawden | 30 |
| Thomas Grant | 40 |
| Richard Putt | 25 |

### South Brent
*[Brent]*
SAILORS

| | |
|---|---|
| Peter Braddon | 40 |
| John Ferrys | 27 |
| Solomon Harvy | 20 |
| Thomas Harvy | 30 |
| John Maddock | 22 |
| Stephen Maddock | 30 |
| Philip Philips | 40 |
| Walter Pulford | 30 |
| James Sharow | 16 |
| Roger Sowton | 30 |
| John Stidston | 31 |

### Diptford
*[Dypford]*
SAILORS

| | |
|---|---|
| Thomas Dench | 30 |
| Peter Tozer | 20 |

### Holne
*[Hole]*
SAILORS

| | |
|---|---|
| Abel Cater | 30 |
| William Cowyck | 31 |

### Rattery
*[Ratterye]*
SAILORS

| | |
|---|---|
| John Michell | 32 |
| Samuel Searle | 36 |
| Richard Wootton | 35 |

### Dartington
SAILOR

| | |
|---|---|
| Michael Kelland | 36 |

### Buckfastleigh
*[Buckfastlye]*
SAILORS

| | |
|---|---|
| Nicholas Cuff | 40 |
| Richard Madock | 22 |
| Oliver Pettiven | 23 |

### Moreleigh
*[Moorley]*
SAILOR

| | |
|---|---|
| Michael Sugar | 32 |

### Chivelstone
*[Chilston]*
SAILORS

| | |
|---|---|
| John Apter | 30 |
| William Boys | 46 |
| Jaspar Chopp | 46 |
| John Chopp | 30 |

**Chivelstone cont'd**

| | |
|---|---|
| William Comming | 38 |
| Edward Dad | 46 |
| Estick Gould | 22 |
| John Grant | 34 |
| Robert Grant | 55 |
| Richard Joye | 20 |
| Roger Kitt | 24 |
| Peter Madick | 24 |
| Nicholas Paunton | 38 |
| Andrew Pethibridg | 42 |
| John Seamen | 50 |
| Robert Shepherd | 58 |
| Peter Stidston | 35 |
| Richard Torring | 50 |
| John Torringe | 58 |
| Bennet Wills | 35 |
| Michael Wills | 40 |

SHIPWRIGHTS

| | |
|---|---|
| George Pownd | 30 |
| Edward Snelling | 50 |
| Roger Weekes | 34 |

## South Pool

### [*South-poole*]

SAILORS

| | |
|---|---|
| Nicholas Cole | 24 |
| Edward Comming | 46 |
| Richard Comming | 32 |
| John Comminge | 45 |
| Richard Comminge | 26 |
| Richard Pill | 30 |
| Anthony Roper | 34 |
| Robert Simons | 20 |
| John Tucker | 31 |
| John Weeke | 44 |

## Stokenham

### [*Stoken-ham*]

SAILORS

| | |
|---|---|
| John Bastard | 54 |
| Mark Cawker | 22 |
| William Cawkyer | 54 |
| Michael Cherswill | 24 |
| Peter Cleffe | 52 |
| Thomas Cooke | 33 |
| Robert Cornish | 35 |

| | |
|---|---|
| Richard Cotmore | 50 |
| Richard Cowles | 24 |
| John Dedlake | 21 |
| Michael Dedlake | 50 |
| Robert Denche | 55 |
| William Derrye | 33 |
| Nicholas Drew | 32 |
| John Edwards sen. | 55 |
| John Edwards jun. | 23 |
| Thomas Eton | 23 |
| John Ewne | 27 |
| Thomas Ewne | 54 |
| John Foxe | 26 |
| John Fyall | 30 |
| Edward Garland | 26 |
| John Garland | 26 |
| Mark Garland | 28 |
| Robert Garland | 50 |
| William Garland | 57 |
| William Garland | 54 |
| William Garland jun. | 52 |
| John Gold | 70 |
| Nicholas Gold | 50 |
| Nicholas Goodyer | 50 |
| Richard Goodyer | 59 |
| Michael Gould | 37 |
| Peter Gould | 40 |
| Richard Gould | 35 |
| Robert Gould | 55 |
| William Gould jun. | 39 |
| William Gould | 44 |
| Thomas Grymetonn | 46 |
| John Harrys | 30 |
| Peter Harrys | 44 |
| Richard Harrys | 58 |
| John Helman | 26 |
| John Holland | 25 |
| John Horswell sen. | 30 |
| John Horswell jun. | 27 |
| Thomas Hynde | 22 |
| Michael Jeffery | 56 |
| Robert Jeffery | 18 |
| William Jeffery | 26 |
| Andrew Jest | 51 |
| John Jest | 23 |
| Peter Jyllard | 21 |
| Philip Kingsto[n] | 34 |
| John Lee | 30 |
| John Lee | 27 |
| William Lee | 30 |

| | | | |
|---|---|---|---|
| John Loine | 53 | John Cutland | 43 |
| Thomas Lowde | 41 | Peter Edwards | 47 |
| Paster Lust | 24 | Hercules Helma[n] | 49 |
| Henry Madock | 32 | Michael Jeffery | 35 |
| John Martin | 25 | John Lust | 19 |
| John Matbrow | 49 | Nicholas Lust | 23 |
| Andrew Matscomb | 44 | William Lust sen. | 66 |
| Andrew Moore | 35 | William Lust jun. | 43 |
| John Moore | 22 | Nicholas Lyff | 26 |
| Michael Mortimer | 30 | Anthony Philip | 45 |
| John Newman | 20 | | |
| Thomas Newman | 58 | | |
| Nicholas Ovant | 26 | **East Portlemouth** | |
| William Panton | 40 | *[East-portlemouth]* | |
| John Peake | 45 | MARINERS | |
| John Philip | 40 | Walter Small | 52 |
| Michael Philip sen. | 54 | William Small | 34 |
| Michael Philip jun. | 23 | | |
| Nicholas Philip | 33 | SAILORS | |
| Nicholas Pinwell | 30 | John Avenn | 36 |
| Nicholas Planke | 28 | Ambrose Cheswell | 22 |
| William Pollye | 20 | William Cleane | 50 |
| Michael Popp | 33 | Walter Cornish | 42 |
| Richard Popp | 29 | John Cuttmore | 30 |
| Thomas Popp | 30 | Nicholas Grey | 40 |
| Thomas Popp sen. | 35 | Christopher Greye | 30 |
| Thomas Popp jun. | 33 | Thomas Lamboll | 25 |
| William Popp | 23 | Walter Nichols | 21 |
| John Preti-John | 32 | William Nichols | 52 |
| Nathaniel Preti-John | 39 | Robert Preti-John | 40 |
| Jaspar Pulsiver | 50 | Francis Stone | 23 |
| Richard Randall | 52 | John Stone | 22 |
| Michael Shane | 30 | Nicholas Stone | 23 |
| Thomas Shepheard | 40 | Bennet Thomas | 22 |
| Thomas Slome | 26 | John Willinge | 27 |
| Nicholas Still | 36 | | |
| Michael Stone | 25 | | |
| Vincent Towler | 28 | **Sherford** | |
| William Towler | 25 | *[Shereford]* | |
| John Towley | 45 | SAILORS | |
| William Warde | 22 | Peter Lamsedd | 40 |
| Nicholas Watts | 34 | William Pernell | 31 |
| Nicholas White | 30 | John Snelling | 40 |
| Edmund Wills | 50 | | |
| John Wills | 23 | **Dodbrooke** | |
| SHIPWRIGHTS | | SAILORS | |
| John Burgin | 25 | Philip Baker | |
| Water Burgin | 32 | Benjamin Hill | |
| William Burgin | 27 | Edward Smyth | |

## Charleton
### [*Charletonn*]

SAILOR

| | |
|---|---|
| John Tabb | 24 |

## Slapton
### [*Slaptonn*]

SAILORS

| | |
|---|---|
| John Androw | 36 |
| John Beele | 36 |
| Richard Boorde | 45 |
| John Brooden | 44 |
| Andrew Curmmin | 38 |
| William Dennys | 19 |
| John Dodd | 31 |
| John Drew | 63 |
| John Edmund | 43 |
| William Edmund | 38 |
| Bennett Grant | 30 |
| Richard Grant | 33 |
| William Grant | 30 |
| Richard Harrys | 20 |
| Robert Harrys jun. | 22 |
| William Harrys | 20 |
| Richard Hawkins | 44 |
| Robert Hawkins | 28 |
| William Hinde jun. | 24 |
| Hercules J[e]llard | 43 |
| Peter J[e]llard | 64 |
| William Lee | 38 |
| Hugh Martin | 30 |
| John Martin | 18 |
| John Martin sen. | 28 |
| Simon Mingo | 28 |
| Roger Snelling | 36 |
| John Tucker | 40 |
| Walter Tucker | 20 |
| William Tucker | 50 |
| William Tucker jun. | 20 |
| Edmond Wills | 40 |
| John Wills | 48 |
| Richard Wills | 19 |
| Robert Wills | 19 |
| John Wood | 66 |

## Blackawton
### [*Black-auton*]

MARINERS & SAILORS

| | |
|---|---|
| Robert Austen | 26 |
| John Bowden | 18 |
| John Campe | 23 |
| Richard Collyn | 22 |
| Walter Cowle | 27 |
| Bennet Downing | 22 |
| Robert Downinge | 21 |
| William Feay | 26 |
| Edmund Hinxton | 19 |
| Robert Holland | 34 |
| Tristram Hollocombe | 30 |
| John Holocombe | 26 |
| Richard Horswell | 34 |
| John Lane | 34 |
| Michael Madsco[m]be | 30 |
| Henry Martin | 24 |
| Edmund Page | 19 |
| John Paton | 25 |
| Nicholas Pooliim | 20 |
| Walter Poolimm | 24 |
| William Pope | 29 |
| Arthur Pyke | 18 |
| Edmond Rider | 20 |
| Richard Skinner | 23 |
| Richard Spark | 19 |
| John Stone | 16 |
| Arthur Tucker | 30 |
| Richard Tucker | 17 |
| Richard Turke | 20 |
| John Udye | 28 |
| Henry Willinge | 22 |
| Peter Winchester | 40 |

FISHERMEN

| | |
|---|---|
| Ambrose Andrew | 29 |
| William Beate | 41 |
| Richard Burgess | 52 |
| Bennet Collin | 55 |
| Thomas Collin | 40 |
| Robert Collys | 23 |
| John Combe | 21 |
| Nicholas Combe | 47 |
| Robert Constable | 50 |
| Thomas Diamonde | 50 |
| John Everye | 40 |
| John Faye | 20 |

| | | | | |
|---|---|---|---|---|
| Tristram Hollocomb | 60 | SAILORS | | |
| Anthony Holmes | 35 | John Austen | 30 |
| Edmond Horswell | 26 | Roger Badiford | 23 |
| Edward Leach | 18 | Thomas Badiford | 30 |
| John Marrick | 30 | John Baker | 33 |
| Richard Mychamoore | 42 | Brian Bennett | 23 |
| Thomas Mychamoore | 19 | John Bennett jun. | 20 |
| Robert Pownd | 46 | Brian Browne | 25 |
| Thomas Rider | 18 | Walter Dunning | 20 |
| William Rider | 16 | Nicholas Dunninge | 30 |
| William Rider sen. | 52 | Thomas Edwards | 45 |
| William Sharpham | 15 | Richard Foord | 23 |
| John Skinner | 19 | Ambrose Graye | 25 |
| Robert Spark | 20 | John Graye | 30 |
| George Sparke | 63 | George Hinxton | 20 |
| Edward Woodocombe | 34 | John Hinxto[n] | 25 |
| Thomas Woorde | 20 | John Hole | 40 |
| | | Ellis Hoyle | 40 |
| SOUNDERS | | Simon Humpston | 30 |
| Robert Bale | 27 | John Johns | 43 |
| Robert Connett | 27 | Henry Lange | 30 |
| Nicholas Garner | 30 | Robert Lange | 40 |
| Nicholas Spark | 34 | John Lucke | 35 |
| Robert Steele | 34 | Richard Lyne | 45 |
| | | William Morrice | 20 |
| SHIPWRIGHTS | | Peter Mynerye | 30 |
| William Bidlake | 25 | Giles Parnell | 45 |
| Richard Burgin | 33 | Robert Peeke | 40 |
| Walter Burgin | 30 | John Philpe | 40 |
| Nicholas Derry | 18 | John Quint | 50 |
| John Foster | 19 | Brian Randall | 40 |
| Hugh Heale | 22 | Garrat Raymond | 40 |
| Edward Holcomb | 24 | Richard Row | 35 |
| William Miles | 20 | Giles Rowe | 30 |
| Richard White | 36 | William Rowe | 41 |
| Thomas Wills | 25 | Henry Torren | 45 |
| | | James Tucker | 18 |

## Dittisham

*[Dittsham]*

| | | | | |
|---|---|---|---|---|
| | | John Tucker jun. | 30 |
| | | William Tucker | 35 |
| MARINERS | | George Veale | 30 |
| Gregory Badford | 40 | Robert Veale | 60 |
| John Bennett | 50 | John Warren | 45 |
| Nicholas Howell | 40 | James Yolland | 40 |
| Hugh Hympstone | 50 | | |
| John Lyne | 32 | | |
| Leonard Morrice | 30 | | |
| Thomas Tozer | 35 | | |
| Brian Tucker | 40 | SAILORS | |
| John Tucker | 50 | Leonard Cominge | 34 |
| | | Thomas Downinge | 37 |

## Halwell

## Halwell cont'd

| | |
|---|---|
| John Pitting | 36 |
| Richard Short | 37 |

## Harberton

SAILORS

| | |
|---|---|
| Thomas Austen | 45 |
| Humphrey Beere | 43 |
| Crispin Calago | 35 |
| John Hurst | 34 |
| William Moore | 27 |
| John Peerse | 27 |
| Thomas Shephen | 36 |
| Philip Turpin | 25 |

## Ashprington
### [Ashbrenton]

SAILORS

| | |
|---|---|
| Thomas Austen | 30 |
| Daniel Ferrys | 40 |
| Peter Foorde | 35 |
| Peter Morgan | 20 |
| Henry Shellabeere | 31 |

## Cornworthy
### [Cornwoorthye]

SAILORS

| | |
|---|---|
| Robert Efford | 36 |
| Vincent Harrado[n] | 30 |
| William Humfrye | 40 |
| Richard Parrott | 30 |
| Robert Pyke | 20 |
| John Skinner | 31 |
| John Stephen | 45 |
| John Yollande | 36 |

## Stoke Fleming
### [Stoke-fleminge]

SAILORS

| | |
|---|---|
| Nicholas Bullye | 35 |
| Thomas Bullye | 33 |
| Hercules Farr | 31 |
| John Foorde | 32 |
| Richard Garratt | 45 |
| Nicholas Gaye | 42 |
| John Gowne | 43 |

| | |
|---|---|
| Henry Lidston | 50 |
| William Liston | 40 |
| Gilbert Lydston | 25 |
| Gilbert Reach | 30 |
| Richard Roope | 33 |
| John Rowe | 43 |
| Nicholas Stabbatt | 26 |
| John Tiller | 32 |
| Richard Vitterye | 60 |
| Robert Winter | 45 |
| Richard Woolston | 30 |

SHIPWRIGHTS

| | |
|---|---|
| Morgan Eliott | 30 |
| Nicholas Eliott jun. | 20 |
| Nicholas Elyott | 90 |
| Edward Halswell | 28 |
| Simon Halswell | 24 |
| Thomas Halswell | 38 |
| Vincent Halswell | 41 |
| John Hilley | 90 |
| Edward Knolls | 30 |
| Arthur Lidston | 20 |
| Vincent Longe | 24 |
| Edward Lydston | 30 |
| Richard Lydston | 28 |
| Richard Mallow | 17 |
| Bennett Snelling | 36 |

## Townstall

SAILORS

| | |
|---|---|
| Christopher Beere | 28 |
| Chter [sic] Currye | 24 |
| Robert Ellener | 25 |
| Robert Every | 50 |
| William Matthew | 30 |
| William Packhell | 20 |
| Peter Prentice | 18 |
| John Roope | 25 |
| John Sayer | 24 |
| Nicholas Sharpha[m] | 18 |
| John Smyth | 22 |
| Arthur Staplhill | 20 |
| Philip Strilye | 19 |
| Serenist Tucker | 20 |
| Peter Wakeham | 18 |
| Daniel Walter | 32 |
| Andrew Waltham | 20 |
| Robert Young | 53 |

## Dartmouth

### [Dart-mouth]

MARINERS AT HOME

| | |
|---|---|
| Peter Bastard | 35 |
| John Bennett | 37 |
| John Blackaller | 55 |
| Thomas Browne | 35 |
| William Constable | 50 |
| Alexander Cuttrill | 49 |
| William Eliott | 36 |
| Nicholas Escott | 48 |
| Edmund Follett | 36 |
| Edward Follett | 45 |
| James Fo[rte]scue | 52 |
| James Goodridg | 51 |
| Thomas Hodge | 54 |
| John Holigrove | 25 |
| William Leach | 31 |
| John Lomer | 32 |
| John Lucomb | 45 |
| Peter Luscomb | 52 |
| Richard Mayne | 30 |
| Henry Mill | 34 |
| John Newman | 28 |
| Arthur Richard | 42 |
| William Sherrom | 42 |
| William Simons | 45 |
| Robert Sparke | 43 |
| Robert Squarye | 43 |
| Christopher Tapley | 31 |
| Gregory Taply | 28 |
| Peter Tyrrye | 38 |
| Richard Waterdonn | 33 |
| Edward Winchester | 52 |
| Vincent Winchester | 25 |
| Gilbert Wreyford | 40 |

SAILORS AT HOME

| | |
|---|---|
| Henry Abraham | 19 |
| George Adgeney | 28 |
| Thomas Adrescott | 40 |
| Thomas Alford | 23 |
| William Alkens | 20 |
| William Allen | 28 |
| John Amell sen. | 40 |
| John Amell jun. | 22 |
| Robert Archer | 20 |
| William Ashe | 25 |
| William Ashfoord | 28 |
| George Axford | 28 |

| | |
|---|---|
| Michael Babbage | 33 |
| Thomas Bagg | 20 |
| Christopher Bande | 30 |
| Engram Banes | 19 |
| Andrew Barter | 40 |
| William Basill | 22 |
| John Bastard | 18 |
| Henry Baston | 18 |
| William Beard | 42 |
| Richard Beere | 20 |
| James Bennett | 27 |
| Thomas Bennett | 25 |
| John Blackaler | 22 |
| Nicholas Blackaler | 29 |
| Nicholas Blackaler | 18 |
| Ralfe Blackaler | 30 |
| Robert Blackaler | 26 |
| Thomas Blackaller | 26 |
| John Bonner | 54 |
| Joseph Bowden | 40 |
| Peter Bowhey | 25 |
| John Bowmann | 22 |
| Daniel Boyes | 23 |
| Philip Boys | 40 |
| John Bremblecomb | 35 |
| John Brooke | 18 |
| Thomas Brooking | 24 |
| James Browne | 30 |
| Christopher Cade | 39 |
| Robert Cally | 35 |
| Thomas Cane | 32 |
| William Canter | 45 |
| Christopher Carey | 19 |
| John Chop | 36 |
| William Church-ward | 19 |
| Robert Churchward | 18 |
| William Churchward | 22 |
| Stephen Cockwell | 35 |
| Nicholas Collyns | 32 |
| William Coombe | 20 |
| Fletcher Corney | 20 |
| John Corney | 35 |
| John Cornish | 24 |
| William Cornish | 22 |
| Richard Cosens | 36 |
| Nicholas Coyte | 43 |
| Humphrey Cross | 54 |
| Abel Cruse | 19 |
| John Cutt | 25 |
| John Cutt | 50 |

**Dartmouth cont'd**

| | | | |
|---|---|---|---|
| William Cutt | 25 | William Hallye | 19 |
| John Cutty | 30 | Richard Haradonn | 42 |
| Edmond Davys | 40 | Thomas Harewood | 23 |
| John Davys | 23 | Christopher Harper | 43 |
| Richard Davys | 20 | Edward Harvy | 20 |
| Vincent Davys | 36 | John Harvye | 31 |
| William Dennys | 40 | Robert Harvye | 23 |
| Christopher Dick | 25 | Lewis Hawkins | 20 |
| Christopher Dick | 28 | Barnard Heninge | 20 |
| Thomas Dick | 35 | John Hill | 55 |
| John Dollinn | 36 | Peter Hill | 20 |
| Nicholas Dominey | 41 | Richard Hill | 23 |
| Richard Downe | 32 | Robert Hill | 22 |
| Thomas Drewe | 23 | Thomas Hinxton | 35 |
| John Duck | 40 | John Hodg | 30 |
| George Earle | 26 | Thomas Hodge | 28 |
| George Earle | 18 | William Hoggett | 25 |
| Hext Egbeere | 35 | James Hole | 27 |
| Edward Evans | 35 | George Holigrove | 20 |
| Thomas Fabese | 45 | Edward Holocomb | 21 |
| Robert Farewell | 22 | John Holocomb | 18 |
| James Farr | 30 | David Hoper | 35 |
| Anthony Fletcher | 32 | Gregory Huett | 22 |
| William Flute | 23 | William Irish | 23 |
| Robert Follet | 28 | John Jackmann | 22 |
| Anthony Follett | 30 | William Jakemann | 23 |
| Gilbert Follett | 25 | Nicholas James | 27 |
| Andrew Foord | 30 | William Jefferye | 35 |
| Owen Foord | 24 | Thomas Jewell | 24 |
| John Foorde | 23 | Thomas Jewell | 20 |
| William Foster | 23 | John Jones | 30 |
| John Fosterd | 29 | William Jones | 35 |
| Thomas Francis | 28 | Abraham Kellye | 30 |
| Bartholomew Frye | 56 | William Kellye | 18 |
| William Fursmann | 20 | William Kemp | 22 |
| Michael Gamon | 20 | John Kempe | 18 |
| Thomas Giles | 30 | William Kennicott | 28 |
| Andrew Gillye | 24 | William Labye | 40 |
| Andrew Glanvild | 29 | Henry Langdon | 18 |
| William Godferye | 18 | John Lash | 36 |
| Charles Good | 45 | Stephen Lash | 21 |
| Robert Good | 18 | Walter Leach | 28 |
| Nicholas Goodridg | 22 | John Lepreye | 46 |
| John Goodridge | 20 | Robert Lernigate | 45 |
| Thomas Goss | 22 | Samuel Ley | 25 |
| William Goss | 24 | Hugh Lighte | 19 |
| Thomas Gosse | 31 | Anthony Lomer | 20 |
| John Grappinge | 28 | Robert Lomer | 19 |
| Edward Hallye | 20 | John Loven | 30 |
| | | Benjamin Luxe | 30 |

| | | | | |
|---|---|---|---|---|
| Robert Malborow | 45 | | Walter Rounsevall | 45 |
| Edward Maninge | 19 | | John Rowe | 53 |
| William Mann | 30 | | John Rowe jun. | 19 |
| Paschoe Matthew | 40 | | John Rowe | 26 |
| Paschoe Matthew | 33 | | Christopher Rowland | 19 |
| William Matthew | 18 | | John Salter | 30 |
| Thomas Mayde | 56 | | John Salter | 40 |
| George Mayne | 24 | | John Sayer | 28 |
| John Meade | 25 | | Richard Scover | 40 |
| Thomas Moone | 20 | | George Sheeres | 26 |
| William Moore | 20 | | John Shutland | 18 |
| James Mortimer | 27 | | Nicholas Skinner | 39 |
| Robert Muddye | 37 | | Robert Skinner | 36 |
| John Naracott | 23 | | Vincent Skinner | 30 |
| Euan Necke | 49 | | John Smyth | 28 |
| Richard Norber | 40 | | Nicholas Smyth | 28 |
| Euan Norman | 20 | | Richard Sofilde | 18 |
| William Norman | 20 | | George Sowton | 20 |
| Robert Norris | 24 | | Peter Sparke | 20 |
| Zachary Norrys | 18 | | William Spurring | 39 |
| Henry Olding | 40 | | John Squyre | 19 |
| Robert Oldman | 23 | | Thomas Stephens | 21 |
| John Oliver | 29 | | John Stone | 35 |
| Robert Oliver | 20 | | Philip Stratchly | 19 |
| Richard Parker | 21 | | Humphrey Street | 18 |
| William Payne jun. | 20 | | Robert Street | 29 |
| William Payne | 24 | | Thomas Street | 26 |
| John Pennye | 18 | | Robert Streete | 25 |
| George Peperill | 20 | | Andrew Swaddle | 25 |
| Lawrence Pepperell | 23 | | John Tabb | 30 |
| John Perinn | 20 | | John Tapley | 20 |
| John Perynn | 20 | | John Thomas | 28 |
| Nicholas Perynn | 20 | | Richard Tirry | 24 |
| Thomas Perynn | 42 | | John Tirrye | 25 |
| Nicholas Philips | 19 | | Richard Toll | 35 |
| William Pickell | 18 | | Richard Tony | 22 |
| William Plumley | 35 | | George Tonye | 26 |
| Nicholas Porke | 30 | | Henry Tozer | 18 |
| Thomas Porke | 32 | | Thomas Tozer | 25 |
| Francis Porter | 31 | | John Trelawny | 18 |
| James Prowt | 35 | | Peter Treveser | 30 |
| Thomas Pullyn | 28 | | Henry Tucker | 18 |
| Henry Pyke | 28 | | Thomas Tucker | 23 |
| James Pyke | 53 | | Walter Tucker | 40 |
| Nicholas Pymble | 35 | | William Tucker | 33 |
| Nicholas Risdon | 18 | | William Vincent | 34 |
| William Risdon | 23 | | Walter Viney | 22 |
| Christopher Roach | 33 | | John Voysye | 19 |
| Henry Roberts | 18 | | Robert Wadland | 42 |
| James Roberts | 20 | | Adrian Wakeham | 23 |

**Dartmouth cont'd**

| | |
|---|---|
| Peter Wakeham | 18 |
| Thomas Wakeham | 18 |
| John Walch | 42 |
| Christopher Walter | 19 |
| John Waye | 28 |
| John White | 26 |
| Robert Whyte-heare | 19 |
| William Widgarr | 28 |
| Robert Wilkins | 20 |
| John Williams | 19 |
| John Wills | 40 |
| Samuel Wills | 30 |
| Robert Windiett | 32 |
| John Winter | 24 |
| William Winter | 24 |
| Alexander Withicombe | 30 |
| Christopher Wood | 58 |
| Henry Woolcott | 37 |
| Nathaniel Wostard | 20 |
| Edward Wright | 36 |

SHIPWRIGHTS

| | |
|---|---|
| Nicholas Adams | 20 |
| John Austinn | 33 |
| Richard Austinn | 19 |
| Thomas Beere | 28 |
| Thomas Colliver | 31 |
| John Constable | 18 |
| John Cooke | 18 |
| William Cutt | 45 |
| Henry Daye | 42 |
| William Evans | 24 |
| John Feater | 18 |
| John Gibbons | 38 |
| John Golborne | 38 |
| Richard Harvye | 38 |
| Richard Hilley | 30 |
| Nicholas Jefferye | 18 |
| Richard Leane | 44 |
| Robert Lome | 41 |
| Nathaniel Martin | 27 |
| Henry Milcomb | 35 |
| Nicholas Moorton | 34 |
| Christopher Pepperell | 19 |
| Peter Philpott | 27 |
| William Raymonde | 30 |
| John Rossmond | 20 |
| Samuel Salter | 23 |
| Nicholas Sanders | 34 |

| | |
|---|---|
| William Scotch | 43 |
| John Sheere | 19 |
| Nicholas Snelling | 33 |
| John Snellinge | 42 |
| Thomas Snellinge | 18 |
| John Spark jun. | 25 |
| John Sparke jun. | 18 |
| John Sparke | 42 |
| John Stagge | 35 |
| John Stoakes | 20 |
| William Tozer | 22 |
| John Tricky | 52 |
| Robert Weekes | 25 |

COOPERS FOR THE SEA

| | |
|---|---|
| Edward Gribble | 18 |
| Henry Gribble | 22 |
| Andrew Harewood | 26 |
| Stephen Harwood | 32 |
| Thomas Harwood | 20 |
| Nicholas Knolls | 25 |
| John Lapthorn | 18 |
| Henry Lowse | 20 |
| Richard Luke | 19 |
| Thomas Lynes | 20 |
| Thomas Manfeild | 20 |
| Nicholas Pascho | 26 |
| Edward White | 20 |
| Henry Widgarr | 26 |

SURGEONS AT SEA

| | |
|---|---|
| James Band | 35 |
| Henry Lumlye | 27 |
| Nicholas Towss | 32 |

MARINERS & SAILORS FROM HOME

| | |
|---|---|
| James Bande | 26 |
| James Bennett | 20 |
| Thomas Bennett | 18 |
| John Bradford | 18 |
| William Bradford | 28 |
| John Broker | 27 |
| Roger Browne | 33 |
| John Carter | 28 |
| Peter Caselye | 30 |
| Stephen Chappen | 40 |
| Bartholomew Clinton | 26 |
| Richard Crocker | 32 |
| William Dennys | 18 |
| George Dyer | 20 |
| William Evans | 30 |

| | |
|---|---|
| Richard Follett | 31 |
| Richard Hackerell | 21 |
| Thomas Harwood | 22 |
| Robert Huddy | 24 |
| Lewis Hullett | 22 |
| Richard Hullett | 29 |
| Robert Hullett | 60 |
| Nicholas Jeffery | 38 |
| John Jefferye | 30 |
| John Jefferye | 26 |
| Thomas Jerome | 30 |
| Edward Johnson | 38 |
| William Kinge | 22 |
| Adrian Lacye | 40 |
| John Langworthy | 20 |
| Richard Leprey | 28 |
| Richard Lomer | 27 |
| Robert Narbir | 35 |
| Jaspar Oliver | 20 |
| John Paddon | 35 |
| John Painter | 23 |
| William Roberts jun. | 28 |
| John Rockett | 26 |
| John Ronsevall | 51 |
| William Simons | 35 |
| John Starr | 18 |
| Lawrence Street | 28 |
| Richard Tack | 30 |
| John Thorne | 23 |
| Nicholas Tozer | 19 |
| Jeffery Triggen | 23 |
| Mathew Tucker | 38 |
| William Walker | 23 |
| John Walter | 19 |
| Edward Ward | 22 |
| John Watson | 26 |
| John Waymouth | 35 |
| Thomas Webber | 60 |
| William White | 40 |
| William Winchester | 44 |
| Henry Wood | 24 |
| Robert Wood | 28 |

## Totnes
### [*Tottnes*]
MARINERS & SAILORS
*These are between 25 & 45.*
Thomas Berd

Thomas Bryan
Christopher Casewell
Hugh Commin
Walter English
Walter Fair-child
Thomas Ferrys
Thomas Fursen
Richard Harvy
Leonard Langton
William Littell
Henry Merdo[n]
Richard Mortimer
Timothy Peirce
John Perdu
Daniel Prouse
Peter Stevens
Osmond Taper
Robert Young

BARGEMEN
*These are between 30 & 50.*
Peter Blackaler
Luke Buttler
John Coxeworthy
John Dever
William Eliott
John Manning sen.
John Manning jun.
Thomas Manning
Edward Perrett
Walter Sheerma[n]
Peter Sherman

## Berry Pomeroy
### [*Berrye-pomrye*]
SAILORS

| | |
|---|---|
| Nicholas Cater | 24 |
| George Cawsye | 30 |
| William Commett | 26 |
| John Corindon | 38 |
| John Duport | 30 |
| John Goodridg | 35 |
| John Gregory | 23 |
| Thomas Hind | 36 |
| Peter House | 24 |
| Henry Light | 20 |
| Samuel Shifrick | 26 |
| John Squyre | 21 |
| Thomas Tucker | 30 |

## Dartmouth [*Dart-mouth*] the Shipping

| Names | Tuns | Ages | Ordnance | Absent |
|---|---|---|---|---|
| The | | | | |
| *Frendshipp* | 40 | 12 | 0 | |
| *Pellican* | 28 | 18 | 0 | |
| *Blessinge* | 75 | 16 | 6 | |
| *Guyft* | 45 | 22 | 0 | |
| *Edward Bonaventure* | 70 | 20 | 4 | |
| *John Winchester* | 50 | 24 | 0 | |
| *Edith* | 20 | 6 | 0 | At La Rochelle [*Rochell*] |
| *Johan* | 50 | 8 | 0 | |
| *Little Guift* | 28 | 15 | 0 | At Spain [*Spayne*] |
| *Jonas* | 32 | 10 | 0 | |
| *Richard* | 28 | 4 | 0 | |
| *Hope-well* | 100 | 24 | 4 | |
| *Hand-maid* | 80 | 30 | 2 | |
| *Faulconn* | 50 | 8 | 0 | |
| *Prym-rose* | 35 | 6 | 0 | At [the Atlantic] Islands |
| *Gabriel* | 28 | 6 | 0 | At Portugal [*Portingall*] |
| *Valentine* | 28 | 14 | 0 | |
| *Ann* | 60 | 8 | 5 | |
| *Christopher* | 80 | 24 | 4 | |
| *Prosperous* | 80 | 25 | 6 | |
| *Revenge* | 100 | 16 | 8 | |
| *William* | 24 | 1 | 0 | |
| *Samuel* | 28 | 12 | 0 | |
| *Sillfyne* | 35 | 10 | 0 | |
| *Phenix* | 18 | 15 | 0 | |
| *Maduse* | 15 | 10 | 0 | |
| *Eagle* | 26 | 12 | 0 | At St Malo [*Malloes*] |
| *Unitye* | 54 | 11 | 0 | |
| *John Bonaventure* | 35 | 9 | 0 | |
| *Rebecca* | 45 | 14 | 0 | |
| *Grace of God* | 80 | 11 | 3 | |
| *Holligrove* | 50 | 5 | 3 | |
| *The Mynikinn* | 50 | 30 | 0 | |
| *Little Content* | 20 | 10 | 0 | |
| *John Baptist* | 45 | 40 | 0 | |
| *Hopewell* | 55 | 16 | 2 | |
| *Prym-rose* | 35 | 7 | 0 | In Spain [*Spayne*] |
| *George* | 28 | 18 | 0 | |
| *Diana* | 25 | 12 | 0 | |
| *Content* | 140 | 24 | 2 | |
| *Rose* | 120 | 15 | 8 | |
| *Sweepe-stake* | 56 | 20 | 0 | |
| *Nicholas* | 35 | 6 | 0 | |
| *Marye* | 16 | 17 | 0 | At Southampton |
| *Dove* | 16 | 8 | 0 | At London |
| *Marye* | 25 | 10 | 0 | |
| *Grace* | 50 | 10 | 0 | |

| Names | Tuns | Ages | Ordnance | Absent |
|---|---|---|---|---|
| *George* | 50 | 16 | 0 | |
| *Philip* | 35 | 20 | 0 | |
| *Swyft-sure* | 40 | 40 | 0 | |
| *Katherine* | 15 | 15 | 0 | At St Malo [*St Malloes*] |
| *Hope-well* | 15 | 1 | 0 | At Ireland |
| *Grace of God* | 35 | 9 | 0 | |
| *Jane* | 18 | 7 | 0 | At *Lantrego* |
| *Lawrell* | 20 | 6 | 3 | At [the] West Indies [*India*] |
| *May-flower* | 60 | 40 | 0 | |
| *Comfort* | 35 | 8 | 0 | |

## In the harbour of Dartmouth, the owners of Totnes [*Tottnes*]

| | | | | |
|---|---|---|---|---|
| *Guift* | 150 | 18 | 10 | |
| *Amitye* | 120 | 20 | 12 | |
| *Consent* | 60 | 12 | 2 | |
| *Robert* | 28 | 10 | 0 | San Lúcar [*Lucas*] |
| *Jane* | 15 | 10 | 0 | |

## In Dartmouth, the owners of Dittisham [*Dittesham*]

*The*

| | | | |
|---|---|---|---|
| *Minyon* | 28 | 14 | 0 |
| *Samuel* | 85 | 16 | 6 |
| *Hope* | 60 | 2 | 4 |
| *Marye* | 18 | 6 | 0 |

## Owners of Kingswear [*Kingswere*]

| | | | |
|---|---|---|---|
| *Jonas* | 80 | 10 | 6 |
| *Jonas* | 20 | 12 | 0 |
| *Blessing* | 100 | 9 | 4 |
| *Blessinge* | 35 | 4 | 0 |
| *William* | 14 | 7 | 0 |

## Owners are of Churston Ferrers [*Churston Ferrys*]

| | | | |
|---|---|---|---|
| *Prosperous* | 50 | 6 | 0 |
| *John* | 35 | 7 | 0 |
| *Falcon* | 28 | 9 | 0 |

## Owners are of Torbay [*Tor-baye*]

| | | | |
|---|---|---|---|
| *Ann-mayde* | 85 | 19 | 7 |
| *Supplye* | 50 | 15 | 0 |
| *John* | 45 | 12 | 0 |
| *Grace* | 45 | 10 | 0 |
| *Peter* | 50 | 13 | 2 |
| *Returne* | 50 | 9 | 2 |
| *True-love* | 24 | 6 | 0 |
| *Talent* | 15 | 10 | 0 |
| *Providence* | 70 | 1 | [blank] |

## Brixham

### [Brix-ham]

| | Age |
|---|---|
| **MARINERS** | |
| John Ellyott | 40 |
| Richard Griggs | 40 |
| John Hullett | 30 |
| Edward Mychelmore | 60 |
| Lewis Scrivener | 33 |
| Robert Wallys | 32 |
| Davye Wooddy | 45 |
| **SAILORS** | |
| John Abraham | 50 |
| John Augar | 27 |
| Nicholas Bickford | 20 |
| Gilbert Blackaler | 27 |
| John Blackaler | 20 |
| Nicholas Blackaler | 46 |
| Pascho Blackaler | 29 |
| Peter Blackaler sen. | 20 |
| Thomas Bockaram | 40 |
| Francis Brimble | 20 |
| Nicholas Brimble | 20 |
| Peter Burgess | 23 |
| John Burnerd | 30 |
| William Burridg | 26 |
| Peter Came | 23 |
| Rennel Churchyard | 30 |
| William Church-ward | 25 |
| Peter Clarke | 36 |
| George Coite | 52 |
| William Coite | 20 |
| William Cole | 28 |
| John Colton | 50 |
| Azarias Condett | 30 |
| John Condett | 30 |
| Vincent Condett | 24 |
| Henry Corne | 36 |
| Thomas Coyde | 20 |
| John Coyte | 25 |
| George Crocker | 26 |
| Thomas Crocker | 37 |
| Nicholas Crout | 20 |
| Peter Crout | 22 |
| John Cruse | 26 |
| Leonard Cruse | 22 |
| Richard Cruse | 20 |
| Andrew Earne | 30 |
| John Evanns | 25 |

| | |
|---|---|
| Richard Field jun. | 18 |
| Richard Fielde | 34 |
| John Fillye | 36 |
| Walter Finmoore | 30 |
| John Gale | 20 |
| James Galmton | 30 |
| Richard Galmton | 36 |
| Richard Galmton | 18 |
| Thomas Galmton | 40 |
| John Garner | 40 |
| John Garratt | 20 |
| John Garratt | 46 |
| Nicholas Garratt | 24 |
| Francis Gillard | 16 |
| George Gillard jun. | 22 |
| Thomas Glover | 30 |
| William Glover | 31 |
| Thomas Godemm | 18 |
| John Gray | 40 |
| Richard Griggs | 18 |
| Peter Hammett | 36 |
| Andrew Hanniferr | 40 |
| Nicholas Hannifer | 19 |
| John Harrys | 28 |
| Peter Hayman | 24 |
| John Jane | 20 |
| Robert Janes | 18 |
| Thomas Kellye | 26 |
| John Lamb-sedd | 34 |
| John Lamb-sedd | 22 |
| Philip Lemm | 34 |
| John Lewys | 50 |
| Thomas Lewys | 18 |
| Peter Lockram | 20 |
| Andrew Luscomb jun. | 23 |
| John Luscomb | 20 |
| William Luscomb | 16 |
| Edward Maddock | 40 |
| Lewis Maddock | 20 |
| John Maye | 36 |
| Michael Moore | 31 |
| Nicholas Morris | 20 |
| William Mugd | 20 |
| John Nicholls | 28 |
| John Nowell | 36 |
| Philip Nowell | 45 |
| John Peepe | 34 |
| Robert Periman | 26 |
| Bartholomew Peter | 24 |
| William Peter | 20 |

| | | | | |
|---|---|---|---|---|
| Nicholas Pettegue | 19 | Roger Crocker | 60 |
| William Philp | 20 | William Cuntryman | 57 |
| John Pomroye | 27 | Thomas Hardye | 36 |
| Peter Pomroye | 20 | George Herniman | 60 |
| William Potter | 40 | Henry Herniman | 20 |
| John Price | 24 | John Herniman | 16 |
| Thomas Quynt | 26 | George Norrocot | 40 |
| Thomas Raddon sen. | 60 | Thomas Romett | 50 |
| Thomas Raddon jun. | 20 | Vincent Sherwel | 40 |
| Richard Randall | 33 | Humphrey Stevens | 40 |
| Edward Reave | 20 | William Tapley | 60 |
| Richard Rewe | 30 | | |
| Andrew Romatt | 40 | | |
| William Scrivener | 18 | | |
| Richard Seaton | 24 | | |
| William Shemmer | 40 | | |
| Henry Shettoch | 46 | | |
| John Skeine | 30 | | |
| Bartholomew Skinner | 33 | | |
| Thomas Skinner | 30 | | |
| Peter Sterte | 30 | | |
| John Stanning | 40 | | |
| John Stone | 30 | | |
| Arthur Stramer | 20 | | |
| Clement Street | 34 | | |
| Barnard Strow | 32 | | |
| Thomas Sweet jun. | 20 | | |
| Richard Tapley | 24 | | |
| Lewis Taylour | 25 | | |
| Nicholas Terrow | 30 | | |
| William Toak | 18 | | |
| Richard Trout | 18 | | |
| Francis Tryumph | 44 | | |
| Edward Vittery | 20 | | |
| John Vitterye | 26 | | |
| Robert Wallys | 32 | | |
| Peter Wheato[n] | 30 | | |
| Robert White | 16 | | |
| Lewis White-hed | 36 | | |
| Thomas Wills | 30 | | |
| John Wyatt | 20 | | |
| Richard Wyatt | 15 | | |
| William Wyatt | 24 | | |
| Hugh Yabb | 60 | | |
| Allen Yarne | 26 | | |
| Peter Yoldonn | 50 | | |
| William Yoldonn | 30 | | |

FISHERMEN

| | |
|---|---|
| Daniel Coyde | 60 |

## Kingswear
### [*Kings-weare*]

MARINERS

| | |
|---|---|
| John Filly | 60 |
| John Garland | 50 |
| Robert Hammett | 26 |
| William Hammett | 26 |
| Edward Hardy | 50 |
| Michael Hawlye | 30 |
| John Hichins jun. | 45 |
| George Madriga[n] | 58 |
| John Melburye | 35 |
| Peter Payne | 30 |
| William Philpe | 50 |
| James Trewoorgy | 30 |

SAILORS

| | |
|---|---|
| William Anger | 30 |
| William Babbedg | 27 |
| John Bannell | 35 |
| Arthur Baylye | 30 |
| Nicholas Blackaler | 30 |
| John Bortemm | 45 |
| Thomas Bortynn | 45 |
| Richard Bowhay | 18 |
| John Cheblye | 23 |
| Thomas Chickey | 20 |
| Walter Churchward | 18 |
| Edward Clarke | 19 |
| Robert Clyff | 36 |
| Nicholas Cooke | 50 |
| Philip Crocker | 18 |
| William Crowberd | 30 |
| William Cully | 17 |
| Simon Cumberland | 30 |
| Alexander Dorchester | 35 |
| John Earle | 40 |

**Kingswear cont'd**

| | |
|---|---|
| John Efford | 22 |
| Peter Ellyot sen. | 45 |
| Peter Ellyot jun. | 19 |
| William Ellyott | 17 |
| Robert Evans | 22 |
| John Follett | 30 |
| Edward Foord | 20 |
| John Fovett | 40 |
| Anthony Foxe | 30 |
| Gregory French | 26 |
| Robert French | 18 |
| Peter Gawden | 23 |
| William Gee | 76 |
| Mark Glory | 40 |
| William Griffin | 40 |
| Gilbert Grove | 35 |
| Alexander Hammett | 19 |
| Stephen Hammett | 17 |
| John Hardye | 20 |
| Thomas Hayman | 22 |
| John Hitchins sen. | 50 |
| Charles Hutchins | 18 |
| Alexander Lambert | 30 |
| George Lane | 20 |
| Jeffery Langford | 35 |
| John Little-John | 24 |
| William Little-John | 26 |
| John Maddick | 23 |
| Thomas Mallerye | 26 |
| Bennett Manlye | 18 |
| Roger Manlye | 16 |
| Stephen Morrys | 35 |
| John Oates | 25 |
| William Oliver | 20 |
| Andrew Perry | 60 |
| William Philp | 30 |
| John Philpe | 16 |
| William Row | 55 |
| Henry Rowe | 28 |
| Mr Alexander Shaply | 44 |
| Alexander Shaplye jun. | 17 |
| David Stanning | 26 |
| Josias Stevens | 25 |
| George Summers | 18 |
| Lewis Tellman | 25 |
| William Thomas | 50 |
| Henry Trewant | 38 |
| John Tucker | 20 |
| John Vitterye | 60 |

| | |
|---|---|
| Bartholomew Voysey | 22 |
| Gregory Vryn | 28 |
| Humphrey Watkins | 24 |
| Richard Webber | 30 |
| Alexander Wills | 35 |
| John Woollytonn | 26 |

SHIPWRIGHTS

| | |
|---|---|
| Robert Crowbeard | 40 |
| William Head-ache | 30 |
| Robert Hooper | 40 |
| James Horswell | 30 |
| George Smith | 20 |

SURGEON

| | |
|---|---|
| John Briggs | 55 |

# Churston Ferrers
## [*Churstone*]

MARINERS

| | |
|---|---|
| John Boyen | 55 |
| John Catton | 40 |
| Edward Hardy | 50 |
| Walter Lambshed | 40 |

SAILORS

| | |
|---|---|
| Robert Band | 45 |
| William Cardy | 50 |
| Henry Cardye | 20 |
| John Cardye | 30 |
| Richard Cardye | 18 |
| William Chard | 20 |
| John Churchyett | 30 |
| William Clarke | 20 |
| Gilbert Clawter | 40 |
| John Clawter | 30 |
| John Clowter | 30 |
| Peter Clowton | 50 |
| Peter Dyer | 30 |
| Richard Farewell | 20 |
| John Ferrys | 20 |
| Walter Garner | 18 |
| Andrew Gotobedd | 51 |
| James Haynes | 40 |
| William Hayward | 30 |
| Walter Hunt | 24 |
| Jeffery Langdon | 41 |
| Emanuel Lawrence | 40 |
| Henry Lewys | 20 |
| Nicholas Lewys | 24 |

| | |
|---|---|
| John Martin | 40 |
| Hugh Mayne | 40 |
| John Moore | 40 |
| Gregory Nosworthy | 25 |
| Edward Owen | 30 |
| James Pett | 27 |
| John Reynolds | 20 |
| Humphry Sheare | 16 |
| Henry Skyrdon | 20 |
| Richard Skyrdon | 25 |
| George Stankha[m] | 30 |
| Richard Stankham | 20 |
| Robert Stone | 42 |
| Christopher Torr | 25 |
| Peter Wells | 15 |
| Henry Wise | 25 |

FISHERMEN

| | |
|---|---|
| William Church-ward | 71 |
| William Cornish | 60 |
| Nicholas Lewys | 50 |

## Paignton

[*Paynton, Painton*]

MARINERS

| | |
|---|---|
| John Berrye | 33 |
| John Deane | 33 |
| Ellis Drew | 30 |
| John Drew | 62 |
| Thomas Lymbry | 40 |
| Robert Mediar | 30 |
| William Neck | 57 |
| Andrew Sexton | 34 |
| William Smyth | 54 |
| Thomas Tobow | 53 |
| Thomas Trend | 40 |
| James Tucker | 45 |
| William Young | 57 |

SAILORS

| | |
|---|---|
| Edward Adams | 34 |
| William Adams | 40 |
| William Adams | 30 |
| William Adams | 33 |
| John Austinn | 20 |
| Christopher Averye | 30 |
| Hugh Baker | 30 |
| Richard Barons | 28 |
| William Barons | 32 |
| Peter Bartley | 26 |
| Warren Bickford | 30 |
| Thomas Blackaler | 22 |
| John Burgyn | 23 |
| John Butland | 30 |
| Robert Butlande | 23 |
| Thomas Buttland | 30 |
| Allen Cole | 24 |
| Edward Cole | 30 |
| William Collier | 24 |
| John Cumming | 34 |
| John Curtesse | 20 |
| Henry Downing | 34 |
| Henry Dunnett | 30 |
| John Durborn | 26 |
| Joseph Durborn | 40 |
| Simon Dyer | 38 |
| Thomas Eales | 30 |
| Adam Furnis | 23 |
| Robert Furnis | 26 |
| Edward Goodridg | 50 |
| William Green | 24 |
| George Gregory | 26 |
| Nicholas Hole | 30 |
| John Horwell | 30 |
| Thomas Jeffery | 32 |
| John Lakely | 35 |
| John Lane sen. | 52 |
| John Lane jun. | 23 |
| John Lange | 28 |
| Robert Langery | 30 |
| John Lawrence | 32 |
| John Maurice | 26 |
| Richard Maye | 26 |
| John Mountayn | 34 |
| John Moysey | 19 |
| John Mudge | 24 |
| Mathew Norrys | 23 |
| Simon Norrys | 30 |
| Richard Orrick | 30 |
| William Pope | 24 |
| Rogert [sic] Poynt | 40 |
| William Quyvier | 32 |
| Walter Radford | 27 |
| Hugh Rider | 31 |
| John Rider | 36 |
| William Rogers | 36 |
| Thomas Rundell | 31 |
| John Saye | 31 |
| William Smyth | 28 |
| Philip Sparke | 23 |

**Paignton cont'd**

| | |
|---|---|
| Thomas Staddonn | 32 |
| John Studdon | 33 |
| Thomas Tobow jun. | 22 |
| Nicholas Torr | 23 |
| Henry Tudd | 42 |
| William Turprin | 38 |
| Peter Webber | 24 |
| Thomas Webber | 24 |
| Martin Young | 22 |
| Richard Young | 27 |
| John Younge | 30 |

FISHERMEN

| | |
|---|---|
| John Cock | 60 |
| Simon Durburn | 45 |
| Robert Gregory | 40 |
| Thomas Martin | 38 |
| Thomas Miller | 30 |
| John Molton | 53 |
| John Pass | 30 |
| Robert Rider | 46 |
| Thomas Smith | 40 |
| John Smyth | 32 |
| Charles Tapley | 50 |
| Richard Thorne | 49 |
| Richard Tomlynn | 40 |
| Richard Webber | 62 |

SHIPWRIGHTS

| | |
|---|---|
| John Langaller | 34 |
| Richard Langaller | 38 |

## Marldon
### [*Mareldonn*]

MARINERS          [ages not given]

Thomas Drewe
Edmond Graye
George Luscomb
Toby Pomerye
Titus Taplye
Henry Wallys
Nicholas Wallys

SAILORS

George Abram
John Abram
Thomas Bickha[m]
John Clyff
John Courtes

Thomas Cullyn
Thomas Cutter
Christopher Daws
Christopher Drew
Barnard Hole
John Lundye
Richard Miller
John Mounts
John Osborne
Odes Peter
William Peter
Richard Rade
George Randall
Richard Rave
Roger Satterlye
George Snell
Alexander Stephe[n]
Richard Tobow
William Tremells
Edward Tuckma[n]
Thomas Wallys
John Windsor

## St Marychurch
### [*St Marye-Church*]

MARINERS & SAILORS

| | |
|---|---|
| George Adams | 32 |
| John Aleword jun. | 20 |
| John Allward | 50 |
| William Allward | 60 |
| John Baker | 35 |
| John Bardar | 36 |
| Mathew Bardens | 50 |
| George Baron | 20 |
| Steven Barren | 25 |
| John Bartar | 18 |
| Michael Bartar | 45 |
| Michael Bartar | 20 |
| Thomas Bartar | 40 |
| William Bartar | 40 |
| William Bartar | 20 |
| John Barter | 28 |
| William Barter | 40 |
| John Basse | 24 |
| John Beard | 18 |
| Richard Bearde | 40 |
| Peter Bennett | 30 |
| Philip Bennett | 43 |

| | | | |
|---|---|---|---|
| Gregory Bickford | 32 | Michael Goodridg | 44 |
| Robert Blanke | 35 | William Goorde | 20 |
| Gabriel Braddon | 30 | John Gowrde | 60 |
| John Brooken | 55 | Humphrey Grewer | 30 |
| Steven Brown | 20 | Peter Haywood | 40 |
| John Browne | 51 | William Hollye | 30 |
| Oliver Browne | 24 | Edward Hore | 40 |
| Thomas Bullye | 40 | Philip Hore | 45 |
| William Burgen | 35 | John Hunnye | 20 |
| John Burring | 60 | William Hunnye | 50 |
| Edward Callye | 24 | John Huswaye | 44 |
| Thomas Card | 20 | William Huswife | 40 |
| Stephen Carell | 30 | Christopher Leaman | 32 |
| Christopher Carrell | 23 | Michael Leaman | 33 |
| John Carrell | 20 | Richard Luxe | 35 |
| William Carrell | 20 | John Mansell | 32 |
| William Cater | 32 | Sander Marrodd | 30 |
| John Cattlefoord | 35 | John Marshall | 60 |
| John Chapter | 22 | Peter Marshall | 24 |
| Bartholomew Cleffe | 40 | William Marshwell | 60 |
| Anthony Codner | 30 | William Marshwell jun. | 30 |
| Christopher Codner | 22 | John Martinn | 36 |
| William Codner | 20 | Richard Moone | 20 |
| George Colcott | 20 | Peter Newcomb | 40 |
| John Cole | 40 | Anthony Parker | 25 |
| William Cole | 30 | William Peatell | 34 |
| Richard Coll | 60 | William Peatell | 30 |
| Richard Coll | 20 | John Pettman | 55 |
| Richard Cook | 40 | William Pettman | 20 |
| Bartholomew Cooke | 45 | John Philpe | 25 |
| William Cooke | 35 | Richard Pitt | 24 |
| John Cookerey | 30 | William Pitt | 60 |
| Thomas Cooper | 30 | John Rider | 30 |
| Robert Corde | 40 | Robert Row | 20 |
| John Courtess | 22 | Gregory Rowe | 18 |
| James Curtys | 35 | John Rowe | 25 |
| Edward Cuttiford | 40 | John Rowe | 50 |
| John Cuttiford | 50 | John Sanders | 50 |
| Stephen Cuttiford | 23 | William Scapter | 35 |
| Thomas Cuttiford | 60 | William Searle | 25 |
| Edward Davye | 30 | William Streamer | 20 |
| John Davye | 30 | John Tapley | 30 |
| John Downinge | 20 | Humphrey Taylor | 20 |
| Christopher Drew | 20 | Michael Taylor | 18 |
| Thomas Drew | 20 | William Taylor | 45 |
| John Euill | 40 | John Taylour | 25 |
| Thomas Exton | 50 | William Taylour | 24 |
| Edward Foxe | 40 | Richard Trype | 50 |
| William Garver | 30 | Christopher Tucker | 40 |
| Robert Good | 19 | John Vitterye | 35 |

**St Marychurch cont'd**

| | |
|---|---|
| Andrew Waymouth | 22 |
| Anthony Waymouth | 20 |
| Christopher Waymouth | 25 |
| Christopher Waymouth | 30 |
| Digory Waymouth | 32 |
| George Waymouth | 18 |
| Richard Waymouth | 60 |
| Richard Waymouth | 35 |
| Robert Waymouth | 30 |
| Robert Waymouth | 30 |
| William Waymouth | 60 |
| William Waymouth | 35 |
| William Waymouth | 34 |
| William Waymouth | 28 |
| John Webber | 22 |
| Robert Webber | 33 |
| Stephen White | 50 |
| Leonard Widdico[m]b | 30 |
| Thomas William | 40 |
| John Witch-hals | 71 |
| John Woolcott | 30 |
| Richard Woolcott | 25 |

## Kingskerswell
### [*Kgs Kerswell*]
MARINERS & SAILORS

| | |
|---|---|
| John Ball | 24 |
| Richard Ball | 24 |
| Thomas Bartar | 18 |
| Walter Bartar | 30 |
| Nicholas Beard | 54 |
| John Bickford | 50 |
| Thomas Braunde | 22 |
| William Clamaford | 50 |
| William Clamaford jun. | 15 |
| Gilbert Cobble | 26 |
| John Coble | 23 |
| Jaspar Codner | 18 |
| John Codner | 22 |
| John Codner | 24 |
| Thomas Codner | 23 |
| William Codner | 18 |
| John Cole | 30 |
| Philip Cole | 21 |
| Edward Crockwell | 30 |
| Christopher Cross | 32 |
| John Drew | 20 |

| | |
|---|---|
| Nicholas Drew | 24 |
| Christopher Glanfeild | 26 |
| John Glanfeild | 28 |
| Silvester Hext | 34 |
| Michael Ladimore | 30 |
| Richard Lamball | 28 |
| Richard Longe | 28 |
| Robert Miller | 26 |
| Roger Miller | 30 |
| Philip Mudge | 20 |
| Nicholas Oxenham | 22 |
| Warren Paule | 22 |
| John Philipp | 20 |
| Richard Philipp | 24 |
| Simon Rodd | 58 |
| Gregory Sampson | 22 |
| Jaspar Sampson | 35 |
| John Satterly | 30 |
| John Saxton | 34 |
| Nicholas Sheere | 25 |
| William Sheere | 23 |
| Robert Taplye | 18 |
| James Underhay | 30 |
| Henry Weare | 40 |
| Anthony Wills | 35 |
| Bartholomew Wills | 20 |
| John Wills | 26 |
| Philip Wills | 24 |
| Roger Wills | 38 |
| John Wincott | 30 |
| William Wood | 26 |
| David Yoe | 22 |
| George Yoe | 50 |
| Thomas Yoe | 20 |

## Tormohun
### [*Tormo-ham*]
MARINERS & SAILORS

| | |
|---|---|
| Bartholomew Bartar | 45 |
| James Bartar | 20 |
| William Bartar | 50 |
| Oliver Blackston | 40 |
| Thomas Bomery | 22 |
| Robert Bomerye | 16 |
| Valentine Bomry | 18 |
| John Burrin | 30 |
| Thomas Caddy | 22 |
| John Cock | 30 |

| | |
|---|---|
| John Cocke | 50 |
| William Colcott | 35 |
| Robert Courtys | 20 |
| William Courtys | 35 |
| George Cross | 35 |
| John Drew | 30 |
| William Dyar | 30 |
| Michael Follett | 40 |
| William Follett | 34 |
| William Follett [sic] | 34 |
| Peter Gabreck | 45 |
| Roger Game | 18 |
| William Gotobedd | 18 |
| Anthony Gowrd | 50 |
| Robert Gowrd sen. | 55 |
| Robert Gowrd jun. | 35 |
| John Hinxton | 18 |
| Samuel Hinxton | 24 |
| John Hore | 18 |
| John Horne | 30 |
| Thomas Lance | 40 |
| John Lange | 30 |
| William Lange | 30 |
| John Leach | 25 |
| Robert Leach | 22 |
| William Leach | 35 |
| Robert Lock | 22 |
| Thomas Manfeild | 28 |
| Jeffery Milbury | 23 |
| Balthasar Molagan | 45 |
| John Neck | 35 |
| George Osborne | 18 |
| Henry Peaze | 30 |
| William Pittman | 22 |
| Michael Row | 25 |
| William Row | 50 |
| John Satterly | 35 |
| Samuel Satterly | 22 |
| Gregory Sevye | 20 |
| Richard Sevye | 16 |
| William Tapley | 24 |
| George Teasye | 22 |
| Bennet Trent | 45 |
| Roger Tucker | 42 |
| William Vittery | 18 |
| Thomas Waymouth | 25 |
| Nicholas Webber | 26 |
| Vncy Weekes | 25 |
| Christopher White | 18 |

| | |
|---|---|
| Christopher White [sic] | 18 |

## Cockington
MARINERS & SAILORS

| | |
|---|---|
| Walter Adams | 42 |
| Nicholas Agarye | 28 |
| Henry Aydie | 40 |
| William Baker | 28 |
| John Ball | 40 |
| Thomas Ball | 38 |
| Will Ball | 38 |
| Bonadventur Barns | 30 |
| Humphrey Barns | 31 |
| John Barons | 35 |
| John Bartone | 23 |
| George Bennett | 41 |
| Henry Bennett | 30 |
| Richard Bess | 30 |
| Walter Bess | 31 |
| Robert Bownd | 39 |
| George Brown | 22 |
| William Browne | 35 |
| Hugh Butcher | 29 |
| Thomas Butcher | 31 |
| William Callinge | 49 |
| John Churchward | 26 |
| George Cooke | 38 |
| John Cross | 30 |
| Richard Cross | 60 |
| Zachary Cullen | 59 |
| Philip Cumming | 29 |
| John Ditch | 25 |
| Richard Follett | 40 |
| William Follett | 30 |
| Richard Hodg | 61 |
| Ellis Jefferye | 48 |
| John Keyman | 40 |
| Samuel Kinge | 29 |
| George Knight | 42 |
| Richard Lander | 30 |
| Edward Legar | 30 |
| Thomas Love | 40 |
| Barnard Osburn | 31 |
| John Pass | 44 |
| Robert Peatrell | 61 |
| George Peter | 31 |
| James Peter | 61 |
| Jarvys Philpe | 30 |

**Cockington cont'd**

| | |
|---|---|
| John Prize | 42 |
| Richard Sampson | 39 |
| Robert Searl | 22 |
| Robert Searle | 24 |
| William Simons | 60 |
| William Smith | 25 |
| Robye Squarr | 30 |
| Henry Stone | 29 |
| Toby Sullinge | 25 |
| Odes Tapley | 60 |
| George Way | 20 |
| George White | 30 |
| Andrew Windsor | 27 |
| Thomas Ylls | 20 |
| Ellis Young | 32 |

## Coffinswell

### [*Coffins-well*]

MARINERS & SAILORS

| | |
|---|---|
| William Baker | 20 |
| John Bennett | 35 |
| George Bickfoord | 30 |
| Daniel Bickford | 32 |
| Michael Bickford | 32 |
| Jaspar Bobis | 25 |
| John Boord | 30 |
| Richard Carell | 23 |
| Nathaniel Chaplinn | 25 |
| Richard Ellyott | 18 |
| Richard Ferrise | 35 |
| Henry Goodman | 35 |
| Richard Goodman | 30 |
| Roger Goodman | 21 |
| Emanuel Goodridg | 21 |
| William Harris | 35 |
| John Haywood | 16 |
| John Haywood | 20 |
| Michael Haywood | 23 |
| Richard Haywood | 20 |
| Richard Haywood | 30 |
| Roger Haywood | 18 |
| Thomas Haywood | 25 |
| William Haywood | 32 |
| Walter Lange | 35 |
| Walter Lange | 31 |
| Robert Lewys | 25 |
| Roger May | 39 |

| | |
|---|---|
| Thomas Michell | 36 |
| William Miller | 18 |
| Richard Mudg | 17 |
| John Mudge | 18 |
| William Nills | 30 |
| Hugh Philip | 28 |
| Jarvys Sampson | 30 |
| Michael Sampson | 25 |
| William Sheere | 22 |
| John Tapley | 23 |
| Rich Tapley | 21 |
| John Wooton | 31 |
| William Yabsley | 40 |

## Newton Abbot

### [*Newtonn Abbott*]

MARINERS & SAILORS

| | |
|---|---|
| Christopher Archer | 30 |
| Richard Archer | 42 |
| William Ash | 40 |
| Hugh Babb | 46 |
| Philip Barrye | 27 |
| Richard Beaumo[nt] | 24 |
| John Boles | 42 |
| John Bowden | 40 |
| Thomas Brese | 24 |
| John Chapter | 31 |
| John Combe | 50 |
| Anthony Couse | 35 |
| John Easton | 18 |
| Thomas Finson | 46 |
| John Foorde | 23 |
| Roger Gotham | 50 |
| Philip Harris | 20 |
| Samuel Harris | 23 |
| John Hayman | 30 |
| John Hell-more | 20 |
| William Hutchins | 34 |
| James Lambshed | 44 |
| George Langaller | 38 |
| John Lange | 46 |
| Moses Logg | 18 |
| James Mann | 16 |
| Mathew Mann | 42 |
| Thomas Moses | 20 |
| Gilbert Nichols | 20 |
| William Oxenham | 41 |
| Peter Pake | 31 |

| | | | |
|---|---|---|---|
| Philip Paul | 22 | Richard Ball | 26 |
| Richard Rew | 38 | John Beare | 47 |
| Martin Snow | 46 | John Bickford | 26 |
| Henry Tillar | 18 | John Blaxton | 44 |
| Robert Wallys | 35 | Simon Bright | 35 |
| Richard Webber | 28 | John Graye | 52 |
| John Weygar | 30 | Lawrence Hutchin | 46 |
| Robert Whiting | 16 | George May | 19 |
| | | William Wright | 24 |

## Abbotskerswell
### [*Abbotts Kerswell*]
MARINERS & SAILORS
Robert Averye                    20

## Shipping of Cockington

| Names | Tons | Ages | Ordnance |
|---|---|---|---|
| The | | | |
| *Handmayd* | 80 | [blank] | [blank] |
| *John* | 40 | do | do |
| *Supplye* | 40 | do | do |
| *Returne* | 60 | do | do |
| *Providence* | 70 | do | do |
| *Grace* | 40 | do | do |

## Tormohun

| | | | |
|---|---|---|---|
| Two ships of | 30 [tons] | do | do |

## Staverton
### [*Stavertonn*]

| | Age |
|---|---|
| MARINERS & SAILORS | |
| Eustice Cobell | 24 |
| John Narwood | 22 |
| John Pack | 23 |
| Thomas Wager | 34 |

## Woodland
MARINERS & SAILORS

| | |
|---|---|
| Francis Tucker | 30 |
| Roger Tucker | 35 |
| William Tucker | 20 |

## Torbryan
### [*Torrbryan*]
MARINERS & SAILORS

| | |
|---|---|
| Andrew Barkwell | 24 |
| William Foord | 26 |
| John Heale | 40 |
| Thomas Reynell | 30 |

## Ipplepen
### [*Ipplepenn*]
MARINERS & SAILORS [ages not given]

Nicholas Bartar
Jeffery Bartor
John Butt

## Ipplepen cont'd
John Damerell
Peter Evans
Richard Foorde
Richard Peeter
Robert Peter
Richard Philipps
Richard Pope
Andrew Preston
Philip Searle
Richard Smardon
Robert Wilston

## Littlehempston
### [*Little-hempston*]
MARINERS & SAILORS
| | |
|---|---|
| Lawrence Foster | 34 |
| John Frost | 30 |
| Edward Smyth | 36 |

## Broadhempston
### [*Broadhemston*]
MARINERS & SAILORS
| | |
|---|---|
| Samuel Burring | 30 |
| Nicholas Cole | 31 |
| Richard Kennicott | 24 |
| William Longe | 40 |
| James Lowman | 30 |

## Kingsteignton
### [*Kings-taynton*]
MARINERS & SAILORS
| | |
|---|---|
| John Alforde | 28 |
| Arthur Avent | 30 |
| Philip Bedlake | 50 |
| Robert Blackford | 33 |
| Roger Collyn | 22 |
| Christopher Crowt | 45 |
| John Goddart | 35 |
| Richard Keymann | 45 |
| Richard Martin | 36 |
| Michael Morrye | 18 |
| Abram Mudg | 26 |
| Anthony Mudg | 40 |
| Anthony Norrocott | 20 |

| | |
|---|---|
| Henry Rowe | 35 |
| William Swanson | 26 |
| Gilbert Underhill | 28 |
| Martin Vinninge | 25 |

## Bishopsteignton
### [*Byshops Taynton*]
MARINERS & SAILORS
| | |
|---|---|
| Gregory Babb | 32 |
| Robert Babb | 30 |
| Thomas Babb | 25 |
| Francis Cumminge | 30 |
| Richard Hambridg | 24 |
| Nicholas Leake | 25 |
| Nicholas Paddon | 20 |
| Simon Painter | 22 |
| John Rodes | 45 |
| William Simons | 28 |

## West Teignmouth
### [*West-tingmouth*]
MASTERS & MASTERS' MATES & MARINERS
| | |
|---|---|
| Ewen Bickford | 46 |
| James Blaxton | 50 |
| Peter Blaxton | 54 |
| John Boddye | 45 |
| John Bonfeild | 60 |
| Anthony Braddon | 50 |
| Edward Codner | 34 |
| William Cumming | 50 |
| Gilbert Downing | 45 |
| Mathew Foxe | 35 |
| Roger Langford | 40 |
| John Starr | 34 |

SAILORS
| | |
|---|---|
| John Allwill | 35 |
| Benjamin Beard | 32 |
| William Benfield | 30 |
| James Blaxton | 50 |
| John Boddye | 45 |
| John Bonfeild jun. | 20 |
| Martin Boswhiddon | 40 |
| Oliver Bradford | 30 |
| Thomas Brickills | 25 |
| Richard Chilston | 30 |
| John Clarke | 26 |

| | |
|---|---|
| Thomas Clarke | 30 |
| William Clogg | 42 |
| Henry Cominge | 20 |
| William Crockwell | 30 |
| George Crowte | 31 |
| Thomas Cumminge | 57 |
| John Cuttiford | 44 |
| Richard Duringe | 31 |
| John East | 25 |
| Richard Eaton | 24 |
| John Ellwill | 25 |
| Thomas Est-cott | 22 |
| James Estcott | 34 |
| Raymond Finson | 22 |
| Robert Fishmoore | 24 |
| William Furlande | 32 |
| William Gamon | 50 |
| Thomas Gant | 55 |
| Thomas Gant | 55 |
| George Gatratt | 40 |
| John Gaunt | 20 |
| John Gey | 60 |
| William Gibb | 30 |
| John Goss | 40 |
| Richard Goss | 21 |
| Thomas Goss | 50 |
| Roger Grynfeild | 20 |
| Paul Hawkin | 20 |
| John Hill | 40 |
| George Hollock | 30 |
| Richard Knighton | 20 |
| Gregory Langford | 24 |
| William Langly | 41 |
| Stephen Light-foot | 24 |
| Peter Light-foote | 60 |
| Henry Lovett | 29 |
| Peter Martin | 40 |
| Thomas Marvell | 35 |
| Richard Moore | 32 |
| Richard Odlye | 50 |
| Richard Palmer | 20 |
| Thomas Palmer | 22 |
| Henry Pearne | 25 |
| John Pearne | 50 |
| Thomas Poole | 40 |
| John Sibly | 31 |
| William Simons | 20 |
| Richard Smyth | 50 |
| Richard Smyth | 50 |

| | |
|---|---|
| Ewyn Sparke | 40 |
| Samuel Tapley | 20 |
| William Tapley | 50 |
| William Tapley | 50 |
| Richard Tozer | 40 |
| William Tozer | 30 |
| John Wader | 30 |

SHIPWRIGHTS
| | |
|---|---|
| Peter Martin jun. | 31 |
| Andrew Stocker | 41 |
| Henry Stocker | 30 |

# East Teignmouth
## [*East-tingmouth*]

MARINERS
| | |
|---|---|
| William Drew | 40 |
| Nicholas Waymouth | 50 |

SAILORS
| | |
|---|---|
| Ellis Beawarde | 30 |
| Edward Belford | 48 |
| Penticost Beniett | 31 |
| Anthony Braddon | 35 |
| William Cater | 24 |
| William Cock | 41 |
| Humphrey Combe | 20 |
| Walter During | 40 |
| William Ferrys | 40 |
| Peter Filsome | 31 |
| John Gammon | 24 |
| John Hale | 30 |
| Richard Hayett | 40 |
| John Hooper | 32 |
| Philip Kyrtonn | 30 |
| John Lucye | 29 |
| Henry Martin | 31 |
| Bartholomew Michell | 30 |
| William Michell | 55 |
| William Mitchell | 40 |
| John Salke | 29 |
| Richard Shapley | 41 |
| Thomas Shapley | 29 |
| Andrew Thacher | 50 |
| Richard Welkin | 45 |

## West Teignmouth [*West-tingmouth*] Shipping

| Their owners | Names The | Tons | Ages | Ordnance | Voyage |
|---|---|---|---|---|---|
| John Gayt [and] Thomas Braddon | *Jesus* | 80 | 12 | 0 | For New-foundland |
| John Gayre [and] Thomas Braddon | *John* | 30 | 4 | 0 | do |
| William Clogg, John Milberry [and] William Towill | *Vineyard* | 60 | 12 | 0 | do |
| William Clogg [and] John Beardon | *Talent* | 50 | 1 | 0 | do |
| John Smyth | *Richarde* | 12 | 4 | 0 | At home |
| Thomas Bricknoll | *Elizabeth* | 8 | 5 | 0 | do |
| William Taplye | *Marye* | 7 | 3 | 0 | do |

### Dawlish

| | Age |
|---|---|
| MASTERS & MARINERS | |
| John Gibb | 31 |
| Robert Gortlett | 32 |
| Richard Haydon | 42 |
| John Helly | 60 |
| Robert Keyme | 61 |
| Robert Lange | 42 |
| John Murrye | 45 |
| John Perrye | 31 |
| William Scutt | 30 |
| Richard Sullack | 26 |
| Christopher Tapley | 30 |
| John Tapley | 31 |
| Valentine Tozer | 31 |
| John Tutt | 30 |
| John Waymouth | 42 |
| | |
| SAILORS | |
| Thomas Allford | 40 |
| Gawyn Babb | 18 |
| John Babb | 20 |
| John Babb jun. | 26 |
| Richard Babb | 23 |
| William Babb | 42 |
| Edward Ball | 30 |
| Gawyne Barrye | 23 |
| Thomas Barrye | 22 |
| John Bennett | 22 |
| William Bickham | 40 |
| William Bonde | 40 |
| Thomas Branscomb | 30 |
| Edward Branscombe | 41 |
| Christopher Bricknoll | 34 |

| | |
|---|---|
| John Bricknoll | 22 |
| Robert Bricknoll | 33 |
| Robert Bricknoll | 33 |
| Richard Bright | 30 |
| John Burrington | 41 |
| Jaspar Byshop | 25 |
| Richard Clapp | 23 |
| John Clarke | 21 |
| Roger Cock | 18 |
| John Cocke | 20 |
| Emanuel Combe | 25 |
| John Cotscott | 40 |
| John Croote | 40 |
| Richard Davye | 24 |
| William Davye | 34 |
| Henry Ellyott | 18 |
| Emanuel Faringdon | 25 |
| Henry Flood | 42 |
| Richard Foorde | 40 |
| Jeffery Gale | 30 |
| Robert Grigory | 30 |
| William Hall | 30 |
| Benjamim Helliar | 30 |
| John Hellye jun. | 30 |
| William Hillye | 26 |
| Andrew Hobby | 23 |
| William Hodgen | 61 |
| Robert Hodgenn | 30 |
| Pancras Jayle | 20 |
| Roger Jefferye | 30 |
| William Johns | 30 |
| Philip Lane | 61 |
| Richard Langbridg | 42 |
| William Langmead | 29 |
| Jeffery Lympscott | 60 |

| | |
|---|---|
| Henry Lymscott | 25 |
| John Lymscott | 25 |
| Edward Middlton | 39 |
| John Oliver | 16 |
| Thomas Oliver | 20 |
| William Oliver | 50 |
| Thomas Paynter | 22 |
| Thomas Perrye | 15 |
| Gawyn Petherick | 25 |
| John Petherick | 18 |
| Robert Philpe | 41 |
| Peter Pine | 30 |
| Thomas Pope | 40 |
| Peter Pyne | 32 |
| Roger Pynn | 39 |
| John Reade | 32 |
| Giles Ridgman | 23 |
| George Salter | 40 |
| Robert Scute | 30 |
| John Sexton | 40 |
| John Simons | 40 |
| John Smalridg | 30 |
| John Stevens | 41 |
| James Swallow | 61 |
| John Tapley | 32 |
| Nicholas Tapley jun. | 18 |
| Philip Tapley | 41 |
| Richard Tapley | 25 |
| William Tapley | 25 |
| Nicholas Taplye | 44 |
| Richard Taplye | 42 |
| Will Tapp | 42 |
| Richard Temple | 30 |
| Henry Torring | 20 |
| Ambrose Trappam | 42 |
| David Tucker | 50 |
| Lewis Tucker | 36 |
| John Vincent | 40 |
| John Voysey | 41 |
| Henry Voysye | 20 |
| Thomas Waye | 41 |
| Thomas Waye | 30 |
| Thomas Waymouth | 20 |
| Robert Weston | 30 |
| Emanuell Wichalls | 40 |
| Richard Wichalls | 28 |
| John Windsor | 25 |
| Thomas Winklye | 60 |
| Jarvyse Winson | 18 |

| | |
|---|---|
| Christopher Wise | 22 |
| Thomas Wise | 24 |
| Gawyn Woolcott | 32 |
| John Woolcott | 24 |

SEINEMEN

| | |
|---|---|
| Robert Alford | 50 |
| John Babb sen. | 30 |
| Gawyn Baker | 46 |
| John Blanke | 30 |
| John Bowden | 20 |
| Bartholomew Cockram | 35 |
| William Downe | 40 |
| Edward Foote | 30 |
| John Foote | 27 |
| John Gribble | 30 |
| Gawyn Sexton | 25 |
| Thomas Sowden | 41 |
| Thomas Thorne jun. | 24 |
| Roger Wise | 53 |
| Francis Wyatt | 26 |

## Shipping of Dawlish

| Names | Burthen | Voyages |
|---|---|---|
| The | | |
| *Marye* | 20 | Newfoundland |
| *Mayeflower* | 12 | At home |

## Combeinteignhead
### [*Combentin-heade*]
Age

MASTERS & MARINERS

| | |
|---|---|
| Jeffery Babb | 50 |
| Simon Fletcher | 53 |
| Gregory Gardner | 40 |
| Thomas Gotham | 50 |
| Thomas Gottham | 51 |
| Thomas Melburye | 55 |
| Francis Paddon | 40 |

SAILORS

| | |
|---|---|
| George Babb | 40 |
| Peter Baker | 28 |
| Christopher Bickford | 28 |
| Henry Bickford | 25 |
| William Bickford | 24 |
| Elias Bowden | 25 |
| Richard Brown | 26 |

## Combeinteignhead cont'd

| | |
|---|---|
| William Burt | 26 |
| John Cade | 33 |
| Melchisadek Cassier | 26 |
| Edward Cawson | 31 |
| Oliver Chappell | 25 |
| Christopher Clampitt | 24 |
| Edward Cleare | 40 |
| John Cleere | 24 |
| Peter Cleere | 24 |
| Simon Colander | 32 |
| Thomas Couse | 24 |
| James Cryer | 25 |
| Joseph Davye | 26 |
| Christopher Drew | 26 |
| Richard Drew | 30 |
| John Drewe | 24 |
| Oliver Drewe | 30 |
| John Dyer | 28 |
| Bennet Eastbrook | 25 |
| George Fletcher | 28 |
| John Foorde | 43 |
| Andrew Fowell | 34 |
| John Fowell | 35 |
| Christopher Fryer | 24 |
| Reynold Fryer | 22 |
| Thomas Fryer | 26 |
| William Fryer | 30 |
| John Gabriel | 25 |
| John Gabriell | 50 |
| Peter Gotobedd | 41 |
| Rich Gotobedd | 32 |
| Thomas Gotobedd | 30 |
| John Gourd | 42 |
| John Helly | 31 |
| Thomas Hubber | 28 |
| John Kendall | 25 |
| Thomas Lambyth | 40 |
| Richard Larimor | 30 |
| Oliver Larimore | 26 |
| William Melbury | 20 |
| John Melburye | 28 |
| Daniel Overell | 25 |
| Gregory Pooke | 51 |
| Christopher Prouse | 24 |
| Thomas Roberts | 36 |
| John Salton | 20 |
| Roger Thorne | 58 |
| Michael Tropall | 23 |
| Andrew Wallys | 34 |

| | |
|---|---|
| James White | 25 |
| Thomas Wills | 28 |
| William Wills | 40 |

# Stokeinteignhead
## [Stokentinheade]

### MASTERS & MARINERS

| | |
|---|---|
| Robert Allnworth | 31 |
| Christopher Andrew | 26 |
| Thomas Andrew | 35 |
| Nicholas Beard | 60 |
| Thomas Beard | 24 |
| Edward Bickford | 30 |
| William Bickford | 43 |
| John Blackaller | 36 |
| Henry Braddon | 36 |
| Ellis Browne | 60 |
| Christopher Clyffe | 40 |
| James Clyffe | 36 |
| William Couse | 36 |
| William Couse | 58 |
| Thomas Couze | 42 |
| Peter Frowde | 30 |
| John Haydon | 42 |
| William Jaker | 20 |
| George Kellye | 23 |
| Henry Leane | 30 |
| Abram Lodimer | 30 |
| Christopher Luxe | 36 |
| John Luxe | 50 |
| Michell Martin | 30 |
| Richard Martine | 40 |
| John Mounke | 35 |
| John Mudge | 26 |
| James Payne | 60 |
| John Payne | 34 |
| Andrew Raddon | 40 |
| John Rope | 23 |
| John Simons | 20 |
| John Wills | 50 |

### SAILORS

| | |
|---|---|
| William Adams | 40 |
| Ellis Andrew | 40 |
| Henry Andrew | 18 |
| John Andrew | 24 |
| John Arnold | 50 |
| Nicholas Ball | 30 |
| Edward Baron | 26 |

| | | | | |
|---|---|---|---|---|
| Henry Baron | 20 | | Walter Meltonn | 48 |
| John Barter | 52 | | Robert Michell | 40 |
| Richard Bodinge | 24 | | Henry Milburye | 51 |
| Robert Bowden | 24 | | John Paddon | 26 |
| Richard Boylman | 40 | | William Paddon | 24 |
| Ellis Browne | 20 | | William Paddon | 26 |
| John Cade | 60 | | James Poole | 40 |
| Richard Cade | 18 | | William Row | 48 |
| Robert Cade | 30 | | Richard Rowe | 50 |
| John Clampitt | 30 | | Edward Simon | 24 |
| Henry Clement | 30 | | William Simons | 50 |
| John Codner | 46 | | Steven Smith | 30 |
| Alexander Colcott | 45 | | Nicholas Snelling | 33 |
| John Combe | 21 | | Edward Symon | 24 |
| John Cooke jun. | 28 | | Nicholas Tasker | 30 |
| Roger Cooke | 26 | | William Tasker | 28 |
| William Cooke | 30 | | John Taylye | 24 |
| John Corke | 30 | | Richard Varrell | 24 |
| Andrew Couch | 25 | | Peter Webber | 23 |
| James Couse | 21 | | Thomas Wench-foord | 23 |
| John Couse | 50 | | John West-lade | 40 |
| John Couse | 27 | | John Whiddon | 24 |
| Robert Couse | 26 | | John Wills | 22 |
| John Cowse | 16 | | Peter Winefoord | 60 |
| John Dense | 50 | | Richard Wood | 42 |
| John Elliott | 27 | | | |
| Edward Ellyott | 29 | | | |
| Robert Eyde | 51 | | **Stoke Gabriel** | |
| John Flawne | 29 | | _[Stoke-gabriel]_ | |
| Ellis Foorde | 22 | | SAILORS | |
| William Frond | 48 | | George Backeare | 40 |
| Markes Frye | 30 | | William Belsford | 20 |
| Henry Grant | 30 | | Andrew Berrye | 40 |
| John Grant | 28 | | Richard Berrye | 30 |
| Richard Hooper | 40 | | Nicholas Blake | 30 |
| William Hooper | 20 | | Benjamin Boringe | 30 |
| Richard Isaake | 40 | | Thomas Bownd | 20 |
| John Jewell | 30 | | Andrew Churchward | 31 |
| Ellis Kyrton | 30 | | James Churchward | 32 |
| Richard Lange | 28 | | Andrew Crutney | 20 |
| John Leane | 30 | | Augustine Crutnye | 20 |
| John Light-foote | 33 | | John Eastabrock | 32 |
| Henry Luxe | 30 | | Henry Hadd | 34 |
| Christopher Maddock | 20 | | William Hodg | 35 |
| Edward Martin | 23 | | John Hunnye | 20 |
| William Martin | 26 | | John Jacksonn | 23 |
| John Martine | 22 | | Vincent Kinge | 31 |
| Christopher Mayne | 24 | | John Knell | 42 |
| John Melbury | 22 | | William Land sen. | 60 |
| Edward Melburye | 50 | | William Laver | 30 |

**Stoke Gabriel cont'd**

| | |
|---|---|
| John Maddick | 23 |
| Peter Rewles | 21 |
| John Rowe | 50 |
| Benjamin Squyre | 21 |
| Richard Squyre | 33 |
| John Stephen | 60 |
| William Stephen | 32 |
| Edward Torringe | 32 |
| William Torringe | 28 |
| John Trostrom | 52 |

## Kenton

### [*Kentonn*]

MASTERS & MARINERS

| | |
|---|---|
| Juell Babb | 35 |
| John Bobbish | 35 |
| Lawrence Bricknoll | 30 |
| John Burgoyne | 45 |
| William Clarke | 50 |
| George Cove | 31 |
| Richard Dart | 30 |
| John Downe | 35 |
| Nicholas Downe jun. | 37 |
| John Dulinge | 40 |
| William Easton | 30 |
| John Foorde | 30 |
| Richard Frost | 25 |
| Robert Geoles | 34 |
| Thomas Geoles | 30 |
| Andrew Helliar | 30 |
| Richard Mitton | 40 |
| Rich Nicholls | 41 |
| John Rogers | 28 |
| Thomas Russell | 55 |
| Thomas Shapley | 41 |
| John Venner sen. | 50 |
| John Venner | 50 |
| Thomas Venner | 35 |
| William Venner | 35 |

SAILORS

| | |
|---|---|
| Thomas Averye | 18 |
| William Basill | 20 |
| Giles Bobish | 40 |
| Richard Bobish | 42 |
| John Cade | 40 |
| Richard Cheese | 50 |
| Sampson Clefinger | 25 |

| | |
|---|---|
| Robert Court | 35 |
| Peter Crapp | 28 |
| Austin Eastchurch | 25 |
| Richard East-church | 24 |
| John Edwards | 24 |
| Roger Ellyott | 35 |
| John Ewinge | 40 |
| Richard Ewyn | 22 |
| John Ewynn | 22 |
| Emanuel Faringdon | 25 |
| Edward Farr | 35 |
| Richard Farr | 32 |
| William Feature | 38 |
| Simon Fennye | 25 |
| Jeffery Ferrys | 20 |
| Christopher Filpe | 50 |
| Philip Filsome | 35 |
| Richard Furlonge | 50 |
| Robert Geales | 38 |
| John Gibb | 31 |
| Richard Gilbert | 40 |
| John Godwyne | 23 |
| Richard Helly | 25 |
| Richard Helly | 28 |
| John Hempston | 24 |
| Charles Hooper | 31 |
| Richard Hunt | 40 |
| John James | 50 |
| Robert Jarmyn | 22 |
| John Jarvys | 23 |
| Anthony Lange | 32 |
| John Langford | 31 |
| Roger Langford | 30 |
| Richard Langlye | 30 |
| Harry Lawrence | 30 |
| John Lawrence | 25 |
| William Loe | 30 |
| John Lowe | 44 |
| Nicholas Lucombe | 30 |
| Nicholas Luxe | 40 |
| Richard Luxe | 30 |
| William Luxe | 24 |
| John Millett | 30 |
| George Mole | 40 |
| John Moore | 22 |
| Peter Parker | 22 |
| John Parr | 31 |
| James Peryman | 30 |
| Mathew Philp | 30 |
| John Pinsent | 35 |

| | |
|---|---|
| Peter Pope | 26 |
| John Prest | 30 |
| George Rodes | 42 |
| Roger Rodes | 35 |
| Andrew Row | 40 |
| John Seyne | 30 |
| Nicholas Shapley | 20 |
| Thomas Shapley | 40 |
| Jeffery Shaplye | 42 |
| John Shattock | 23 |
| Adam Short | 32 |
| William Simons | 50 |
| Alexander Skinner | 23 |
| Raymond Smith | 50 |
| Emanuel Torringe | 25 |
| James Venner | 35 |
| Walter Venner | 24 |
| Emanuel Warren | 35 |
| Philip Warren | 20 |
| Robert Warren | 35 |
| William Warren | 35 |
| Nicholas Wills | 18 |

## Powderham

MASTERS & MARINERS

| | |
|---|---|
| Nicholas Corworthy | 42 |
| John White | 60 |

SAILORS

| | |
|---|---|
| Richard Averye | 50 |
| Nicholas Boysye | 30 |
| Robert Browne | 37 |
| John Joynt | 49 |
| Tristram Kelly | 26 |
| Robert Kellye | 22 |
| William Kellye | 50 |
| Thomas Kenwood | 23 |
| Nicholas Marshall | 30 |
| William Taylour | 41 |
| John Tross, Owner | 35 |
| William Venner | 20 |
| John Waymouth | 30 |

## Shipping of Kenton

| Owners | Names The | Burthen | Ages | Ordnance | Voyages |
|---|---|---|---|---|---|
| John Hellye | *Godspeed* | 36 | 7 | 0 | At home |
| Thomas Wills, John Barter [and] Emanuel Wichalls | *Marye* | 20 | 12 | 0 | do |
| Thomas Wills, George Brooke Roger Elliott [and] Nicholas Paddon | *Guift* | 20 | 7 | 0 | do |
| Edith Avery, Walter Venner [and] Thomas Avery | *Thomas* | 36 | 2 | 0 | do |
| Nicholas Downe [and] Richard Baynham | *Rose* | 50 | 10 | 3 | In Wales |
| Nicholas Downe, Jesse Vass [and] Widow Vinton | *Pleasure* | 60 | 20 | 4 | For the [Atlantic] Islands |
| William Clarke | *Edward* | 20 | 10 | 0 | In Wales |
| William Gold John Lynn | *Tryall* | 45 | 10 | 0 | For Newfound-land |

## Shipping of Powderham

| Owners | Names | Burthen | Ages | Ordnance | Voyages |
|---|---|---|---|---|---|
| | The | | | | |
| John Tross [and] John Joynt | Remembrance | 36 | 14 | 0 | For Newfound-land |
| John White, John Waymouth [and] Nicholas Coxworthy | Elizabeth | 26 | 16 | 0 | At home |
| Nicholas Coxworthy [and] Joseph Stroebridg | Prosperous | 30 | 13 | 0 | At St Malo [Malloes] |
| John Waymouth [and] Thomas Amye | Cottage | 20 | 8 | 0 | At Newfoundland |

### Exmouth

| | Age |
|---|---|
| MASTERS & MARINERS | |
| John Cross | 35 |
| John Elmer | 34 |
| Simon Loveringe | 28 |
| George Perdon | 35 |
| William Perdon | 25 |
| William Purchase | 20 |
| Thomas Smyth | 30 |
| George Stoke | 29 |
| Robert Temple | 35 |
| John Tucker | 50 |
| SAILORS | |
| John Adgar jun. | 30 |
| Christopher Adger | 25 |
| John Auger sen. | 31 |
| John Bamfeild | 26 |
| Thomas Bamfeilde | 26 |
| John Bull | 33 |
| John Butson | 30 |
| William Cable | 31 |
| Lewis Cheynye | 25 |
| Ellys Creeze | 50 |
| George Cross | 28 |
| Robert Dicker | 35 |
| William Farrant | 22 |
| George Goldsworthy | 40 |
| John Hemlock | 40 |
| Richard Hodder | 25 |
| Thomas Jollye | 28 |
| Philip Knight | 25 |
| Thomas Lamsey | 26 |
| Gregory Levye | 28 |
| Thomas Levye | 26 |
| George Loveringe | 30 |
| Peter Moore | 30 |
| Cyprian Page | 30 |
| George Peirce | 30 |
| Nicholas Perdon | 30 |
| John Stevens | 32 |
| Philip Stouard | 24 |
| Thomas Temple | 19 |
| William Temple | 30 |
| John Tucker | 25 |
| Bartholomew Whitlock | 28 |

### Exminster
#### [Exmister]

| | |
|---|---|
| MASTERS & MARINERS | |
| Mark Golsworthy | 40 |
| Roger Smith | 40 |
| Robert White | 35 |
| SAILORS | |
| Ellis Berrye | 30 |
| John Bickford | 32 |
| John Butsonn | 35 |
| John Collin | 25 |
| John Foster | 24 |
| John Hamlinn | 30 |
| William Hamlyn | 35 |
| Robert Wills | 32 |

### Lympstone
#### [Lymston]

| | |
|---|---|
| MARINERS & SAILORS | |
| Edmund Adams | 25 |
| James Adams | 30 |

| | | | | |
|---|---|---|---|---|
| Henry Bamfeild | 27 | Robert Lovering | 33 |
| Robert Bickford | 43 | William Loveringe | 32 |
| John Brissett | 50 | John Mills | 25 |
| John Brissett | 28 | Robert Morhay | 30 |
| William Browne | 27 | Henry Parker | 22 |
| Zachary Bull | 32 | John Parker | 53 |
| John Byshopp | 30 | Thomas Pulman | 35 |
| Gregory Carvell | 35 | John Rigers | 30 |
| Charles Cooke | 50 | Roger Rule | 35 |
| Richard Cookemay | 45 | John Scott | 35 |
| Philip Downell | 55 | Alexander Shapton | 55 |
| Henry Ellyott | 30 | David Shapton | 25 |
| John Elyott | 22 | John Shepherd jun. | 19 |
| John Hall | 30 | Henry Sprage | 40 |
| George Justing | 18 | Robert Taylor | 19 |
| Richard Kingman | 40 | John Taylour | 50 |
| Christopher Labett sen. | 40 | William Taylour | 24 |
| Edward Labett | 28 | Christopher Warren | 25 |

## Shipping of Exmouth

| Owners | Names | Tuns | Ages | Ordnance | Voyages |
|---|---|---|---|---|---|
| | The | | | | |
| George Perdon | *Due Grace* | 30 | 30 | 0 | Newfoundland |
| John Marshall, Peter Payne [and] Vincent Helman | *True Laborer* | 40 | 26 | 0 | do |
| George Perdon, Philip Stopher [and] John Sheapeard | *Patience* | 40 | 14 | 0 | do |
| Henry Spicer, Robert Turpin, Robert Lovering, George Pearne [and] Philip Stopher | *New Patience* | 30 | 11 | 0 | [blank] |
| George Perdon | Two fisher boats | 20 | 6 | 0 | do |
| Benedict Whitcow | *Patience* | 34 | 14 | 0 | do |

## Shipping of Lympstone [*Lymston*]

| | | | | | |
|---|---|---|---|---|---|
| | The | | | | |
| Stephen Taylour, Philip Stopher [and] Benedict Whitcow | *Constance* | 60 | 12 | 0 | From home |
| John Bass, Philip Stopher, John Sheapheard [and] John Tross | *Dove* | 50 | 16 | 0 | Newfoundland |
| George Perdon, Philip Stopher [and] John Shepeard | *Old Patience* | 40 | 14 | 0 | From home |

## Shipping of Lympstone cont'd

| Owners | Names | Tuns | Ages | Ordnance | Voyages |
|---|---|---|---|---|---|
| Stephen Taylor, Philip Stopher [and] Nicholas Bolt | *Flower* | 40 | 14 | 3 | At the [Atlantic] Islands |
| Thomas Bass [and] John Bryant | *Mynion* | 18 | 16 | 0 | At home |
| Five boats each of 10 [tons] | | | | | All at home |

## Topsham
### [*Topish-ham*]

| | Age |
|---|---|
| **MASTERS & MARINERS** | |
| Nicholas Elston | 24 |
| Thomas Jordan | 34 |
| Richard Langford | 35 |
| John Rowe | 26 |
| Stephen Taylour | 35 |

| SAILORS | |
|---|---|
| Morrice Adams | 22 |
| John Averye | 53 |
| William Bassell | 37 |
| Nathaniel Bawden | 26 |
| George Brodridg | 20 |
| Thomas Brown | 35 |
| Richard Burnard | 26 |
| Richard Call | 20 |
| Richard Carder | 27 |
| John Coggens | 30 |
| John Corbin | 40 |
| Henry Dyer | 22 |
| Thomas Elston | 22 |
| John Elstonn | 23 |
| John Englande | 30 |
| Gilbert Goldsworthy | 36 |
| Christopher Hendye | 50 |
| Amareth Ladye | 24 |
| Thomas Ladye | 40 |
| Richard Lyle | 26 |
| Richard Markar | 30 |
| John Marker | 36 |
| Robert Meere | 30 |
| Richard Mole | 32 |
| Bartholomew Nott | 20 |
| Robert Peach | 30 |
| William Poole | 22 |
| Richard Suer | 22 |

| | |
|---|---|
| William Suer | 26 |
| John Tuckerman | 32 |
| John Tybbye | 23 |
| Peter Varley | 45 |
| William Winter | 58 |
| John Withall | 23 |
| William Withall | 22 |
| William Wootton | 32 |

## Woodbury
### [*Woodburye*]

| MASTERS & MARINERS | |
|---|---|
| Robert Caddy | 54 |
| Roger Favers | 41 |
| Richard Hoppin | 50 |
| William Waye | 40 |
| William Whetcomb | 50 |

| SAILORS | |
|---|---|
| William Baker | 32 |
| Gregory Bayle | 40 |
| James Bayle | 38 |
| John Dabbyn | 34 |
| William Glass | 32 |
| Richard Hethen | 30 |
| William Jermayn | 30 |
| William Kedde | 28 |
| Thomas Payne | 40 |
| John Pittfolde | 50 |
| Robert Robbins | 45 |
| William Soper | 41 |
| Anthony Truscott | 40 |
| James Vincent | 23 |
| John Westcott | 40 |

| SHIPWRIGHTS | |
|---|---|
| Richard Adam | 52 |
| Robert Adam | 32 |
| William Ellys | 40 |

| | | | | |
|---|---|---|---|---|
| John Heath | 40 | | John Kedell | 28 |
| Philip Plymton | 30 | | William Peirce | 50 |
| John Rolsom | 28 | | Robert Taylor | 37 |
| William Till | 41 | | John Warrye | 40 |

SHIPWRIGHTS

## Colaton Raleigh
## [*Collytonn Rawley*]

SAILORS

| | | | |
|---|---|---|---|
| | | Robert Collier | 46 |
| | | Thomas Kinge | 40 |
| | | William Lenmore | 62 |
| William Green | 36 | Richard Midwinter | 37 |
| | | James Tricker | 48 |

## Topsham [*Topish-ham*] Shipping

| Owners | Names | Tuns | Ages | Ordnance | Voyage |
|---|---|---|---|---|---|
| Thomas Amye, Christopher Clarke, [and] Steven Taylor | Angell | 100 | 8 | 3 | In Newfoundland |
| Stephen Taylor, Ezekias Vass, [and] Abram Westlake | Comfort | 40 | 10 | 2 | At San Lúcar [ Lucas] |
| Stephen Taylour, Philip Stopher, [and] Nicholas Bolt | Flower | 35 | 14 | 3 | At the [Atlantic] Islands |
| Richard Sanders, Roger Mallett, [and] John Row | Greater Frendshipp | 28 | 6 | 0 | At home |
| William Elsdon | Mynion | 60 | 12 | 0 | Newfoundland |
| do | Dyamonde | 50 | 10 | 0 | do |
| William Carye [and] Robert Carye | Providence | 60 | 12 | 1 | do |
| Thomas White | Rose-marye | 55 | 16 | 3 | At San Lúcar [ Lucas] |
| do | Violett | 35 | 20 | 2 | At home |
| Ezekias Vass | Delight | 50 | 20 | 0 | Newfoundland |
| Ezekias Vass, Nicholas Downe [and] Julian Vinton | Pleasure | 60 | 28 | 2 | For the [Atlantic] Islands |
| Richard Langford | Hopewell | 40 | 12 | 0 | Newfoundland |
| Richard Langford, Steven Taylor, [and] Robert Adams | Michaell | 45 | 12 | 0 | do |
| Ignatius Jourdan, John Jordan, Richard Langford [and] Thomas Jordan | Virginn | 45 | 1 | 0 | At home |
| Daniel Vass [and] Henry Battifeild | Marye & Margaret | 60 | 2 | 3 | San Sebastian |
| Richard Crowe | Due Returne | 43 | 8 | 0 | At the Madeira [Island]s |
| Abraham Rutter | Greyhounde | 20 | 4 | 0 | At home |

**Topsham Shipping cont'd**

| Owners | Names | Tuns | Ages | Ordnance | Voyage |
|---|---|---|---|---|---|
| Robert Peath | *True meaninge* | 10 | 2 | 0 | do |
| Richard Shacherly, Roger Yoe [and] Thomas Broadmead | *Lesser Frendshipp* | 18 | 8 | 0 | At Seville [ *Sivill*] |
| William Carye | *Little Elizabeth* | 10 | 3 | 0 | At home |
| Abraham Rutter | *Unicorne* | 120 | 6 | 0 | From home |
| John Sheere | *William* | 10 | 3 | 0 | At home |

## Withycombe Raleigh
### *[Withicombe Rawley, Withycombe Rawlye]*

| | Age |
|---|---|
| MASTERS & MARINERS | |
| Edward Bass | 35 |
| Robert Nutt | 31 |
| Robert Parker | 30 |
| William Parker | 60 |
| Richard Smyth | 44 |
| William Westcott | 60 |
| | |
| SAILORS | |
| Francis Brissett | 38 |
| Gabriel Burlye | 34 |
| Richard Cheyny | 30 |
| William Glass | 32 |
| William Gotham | 31 |
| Richard Heathen | 32 |
| John Howsen | 23 |
| William Keed sen. | 51 |
| William Keed | 28 |
| Clement King | 30 |
| William Parker | 22 |
| Thomas Payne | 40 |
| John Pittfold | 50 |
| Richard Pyke jun. | 32 |
| Richard Pyke | 60 |
| Robert Robins | 45 |
| William Toller | 35 |
| Richard Williams | 21 |
| George Woode | 32 |
| Josias Woode | 28 |
| | |
| SHIPWRIGHTS | |
| John Andye | 48 |
| John Parker | 38 |

## East Budleigh
### *[Budleye]*

| SAILORS | |
|---|---|
| Nicholas Bruton | 36 |
| George Cookney | 30 |
| Richard Curtyse | 52 |
| Henry Elliott | 23 |
| Richard Feyter | 42 |
| Richard Harrison | 33 |
| Andrew Hill | 31 |
| William Hill | 40 |
| William Hoppin | 21 |
| Michael Manfeild | 30 |
| Stephen Manfeild | 33 |
| Richard Moody | 42 |
| Thomas Stocker | 22 |
| Robert Walberton | 40 |

## Otterton
### *[Ottertonn]*

| SAILORS | |
|---|---|
| Henry Burgin | 46 |
| Gilbert Ellyott | 28 |
| Richard Gibb | 60 |
| William Gibb | 23 |
| Thomas Goodridg | 50 |
| Richard Heather | 24 |
| Richard Lucas | 30 |
| William Lucas | 34 |
| Philip Manlye | 50 |
| Marmaduke Martin | 40 |
| Robert Pinn | 64 |
| William Reed | 30 |
| Philip Rogers | 31 |

| | |
|---|---|
| William Sherrin | 34 |
| Richard Warren | 25 |
| Edward Wheaton | 24 |

SHIPWRIGHTS

| | |
|---|---|
| John Barnes | 30 |
| John Bayly | 34 |
| John Bayly | 55 |
| Robert Bayly | 29 |
| William Bayly | 30 |
| Simon Baylye | 40 |
| Richard Bugenn | 26 |
| John Clarke | 32 |
| William Dollen | 30 |
| Samuel Gibb | 18 |
| Richard Grindle | 46 |
| Robert Hussy | 36 |
| William Kenwood | 53 |
| Clement Lugg | 32 |
| William Macye | 22 |
| William Moore | 21 |
| Arthur Pyne | 23 |
| Robert Reely | 30 |
| John Rugg | 45 |
| Thomas Tricker | 36 |
| Thomas Williams | 20 |

## Aylesbeare
SAILORS

| | |
|---|---|
| William Bond | 35 |
| Walter Farrant | 36 |
| Edward Haycraft | 23 |
| Bennett Hellen | 34 |
| John Southwood | 29 |
| James Spare | 21 |
| John Spare | 28 |

## Sidbury
### [Sydburye]
SAILORS

| | |
|---|---|
| Francis Bartlett | 23 |
| Robert Penny | 40 |
| Christopher Rogers | 40 |
| Anthony Smyth | 24 |
| Mathew Smyth | 34 |
| John Tree | 38 |

## Branscombe
### [Branscomb]
SAILORS

| | |
|---|---|
| Francis Bartlett | 23 |
| Humphrey Sholdnr | 24 |

## Colyton
### [Culliton]
SAILORS

| | |
|---|---|
| John Clarke | 31 |
| John Hasely | 30 |
| Alexander Hayman | 40 |
| Jacob Samford | 32 |
| Richard Sampson | 32 |
| Bartholomew Spiller | 30 |
| Richard Tapley | 35 |
| John Tyrling | 26 |
| Robert Weekes | 45 |

## Salcombe Regis
### [Saltcombe]
SAILORS

| | |
|---|---|
| John Channon | 32 |
| William Lacye | 46 |
| Robert Simons | 34 |
| Thomas Slade | 28 |

## Uplyme
SAILORS

| | |
|---|---|
| Andrew Cooke | 45 |
| Thomas Hitch-cock | 46 |
| Robert Hore | 30 |
| William Swayn | 20 |
| William Swayne | 54 |

## Sidmouth
### [Sydmouth]
MASTERS & MARINERS

| | |
|---|---|
| Robert Ashlye | 36 |
| Andrew Cawly | 36 |
| Edward Fortune | 20 |
| Thomas Gold | 24 |
| Henry Hayman | 38 |
| George Ladd sen. | 44 |

**Sidmouth cont'd**

| Jarvys Landrake | 46 |
|---|---|
| Jeremy Maior | 31 |
| William Pyke | 40 |
| John Randall | 28 |
| William Row | 42 |
| William Satterly | 30 |
| Stephen Speedwell | 26 |
| Reynold Sprayn | 46 |

SAILORS

| William Cawly | 24 |
|---|---|
| Charles Chano[n] | 22 |
| William Chocke | 30 |
| Richard Crutchard | 26 |
| Edward Fortune | 19 |
| Humphry Gold | 20 |
| Lawrence Justin | 32 |
| Robert Lanilark | 21 |
| Ellis Lydford | 28 |
| Nicholas Lydford | 19 |
| John Peryam | 21 |
| Richard Peryam | 33 |
| Robert Rogers | 30 |
| Richard Scutt | 24 |
| Henry Soper | 22 |
| Nicholas Warren | 20 |

FISHERMEN

| John Ashley | 26 |
|---|---|
| Mathew Ashley | 46 |
| William Ashley | 40 |
| Richard Ashly | 62 |
| Edward Ashlye | 20 |
| John Ashlye | 18 |
| Timothy Badston | 18 |
| William Barlye | 40 |
| Edward Baron | 30 |
| Robert Bennye | 31 |
| William Burlye | 40 |
| Solomon Burt | 24 |
| Simon Bynny | 30 |
| George Carter | 24 |
| John Carter | 30 |
| Walter Carter | 18 |
| Charles Cawly | 26 |
| James Cawly | 24 |
| John Cawlye | 24 |
| William Cawlye | 31 |
| William Cawlye | 26 |

| Edward Chanon | 36 |
|---|---|
| Richard Clapp | 51 |
| John Clarke | 26 |
| John Clarke | 32 |
| Thomas Clarke | 50 |
| Edward Clayter | 41 |
| Edward Clement | 21 |
| John Clement | 40 |
| John Combe | 21 |
| Nicholas Cranmer | 33 |
| Robert Curtiss | 60 |
| Thomas Cuttiss | 32 |
| John Gould | 30 |
| Nicholas Hake | 32 |
| William Hake | 30 |
| Mathew Hayman | 18 |
| Richard Hellien | 40 |
| William Jesse | 46 |
| John Keesclake | 40 |
| Henry Kerslack | 36 |
| Edward Ladd | 40 |
| George Ladd jun. | 26 |
| Henry Ladd | 22 |
| William Langclark | 18 |
| Thomas Maynard | 56 |
| Edmund Nubery | 40 |
| Robert Parker | 40 |
| John Periman | 50 |
| William Periman | 26 |
| William Periman | 20 |
| John Pinsent | 26 |
| Edward Pyke | 30 |
| Nicholas Pyke | 18 |
| Henry Radford | 34 |
| John Robins | 23 |
| Edward Roe | 36 |
| Robert Row | 20 |
| Stephen Row | 25 |
| Thomas Row | 17 |
| John Rugg | 20 |
| Robert Scutt | 26 |
| William Scutt | 40 |
| John Seward | 40 |
| Ellis Slee | 46 |
| Peter Smyth | 25 |
| Thomas Speedwell | 21 |
| John Stocker | 32 |
| Edward Tones | 36 |
| Edward Wheato[n] | 18 |

| | | | |
|---|---|---|---|
| William Wheaton | 22 | John Soundier | 30 |
| John Whytter | 34 | Robert Soundier | 34 |
| Richard Windsor | 60 | Robert Starr | 40 |
| | | John Stockham | 24 |
| | | Barnard Thwyte | 32 |

## Beer and Seaton
### [*Beere & Seaton*]

| | | | |
|---|---|---|---|
| | | Nicholas Welmingto[n] | 30 |
| | | William Wheeker | 18 |
| | | Peter Wooton | 30 |

MASTERS & MARINERS

| | | | |
|---|---|---|---|
| Barnard Babb | 32 | | |
| Humphrey Burrow | 36 | FISHERMEN | |
| Christopher Cally | 28 | Edward Bartlett | 40 |
| Robert Callye | 35 | Richard Bartlett | 36 |
| Zachary Cillenbord | 30 | Peter Benns | 28 |
| John Clapp | 21 | Robert Bonfeid | 45 |
| John Courtys | 21 | John Bonfeild | 40 |
| John Dare | 34 | Edward Burrell | 26 |
| Nicholas Dare | 40 | Barnard Burrow | 20 |
| Robert Dare | 44 | John Cally | 26 |
| William Garratt | 30 | Thomas Cally | 36 |
| John Jey | 35 | John Callye | 38 |
| Richard Lynke | 42 | William Callye | 24 |
| Michael Manston | 30 | Christopher Cyllenbord | 20 |
| John Twytchyn | 34 | John Cyllenbord | 28 |
| Richard Twytchyn | 40 | John Dare | 40 |
| | | Edward Drever | 26 |

SAILORS

| | | | |
|---|---|---|---|
| | | Nicholas Drever | 24 |
| Vincent Babb | 26 | John Garratt | 40 |
| Walter Babb | 50 | Charles Gerrant | 36 |
| Edward Bonfild | 26 | Ellis Gerrant | 46 |
| John Burrow | 25 | John Good | 28 |
| Robert Burrow | 19 | William Good | 22 |
| John Cally | 26 | John Hart | 18 |
| John Callye | 34 | Henry Hooper | 40 |
| Timothy Callye | 28 | John Hooper | 50 |
| John Carter | 24 | John Hull | 34 |
| John Clepitt | 24 | Nathaniel Jels | 25 |
| Jeffery Foord | 20 | John Ley | 20 |
| Thomas Foorde | 20 | John Pole-glaz | 20 |
| Thomas Gray | 30 | Jobe Quintrell | 56 |
| Robert Howse | 40 | John Sheeres sen. | 40 |
| Robert James | 34 | Philip Tuther | 20 |
| Henry Lee | 19 | Robert Wistlade | 23 |
| Barnard Lowma[n] | 36 | | |
| Robert Mell-huiss | 40 | | |
| Amias Mills | 20 | | |

## [Beer and Seaton] Shipping

| John Mills | 44 | Names | Tuns |
|---|---|---|---|
| William Radod | 54 | The | |
| William Seward | 28 | *Robert & John* | 18 |
| John Sheeres | 24 | *Will[iam] & John* | 24 |
| George Soper | 21 | *Ascension* | 12 |

**Beer and Seaton Shipping cont'd**

| Names | Tuns |
|---|---|
| *William* | 18 |
| *Mary* | 14 |
| Twelve fishing boats | |
| of between 5 & 10 [tons] | |

## Axmouth

| | Age |
|---|---|
| SAILORS | |
| John Abbott | 55 |
| John Baker | 54 |
| Richard Casewell | 33 |
| John Clarke | 50 |
| Robert Coade | 35 |

| | |
|---|---|
| Francis Garland | 42 |
| Thomas Seaward | 28 |
| Thomas Stevens | 30 |
| William Webber | 60 |

## Axminster
### [*Axmister*]

| | |
|---|---|
| SAILORS | |
| William Furnis | 33 |
| Peter Michell | 25 |
| John Waller | 40 |

[signed]   W[illiam] Courtenay

Jaspar Swyft

# NORTH CORNWALL, 1626

## FRANCIS BASSET'S SURVEY OF MARINERS AND SHIPS, 1626

[the following two letters preceded the survey]

PRO, SP16/33/69

[dorse] 1626. To the right honourable my master the Duke of Buckingham his grace.

May it please your Grace

Your commands bearing date the 11th of July, for the taking [of] a muster of the Mariners & Fishermen on the North Coast of Cornwall, came not to me until the last of that month. I have exactly, & with as much speed as might be, performed that duty, and have returned (unto Mr Nicholas) a perfect list of them to be presented [to] your Grace. There is not any ship either in or belonging to any of those ports, only three small barques no way capable of ordnance, the biggest not being above twenty ['forty' crossed out] tuns. I know not of any thing worth presenting your Grace but most humbly crave to be enabled by your gracious commands to manifest the duty due, from the humblest of your Grace's servants.

[signed] Francis Bassett

Tehidy [*Tehidie*] this 10th of August 1626


PRO, SP16/33/70

[dorse] For Edward Nicholas esq. my right worthy friend at York House, at the sign of the gate in the Strand, London

R[eceived]. 27 August 1626 Mr Francis Basset Vice-Admiral of the north of Cornwall.

Worthy Sir

I received on the last of July, a command from my Lord (which bore date the 11th of that month) for the taking of a muster of all the Mariners and Fishermen within the jurisdiction of my Vice-Admiralty, which with all the speed that might be I have effected, and return you ['at' crossed out] present a perfect list of them, and beseech you present it my Lord, with my letter inclosed. Sir, you have [been] most friendly, infinitely obliged me by preserving me in my Lords good Grace, which appears to me from himself. Believe me Sir there is not any thing in the world I more desire than to be commanded by him, and to do him service, which in all I can I will ever faithfully manifest, and trust so to serve him, and thank you as you shall not repent you of such favours done unto me. Upon all occasions wherein you shall think me capable of my Lord's command, I beseech you let me receive them: and wherein so poor a man may do you service, rest assuredly you shall really command,

Your most affectionate friend to serve you,

[signed] Francis Basset

Tehidy [*Tehidie*] this 10th of August 1626

53

PRO, SP16/33/70 (i)
[dorse] R[eceived]. 27 August 1626. A List of the Ships, Mariners & Seamen within
the Vice-Admiralty of the north of Cornwall.

A list of Mariners, Sailors and Fisherman belonging unto the port of St Ives in the county of Cornwall taken (by Francis Bassett, esq., Vice-Admiral of the north parts of the said county). ['the 29th July 1626' crossed out]

MASTERS

| | | |
|---|---|---|
| Philip Michell | aged | 35 |
| Richard Nance | | 48 |
| William Pitt | | 54 |

SAILORS OF ST IVES

| | |
|---|---|
| James Barber | 36 |
| Richard Barber | 50 |
| Robert Bolithoe, shipwright | 34 |
| William Clarke | 19 |
| John Cosens, ['36' crossed out] | 50 |
| Thomas Dayow | 41 |
| George Diggins | 24 |
| Peter Goyte, sailor | 18 |
| Richard Hockin | 28 |
| William Jacks | 46 |
| Martin Jordan | 40 |
| John Joste | 22 |
| John Launder sen. | 52 |
| Thomas Lawrie | 22 |
| Nicholas Walkey | 24 |

FISHERMEN OF ST IVES

| | |
|---|---|
| Philip Allen | 45 |
| Richard Allen | 18 |
| Stephen Barber | 50 |
| Henry Baylie | 27 |
| Peter Baylie | 22 |
| John Busephio | 40 |
| Thomas Candrowe | 25 |
| John Carneney | 50 |
| John Cocke | 24 |
| William Coger | 20 |
| John Cooke | 35 |
| William Davie | 30 |
| John Evoa | 35 |
| Robert Foster | 34 |
| Richard Hickes sen. | 28 |

| | |
|---|---|
| Alexander Hockin | 18 |
| Lewis Hockin | 28 |
| George Hutchins | 48 |
| Stephen Kuke | 62 |
| John Launder jun. | 19 |
| John Launton | 20 |
| Thomas Lillie | 34 |
| Philip Luke | 58 |
| Thomas Maffeild | 31 |
| Thomas Nancathen | 28 |
| Michael Nattell | 50 |
| John Oppey | 54 |
| Richard Peence | 42 |
| George Printer | 25 |
| Henry Randall | 34 |
| John Rawe | 35 |
| William Rawe jun. | 21 |
| Henry Shapland | 35 |
| Thomas Solminner | 21 |
| Lewis Stephen | 25 |
| Richard Stephen | 33 |
| Thomas Sterrie | 34 |
| Thomas Tackabird | 22 |
| Christopher Tregarthen | 34 |
| Henry Tregerthen jun. | 45 |
| John Trem=bethoe | 34 |
| John Vallett | 24 |
| James Walkey | 24 |
| James Wattie | 45 |
| John Wattie alias Hyatt | 26 |
| John Wattie | 36 |
| William Woolcocke | 25 |

The names of those Mariners and Sailors which belong unto the said port of St Ives and are now in voyages

MASTERS                    [ages not given]

Giles Hauke
Thomas Sise
Henry Tregenthen sen.

SAILORS

John Barber
William James
John Kittowe

William Launton
John Macroth
William Purchas
Henry Stephens
John Tomkin

A list of [illegible] Mariners, Sailors and Fishermen belonging unto the port of Padstow [Padstowe] in the county of Cornwall taken (by Francis Bassett esq. Vice-Admiral of the North parts of the said county of Cornwall) the first of August, 1626.

MASTERS

| | | |
|---|---|---|
| Jeffery Cornish | aged 60 | at sea |
| Innego Dyer | 60 | do |
| Edward Harris | 50 | do |
| Walter Kettowe | 48 | do |
| John Norman sen. | 61 | |
| John Norman jun. | 27 | at sea |
| Morgan Phillipps | 40 | do |
| Peter Quint | 40 | do |
| Benjamin Skoute | 40 | do |
| William Willson | 40 | do |

SAILORS OF PADSTOW [PADSTOWE]

| | | |
|---|---|---|
| Nicholas Androw | 23 | at sea |
| James Bennett | 40 | do |
| John Bone | 24 | do |
| John Burdwoode | 40 | do |
| John Cornishe | 24 | do |
| Bennet Dandey | 28 | do |
| Philip Dyer | 26 | do |
| John Edwards | 30 | do |
| Erasmus Glover | 40 | do |
| Richard Glover | 35 | do |
| Gregory Hodge | 30 | do |
| Richard Jewells | 30 | do |
| Henry Peter | 24 | do |
| Henry Quinte | 18 | do |
| John Richard | 30 | do |
| John Sare | 40 | do |
| John Tippett | 40 | do |
| John Welshe | 26 | do |

FISHERMEN OF PADSTOW [PADSTOWE]

| | | |
|---|---|---|
| Edward Edwards | 60 | |
| John Garred | 40 | at sea |

| | | |
|---|---|---|
| William Gilbert | 57 | |
| Henry Moyle | 58 | |
| Walter Perkin | | |
| John Saundry | 45 | |
| Reinald Scarbroke | 36 | at sea |

FISHERMEN OF THE PARISH OF ST MERRYN [ST MERRIN]

| | |
|---|---|
| Henry Jley | 26 |
| Henry Jley jun. | |
| John Rawlin | 22 |
| John Roberts | 35 |
| John Tom | 30 |

FISHERMEN OF THE PARISH OF ST COLUMB MINOR [ST COLLOMBE THE LOWER]

| | | |
|---|---|---|
| Charles Beard | 55 | |
| John Cocke | 35 | |
| Christopher Deane | 31 | |
| John Emott | 26 | |
| Robert Emott | 80 | |
| William Emott | 23 | |
| Christopher Kestell | 47 | |
| Humphrey Olde | 23 | |
| John Richard | 50 | |
| Richard Robert | 30 | |
| Nicholas Warrren | 50 | at sea |

FISHERMEN OF THE PARISH OF CRANTOCK [CRANTOCKE]

| | | |
|---|---|---|
| Goyen Cocke | 66 | |
| Philip Harrie | 44 | at sea |
| John Hockin | | |
| Bennet Michell | 63 | |
| John Scovren sen. | 52 | |
| John Scovren jun. | 46 | |
| John Scovren minor | 20 | |
| Thomas Scovren | 20 | |
| William Typpett | 53 | |
| Bennet Wills | 35 | |

FISHERMEN OF THE PARISH OF CUBERT

| | |
|---|---|
| Saundrie Dellbridge | 60 |
| John Emott | |
| James Oates | 48 |

BARGEMEN BELONGING TO THE PARISH OF EGLOSHAYLE [EGLOSEALE] AND ST BREOCK [ST BREAGE]

| | |
|---|---|
| Joseph Beare | 55 |
| Simon Billinge | 27 |
| Thomas Billinge | 20 |

| | | | |
|---|---|---|---|
| John Bligh | 38 | | |
| John Cawlinge | 54 | | |
| John Cocke | 70 | | |
| Thomas Cocke | | | |
| John Corke | 38 | | |
| Frances Couch | 40 | | |
| Edward Ede | 56 | | |
| Humphrey Grosse | 34 | | |
| Nathaniel Hambley | 40 | | |
| Jacob Hellson | 56 | | |
| John ['Hatc' crossed out], | | | |
| Hitchens | 48 | | |
| John Launder | 40 | | |
| Hugh Lawrance | 42 | | |
| Richard Pearse | 30 | | |
| Bartholomew Phillipp | 32 | | |
| Stipio Preler | 28 | | |
| John Scott | 60 | | |
| Clemens Simon | 42 | | |
| Richard Skinner | 40 | | |
| James Skrout | 57 | | |
| Henry Sleepe | 40 | | |
| John ['Trega' crossed out], | | | |
| Tregathen | 70 | | |
| John Trerubie | 55 | | |
| Walter Trerubie | 56 | | |
| Christopher Wolfe | 35 | | |
| Henry Woode | 24 | | |

FISHERMEN OF THE PARISH OF ST MINVER

| | | |
|---|---|---|
| Oliver Ball | 34 | |
| John Hickes | 33 | |
| William Hickes | 60 | |
| Richard Ivy | 35 | |
| John Jackett | 63 | |
| Robert Jackett | 35 | |
| John James | | |
| Walter Jefferie | 40 | |
| Anthony Jenkin | 58 | |
| Ambrose Marke | 48 | |
| Mathew Morrice | 54 | |
| Nicholas Olver | 34 | |
| Raphe Olver | 60 | |
| Otes Pope | 18 | |
| George Shoale | 60 | |
| Humphrey Stile | 29 | |
| Nicholas Stile | 24 | |

FISHERMEN OF THE PARISH OF ENDELLION
[ST ELLION]

| | | |
|---|---|---|
| John Aunger | 46 | at sea |
| Ralph Billinge | 60 | |
| Richard Billinge | 16 | |
| John Bray | 60 | |
| Nicholas Browne | 30 | at sea |
| Richard Browne | 62 | |
| John Browning jun. | 20 | at sea |
| John Browninge sen., | | |
| ['at sea' crossed out] | 70 | |
| Richard Carveth | 37 | |
| John Chevalle | 40 | at sea |
| Thomas Collen | 23 | |
| Ferdinand Collinge | 35 | at sea |
| Robert Davies | 50 | do |
| Nicholas Emott | 68 | do |
| Thomas Emott | 30 | do |
| Richard Forde | 20 | do |
| Raphe Gey | 40 | |
| Thomas Gey | 30 | at sea |
| John Gilbert | 65 | |
| Christopher Grigg | 50 | at sea |
| Francis Grigg | 46 | do |
| William Grigge | 40 | do |
| George Hicks | 45 | |
| William Hickes, | | |
| ['at sea' crossed out] | 35 | |
| Humphrey Jackett | 27 | |
| John James | 50 | at sea |
| Thomas James | 38 | |
| George Jefferie | | |
| Oliver Moyle | 60 | at sea |
| Christopher Olver | 26 | do |
| John Olver | 20 | do |
| Nicholas Parson | 20 | do |
| John Pearse | 60 | do |
| John Rowe | 45 | |
| Anthony Stone | 61 | |
| John Tom | 27 | at sea |
| William Trefry | 24 | do |
| William Trefry | 20 | |
| John Trenden | 25 | at sea |
| Thomas Trenoden sen. | 50 | do |
| John Triplett | 23 | do |
| John Waye | 60 | do |
| Robert Wills | 44 | do |

THE PARISH OF BOSCASTLE [*BOTREAUX CASTELL*]
the Sailors and Fishermen did not appear
Philip Joeile
Edward Joslen
William Popham
Bawden Tincke
John Tincke
William Tincker
John Tubb sen.
John Tubb jun.
Roger Tubb
Charles Stephen
William Stephen
Richard Warren

THE PARISH OF TINTAGEL [*TINTAGELL*],
the Sailors and Fishermen did not appear
John Browne
Thomas Browne
John Hender

John Hender
Thomas Hender
John Lavers
John Parson
John Robins
Richard Robins
Richard Tincke
William Tincke
Hercules Weyles
Clemens Wickett

BARQUES BELONGING UNTO THE PORT OF
PADSTOW [*PADSTOWE*]
Morgan Phillipps owner of a barque called
the *George* of 28 tons
Morgan Phillippes owner of an other
barque called the *Fortune* of 28 tons.
Peter Quinte owner of the *Harrie* of 40
tons or there abouts.

# SOUTH CORNWALL, *c.*1626

SIR JAMES BAGG'S SURVEY

## EAST HUNDRED

PRO, SP16/34/104
[dorse] Cornwall. South. East Hundred

### Place of Abode

### Saltash
### [*Saltashe*]

| Qualitie and Men's Names | Age |
|---|---|
| FISHERMEN | |
| Robert Bennet | 20 |
| William Blake | 30 |
| John Cornelius | 40 |
| William Grills | 34 |
| Elias Harros | 35 |
| John Ridge | 26 |
| Roger Stacy | 25 |
| Edward Stacye | 25 |
| Edmond Whale | 30 |
| | |
| GUNNERS | |
| Thomas Marnolls | 55 |
| James Phillipps | 46 |
| Thomas Rawlinge | 30 |
| | |
| MARINERS | |
| Simon Elliot | 30 |
| Robert Ford | 60 |
| Francis Greepe | 40 |
| Thomas Jago | 30 |
| James Holman | 30 |
| Thomas Paulin | 35 |
| John Traplinge | 40 |
| | |
| SAILORS | |
| Philip Balhatchet | 40 |
| John Bater | 40 |
| Thomas Bennet | 30 |
| John Bonyface | 25 |
| Robert Bonyface | 30 |
| John Boone | 20 |
| Edmond Brend | 35 |
| John Burgin | 40 |
| George Clarke | 30 |
| Robert Clarke | 30 |
| Thomas Collinge | 22 |
| William Crouste | 30 |
| John Foote | 30 |
| Robert Frost | 40 |
| Stephen Garrat | 35 |
| Robert Gatche | 20 |
| John Goyte | 22 |
| Thomas Greynes | 40 |
| Thomas Hoare | 30 |
| Thomas Hole | 30 |
| John Keete | 50 |
| Thomas Kneebone | 40 |
| Richard Marshall | 25 |
| William Martyn | 25 |
| Arthur Meade | 34 |
| Simon Mill | 40 |
| John Mitchell | 30 |
| Edmond Norrinton | 18 |
| Mathew Olvar | 24 |
| William Olvar | 50 |
| Nicholas Parker | 40 |
| Richard Pecoke | 30 |
| Peter Perry | 30 |
| Thomas Perry | 30 |
| Simon Piper | 20 |
| Edmond Skynner | 40 |
| John Snorton | 30 |
| James Stevens | 20 |
| William Stotson | 40 |
| Hugh Sweet | 30 |
| Robert Symons | 30 |
| Richard Teige | 30 |
| Thomas Teige | 34 |

## Saltash cont'd

| | |
|---|---|
| Richard Teite | 25 |
| Mathew Venard | 18 |
| Thomas Venner | 25 |
| Thomas Wattervile: | 24 |
| John Williams | 24 |
| Richard Williams | 46 |
| William Williams | 30 |
| Edmond Wills | 40 |

SAILORS AND SERVANTS

| | |
|---|---|
| William Avent | 20 |
| Richard Bevill | 30 |
| Arthur Coute | 20 |
| John Mill | 20 |
| Walter Petheron | 18 |
| Nicholas Pitt | 18 |
| Richard Rundell | 20 |

SHIPWRIGHTS

| | |
|---|---|
| Leonard Brett | 50 |
| Richard Gaude | 30 |
| John Harbour | 26 |
| Walter Harbour | 18 |
| William Hill | 26 |
| William Hunkin | 30 |
| Walter Stacie | 35 |

## St Stephens-next-Saltash

*[St Stevens juxta Saltashe]*

SAILORS          [ages not given]

John Barnecot
Richard Bonsoll
Richard Cholwell
John Collinge
Archelaus Haukin
William Henden
William Hendy
Edward Hoskins
Mathew Luce
William Sendy
Richard Skelton

## Antony

*[Anthony]*

MARINERS

| | |
|---|---|
| Henry Blake | 50 |
| Emanuel Harris | 30 |

SAILORS

| | |
|---|---|
| Stephen Alley | 30 |
| Thomas Avery | 24 |
| John Barrey | 30 |
| John Best | 30 |
| John Body | 60 |
| Mathew Body | 40 |
| Thomas Body | 24 |
| Peter Burtt | 20 |
| Ambrose Carewe | 20 |
| Edward Collen | 30 |
| Richard Collinge | 24 |
| Peter Corner | 30 |
| Bartamyn Crudicot | 20 |
| Thomas Dwene | 36 |
| Isaac Dweyne | 28 |
| Peter Dweyne | |
| Henry Govett | 20 |
| Walter Greene | |
| Daniel Greete | |
| John Greete | |
| John Harry | 20 |
| John Hendy | 20 |
| Thomas Hockinge | |
| Stephen Hodge | 24 |
| John Holman | 26 |
| John Hoskins | 20 |
| Thomas House | 24 |
| George Hunkin | 30 |
| John Hunkin | 40 |
| Robert Hunkin | 40 |
| Thomas Hunkin | |
| John Leight | 40 |
| John Mitchell | 30 |
| Robert Olver | 28 |
| Pascho Pierce | 30 |
| George Popleston | |
| Philip Popleston | |
| Josias Poplestone | |
| Stephen Poplestone | 20 |
| Walter Poplestone | 23 |
| Richard Relive | 30 |
| Thomas Roache | 20 |
| Stephen Sergeant | 20 |
| Jonathan Stevens | 26 |
| William Stevens | 30 |
| Peter Trappinge | 30 |
| John Treneman | 20 |
| Elias Weringe | 30 |
| Thomas Wilcocke | |

SAILOR SERVANTS
Samuel Coade
John Cole
Henry Corwithy
William Hoake

SAILOR SERVANTS
John Batt jun.
Manides Govet
John Harte
Robert Hill
Amos Peter
John Sergeant

## Sheviock
[*Sheviocke, Shevioke*]

FISHERMEN [ages not given]
John Batt sen.
Dowell Dewstowe
Richard Harle
William Helliar
John Lavers
Richard Lavers
John Lythibie

MARINERS
Elias Barne
George Carkett
Robert Hoskins

SAILORS
John Barne
Peter Berd
Emanuel Bohey
Thomas Briget
William Broad
William Giles
Edward Hawke
Francis Hoskin
David Lythiby
Oliver Maisters
Edward Mooresheed
Henry Nauter
John Nauter
Walter Peake
Thomas Peperel
Oliver Peter
John Ruby
William Sergeant
Thomas Tenny
Coranish Tradinham
John Truscott
Richard Truscott
Stephen Vinton
Ezekiel Warren
John Wicot

## Millbrook
[*Milbrooke*]

GUNNERS
| | |
|---|---|
| William Bound | 44 |
| Nepthaly Mill | 38 |
| John Rawe | 48 |
| John Symon | 48 |
| Thomas Taylor | 38 |

MARINERS
| | |
|---|---|
| John Bartlett | 30 |
| John Charke | 44 |
| John Dwayne | 48 |
| Henry Griddon | 38 |
| John Gruffin | 35 |
| Pascho Lawrey | 32 |
| John Lucas | 32 |
| John Mitchell | 35 |
| William Penticost | 45 |
| George Penticoste | 38 |
| John Pierce | 48 |
| Walter Rawe | 48 |
| Toby Richards | 42 |
| Digory Searle | 32 |
| Richard Taprell | 25 |

PILOTS
| | |
|---|---|
| Edward Bound | 48 |
| John Criffle | 60 |
| Richard Cudlipp | |
| William Evans | 52 |
| George Harris | 46 |
| Jacob Mill | 36 |
| Thomas White | 40 |
| Richard Wood | 54 |

SAILORS AND SERVANTS
John Belly
William Bonsell
William Jennings
John Mitchell
Edward Moreshed

**Millbrook cont'd**
Walter Rawe

SHIPWRIGHTS
William Carne
William Cornishe          40
John Hoop                 28
John Pierce               32
Tristram Westbreake       36
John Winche               30

## Millbrook and Maker
### [*Milbrooke et Maker*]

COOPERS
John Dawe
Philip Dawe

TRUMPETER
James Nicholls

SAILORS
John Adams
Walter Adams
Henry Atkins              38
Arthur Babidge
John Bambury
Joseph Barlett
Peter Bartlett
John Bely
Nicholas Bely
John Blake                28
John Bligh
Cutbert Body
John Brande               34
John Cause                38
William Chappleman
Penticost Charke          38
Michael Clynnicke         38
Richard Collin
Thomas Collin
Samuel Coppenge           28
John Cornishe
Oliver Cornishe           36
Sampson Cornishe          38
Stephen Dalmon            36
Thomas Dawe
Gregory Derry
John Dwayne jun.          24
John Dynner
Peter Edward

Nicholas Farres           44
Pascho Farres
John Gelly                36
Richard Gross             30
Richard Harvy
William Hockin
Ambrose Honycombe
Richard Honycombe
Thomas Honycombe
Clement Hooper
John Hoskinge
John Humfry               36
Walter Hunkin
William Laury             40
Richard Lawry
William Lithby
Walter Marchant           32
John Moone
Stephen Mutterlaige       38
Richard Nicholls
Nehemyas Olver
John Penny
Thomas Phisicke
Almett Prissillicke
Henry Randall
William Rayne
George Riche
Richard Robins
William Rodd              26
Peter Rowe
Edward Russell
Jacob Searle
John Sellcombe
Edward Sergeant
William Skynner
John Stevens
Richard Streeke
Pascho Tannell            40
Charles Teige             40
William Tooker            28
Robert Toule
Walter Trigg
David Tye
Henry Weale               26
Henry Weale
Henry Williams
Robert Wills              44

SAILORS AND FISHERMEN
Thomas Candy

John Crabb
William Mitchell
Walter Randall
Daniel Rasher
Richard Rawe
Daniel Stevens
Edward Symons
Fardinando Trigg
Griffin Truscott

## Botus Fleming
### [Botesflemminge]
MARINER
Samuel Mintren                    40

SAILORS
Richard Barret                    25
Richard Frost                     36
Nicholas Jago                     35
Martin Jagoe                      20
John Knight                       40
Anthony Leane                     24
Nathaniel Mintren                 25
Nicholas Robert                   20
John Sparnoll                     30
Mathew Webb                       20

## Landulph
### [Landulpe]
GUNNERS
John Borrond                      40
Roger Helland                     60
William Jefford                   35
Thomas Knight                     40

FISHERMEN
Jacob Frost                       30
Nicholas Frost                    65
Richard Geast                     55

MARINERS
John Corbin                       40
John Ham                          70

SAILORS
Richard Bond                      35
Francis Emett                     30
Nicholas Guest                    22
Thomas Gullet                     24

Peter Gullid                      32
Richard Gullod                    20
William Ham                       28
John Hunkin                       25
John Hutchin                      24
William Jope                      50
John Lander                       24
Swy-inor Lewes                    20
John Mathewe                      30
Francis Moyse                     30
John Peirce                       35
William Pierce                    40
Francis Smaley                    32
George Tittson                    36

SAILOR FISHERMAN
John Helland                      28

## Landrake
FISHERMEN            [ages not given]
Richard Couche
Thomas Heard
Jeffrey Jope

## St Germans
### [St Jermans]
MARINER
Arthur Hutchins                   46

SAILORS
William Barden                    38
Tristram Chaslyn                  40
John Harsdon                      46
John Hill                         30
William Jeffry                    26
Thomas Lavers                     20
Robert Leane                      26
Richard Lylley                    40
John Mitchill                     22
William Parson                    34
John Russell                      26
William Steven                    28
William Wedge                     30

## St John
### [St Johns]
FISHERMEN
Edward Goyte                      30

**St John cont'd**

| | |
|---|---|
| George Greete | 44 |
| John Moore | 30 |
| William Motton | 26 |
| Robert Raine | 20 |
| John Randle | 30 |

SAILORS

| | |
|---|---|
| John Bondage | 30 |
| Robert Clems | 42 |
| Robert Edley | 38 |
| Richard Head | 46 |
| Andrew Hunkin | 40 |
| Roger Pierce | 50 |
| Thomas Pierce | 21 |
| John Raine | 44 |
| William Randell | 32 |

## Rame

GUNNERS          [ages not given]

Ezechia Anger
Steven Atkins
Thomas Weale

MARINERS

Henry Saunders
Peter Saunders

SAILORS

Peter Beake
John Brone
Nathan Brone
Richard Burges
Thomas Couche
John Dade
John Foote
Malachy Foote
Richard Fose
Richard Foxe
Jeremy Gelly
Zachary Gennys
William Gennys
John Hatch jun.
John Hatche sen.
John Haynes
Digory Hewe
Steven Jane
James Jorey
James Mayne

John Mayne
Isaac Mershall
Daniel Mill
John Mitchell
Ralph Nicholas
Richard Nicholls
Robert Nicolls
Robert Reane
Edward Richards
Richard Richards
John Spredall
John Staman
Richard Vogler

## Calstock
### [*Calstocke*]

SAILORS

| | |
|---|---|
| John Adam | 40 |
| Abel Bond | 40 |
| William Bond | 44 |
| Humphrey Chipman | 35 |
| John Derry sen. | 50 |
| John Derry jun. | 22 |
| Daniel Doble | 44 |
| Anthony Facy | 53 |
| John Facye | 70 |
| Edward Greet | 60 |
| William Harry | 54 |
| Daniel Hawkin | 60 |
| Anthony Honicombe | 54 |
| Edmond Honycombe | 50 |
| James Slade | 36 |
| John Stentaford | 34 |
| Mark Stentaford | 42 |
| Anthony Streek | 33 |
| Roger Symons | 24 |
| Philip Webb | 55 |
| Richard Webb | 48 |
| Richard Wills | 34 |
| Robert Wison | 24 |

## Menheniot
### [*Minhenit*]

FISHERMAN

| | |
|---|---|
| William Bawden | 40 |

## St Mellion
### [*St Mellin*]

SAILOR

Walter Walkey       18

[signed] James Bagg

| The names of the ships | Burthen | Ordnance | Capable to carry | The Owners' names. |
|---|---|---|---|---|
| **Saltash** [*Saltashe*] | | | | |
| Phillipp | 200 tons | 14 | 20 | Thomas Paulinge |
| Isaac | 60 | 0 | 6 | Edmond Herringe |
| True dealinge | 40 | 0 | 2 | do |
| Retorne | 50 | 0 | 4 | Sampson Bond |
| One barque | 35 | 0 | 2 | William Lucas |
| Desire | 15 | 0 | 0 | Margaret Beele |
| **Antony** [*Anthonie*] | | | | |
| Prescilla | 65 | 6 | 8 | Simon Rowe |
| Joane | 55 | 0 | 5 | do |
| White Lyon | 40 | 0 | 4 | Ferdinando Triggs |
| Welfare | 90 | 6 | 8 | do |
| Maye Garland | 50 | 0 | 5 | Henry Sergeant |
| **Sheviock** [*Sheviocke*] | | | | |
| Dayestarr | 50 | 0 | 5 | William Hitchens |
| **Millbrook** [*Milbrooke*] | | | | |
| Portion | 90 | 6 | 10 | Richard Rowe |
| Rebecca | 60 | 0 | 4 | do |
| Pearle | 40 | 0 | 2 | do |
| Prymrose | 20 | 0 | 0 | do |
| Josephe | 20 | 0 | 0 | do |
| William & John | [blank] | [blank] | [blank] | do |
| Retorne | 120 | 0 | 10 | William Rowe |
| Tryall | 130 | 4 | 12 | do |
| Concord | 120 | 2 | 10 | do |
| Amytie | 40 | 0 | 2 | do |
| Expectacon | 80 | 6 | 8 | Peter Rise & Henry Skynner |
| Peter | 40 | 0 | 4 | do |
| Elizabeth | 30 | 0 | 0 | do |
| John | 40 | 0 | 4 | John Blake |
| Symon | 60 | 2 | 4 | do |
| George | 80 | 2 | 8 | Richard Bely |
| Abraham | 80 | 0 | 6 | John Evans jun. |
| **Botus Fleming** [*Botesfleminge*] | | | | |
| Digory | 40 | 0 | 3 | Richard Wills |

[signed] James Bagg

# WEST HUNDRED

PRO, SP16/34/105
[dorse] Cornwall. South. West Hundred.

### Place of Abode

## East Looe

### [East Loe]

**Qualitie and Men's Names**

FISHERMEN            [ages not given]
Thomas Baddock
Jerman Bale
Robert Barker
Nicholas Barret
John Barry
William Beale
Jacob Beare
Michael Blith
Henry Butler
John Butler
John Byllet
Henry Cade
Talland Cardew
Pascho Carlyne
Thomas Carrow
Andrew Caruo
John Chubb sen.
John Chubb jun.
Thomas Clemeans
Henry Collinge
Pascho Colliver
John Colly
Nicholas Collyn
Mathew Couch
Richard Courtes
Peter Criffill
Richard Criyffell
Luke Daddo
Edward Davies
William Desurrent
Thomas Fitswilliames
Thomas Fraucis
Dennis Fryer
Nicholas Glyddon
John Grace
Henry Gray
John Grove
John Gyles

David Harris
John Harris
Richard Harris
Robert Haukings
Henry Hickes
Thomas Hickes
John Higgins
Peter Hilliar
William Hoakey
Thomas Hoaly
William Hodgson
Henry Hoop[er]
Richard Jago
John Jesper
Thomas, John Nott's man
John Kellow
Walter Lallur
Phillip Landro:
Basten Lawellen
David Lory
Pascho Luky
Walter Mathew
Roger Mirracke
Thomas Natkins
Arthur Newton
James Nichols
Israel Parkins
John Penquit
George Perke
John Pike
Thomas Poore
Morrish Prinne
Thomas Russell
Pascho Scull
John Searle
Henry Skinnar
Edward Sleepe
Martin Smith
John Sommer
John Stephen jun.
Thomas Symon jun.
John Trelether
James Trigameur
John Walter
John White
Pethrick White
John Williames,
    son to John Williams, carpenter
Phillip Williames

John Abbott
John Batton
Edward Dabbyn

## The Port
## East Looe
[*East Lowe*]

| The ships' names | Burthen | Ordnance | Capable to carry | Owners' names |
|---|---|---|---|---|
| The *Mayflower* | 40 tons | [blank] | [blank] | William Mayowe |
| The *Successe* | 40 tons | do | do | John and ThomasEger |
| The *Margaret* | 40 tons | do | do | William Pope [and] William Parris |
| The *Qartred* | 40 tons | do | do | Dennis Fitzwilliams [and] Daniel Chubb |
| The *Trinity* | 20 tons | do | do | Philip Hickes |
| The *William* | 18 tons | do | do | Thomas Eger |
| The *Grace* | 16 tons | do | do | Philip Williams |

[signed] James Bagg

## Owners of boats belonging for fishing
## burthen about 8 or 10 tons and some less

| Fishermen | | Masters of shipping |
|---|---|---|
| Thomas Spoore one boat | 1 | Edmond Fitzwilliames |
| Dennis Fitzwilliams one boat | 1 | John Williames |
| John Hyckes one boat | 1 | Philip Hickes sen. |
| Philip Hickes several 2 boats | 2 | John Pope |
| William Parris 2 boats | 2 | Ambrose White |
| John Egar 2 boats | 2 | Thomas Spoore |
| Johan Peke widow 2 boats | 2 | Richard Davies |
| Philip Hyckes jun. 2 boats | 2 | Ezekiel Colman |
| Daniel Chubb 2 boats | 2 | John Nott |
| Robert Spoore one boat | 1 | William Pope, |
| Philip Fitzwilliames one boat | 1 | Master & gunner |
| Thomas Egar one boat | 1 | |
| John Hickes widow one boat | 1 | |
| Thomas Symon 2 boats | 2 | |
| Philip Williames one boat | 1 | |
| Thomas Collynes one boat | 1 | |
| Margaret Pope widow 1 boat | 1 | |
| John Pope one boat | 1 | |
| Edmond Fitzwilliams | | |
| Margaret Fitzwilliams | 1 | |

[*Note*] These boats scarce $^1/_2$ of them are employed for want of men in regard there hath been taken away by the Turks and some other boats with two barks are to the number of 60 men and upwards.

## The names of fishermen and sailors in the port of Polperro [*Polpera*]

Nicholas Cornish     [ages not given]
Lawrence Davye
Lawrence Frethry
Thomas Mark
John Maynard
Thomas Searell
Henry Sawle
Robert Stepp

## Lansallos

| | Ages | |
|---|---|---|
| SEAFARING MEN | | |
| John Bathe | 30 | years |
| Robert Crago | 24 | |
| Pascho Goad | 20 | |
| John Gyddie | 30 | |
| Cornelius Hearle | 60 | |
| Nicholas Hockin sen. | 60 | |
| Nicholas Hockin | 20 | |
| Nicholas Jane | 30 | |
| William Lally | 40 | |
| William Martyn | 40 | |
| John Olyver | 40 | |
| John Palmer | 30 | |
| John Peake | 30 | |
| Thomas Philfe | 40 | |
| George Pope | 46 | |
| Richard Pope | 40 | |
| Thomas Priar | 20 | |
| Ralph Searle | 56 | |
| Thomas Waie | 60 | |
| Mathew Welch: | 20 | |
| Thomas Welch: | 40 | |

Thomas Peake     [?constable]

## Polruan

### [*Polruanport*]

A ship called the *Barnard* with 2 pieces of ordnance
     John Mayone owner

A small bark called the *Successe*
     Francis Bond owner

## The names of fishermen and other sailors in this port

William Allen     [ages not given]
Richard Anger
Edward Barker
Banden Blake
John Boone
John Broade
Richard Broade
Thomas Broade
Mathew Carne
William Carrowe
Thomas Cooke
Raphe Dawe
Robert Dawe
James Denboro
George Downinge
Thomas Gendall
Walter Gendall
John Hannyball
Stephen Holman
Richard Jenking
Thomas Jessopp
Richard John
John Kent
Raphe Leckes
Henry Lewes, shipmaster
John Litle
William Litle
Arthur Little
Nicholas Merrygoe
Richard Moore
John Owne
Richard Parkery
William Parkin
William Pearse
Thomas Pell
Thomas Penwarne
William Perryman
Henry Pill
John Polsew
John Pope
Thomas Poynter
John Rendall
John Sampson
Thomas Smyth
William Stephens
John Teage
Edward Tom

John Tom sen.
John Tom
Robert West
Alexander Willyams
Edward Wymend
Edward Wymond
William Wymond
John Wymouth

## West Looe
### [*West Lowe*]
*Darlyng*, burthen 30 tons, ordnance [blank], owner's name - Simon Peake

**The names of fishermen and other sailors in the port of West Looe [*West Lowe*]**
John Boyne
William Bath
Walter Bodwaye
John Butler
John Carne
Pascoe Chubb
Walter Distin
Walter Fostrett
Stephen Gorge
Richard Hawkins
Robert Nettle
Richard Nicholles
Leonard Pett
Nicholas Stephens
Thomas Vyne
Thomas Ward
Cornelius Warren
John Welsh
John Wenmouth
Henry Wenmouth
John White
Roger White
Ambrose Will
Nicholas Wills

[signed] James Bagg

# POWDER HUNDRED

PRO, SP16/34/108
[dorse] Cornwall. South. Powder Hundred

**Place of Abode**

# Fowey

| Qualitie and Men's Names | Age |
| --- | --- |
| MARINERS | |
| John Batten | |
| John Cade | 52 |
| John Cobb | 52 |
| David Forgesson | |
| Ciprian Goodale | |
| Philip Goodale | |
| William Lucas | 46 |
| Edward Mugford | |
| Lewis Sprye | 36 |
| William Vien | |
| John Vyen | 58 |
| John Williams, | |
| ['gunner' crossed out] | 50 |
| | |
| SAILORS | |
| Michael [blank] | 27 |
| Richard Bowringe | 26 |
| Henry Burn | 33 |
| John Cleere | 40 |
| John Cooke | 26 |
| William Cooke | 34 |
| Richard Couche | 38 |
| Richard Dunn | 24 |
| John Dyer | 20 |
| Robert Forgeson | 26 |
| Frances Hamet | 18 |
| Walter Hamet | 44 |
| Thomas Helman | 36 |
| William Hill | 46 |
| William Hodge | 22 |
| John Holey | 30 |
| Thomas Huio | 56 |
| John Jonsen | 30 |
| Endego Jonson | 55 |
| Michael Kee | 56 |
| William Labes | 34 |
| Edward Marwoode | 52 |
| Edward Neele | 46 |
| William Nobes | 27 |
| Avery Palmer | 38 |
| Richard Pascho | 46 |
| Thomas Phillips jun. | 26 |
| William Pope | 24 |
| John Slyman | 34 |
| Walter Slyman | 25 |

## Fowey cont'd

| | |
|---|---|
| Thomas Stephens | 30 |
| John Tome | 36 |
| Abraham Torant | 38 |
| Oliver Torney | 28 |
| Aaron Walishe | 32 |
| Moses Walishe | 33 |
| Mathew Williams | 50 |
| Nathaniel Williams | 46 |
| Thomas Woolridge | 40 |

GUNNER

| | |
|---|---|
| Peter Cade | 50 |

## Mevagissey
### [Mevagesa]

MARINERS

| | |
|---|---|
| William Blericke | 40 |
| Richard Dunn | 40 |
| Francis Moyle | 40 |
| Barnard Preest | 38 |
| John Tudd | 42 |

FISHERMEN

| | |
|---|---|
| John Badcocke | 40 |
| Roger Ball | 40 |
| William Boond | 40 |
| Edward Cornishe | 40 |
| John Dalley | 40 |
| Michael Dalley | 30 |
| Richard Dalley | 20 |
| William Dalley | 34 |
| Arthur Davye | 40 |
| William Dawe | 30 |
| Charles Decka | 40 |
| Edward Hennowe | 40 |
| Richard Hugo | 40 |
| William Jenkin | 40 |
| Mathew John | 30 |
| Thomas John | 33 |
| John Laingworthy | 40 |
| John Markes | 40 |
| John Rowett | 60 |
| John Russell | 25 |
| John Stephen | 40 |
| Hugh Stephens | 22 |
| Richard Stephens | 50 |
| Richard Syncocke | 50 |
| Luke Thomas | 22 |
| Michael Williams | 40 |

## Philleigh
### [Phylleigh]

MARINER

| | |
|---|---|
| John Levy | 55 |

## Truro

MARINER

| | |
|---|---|
| Edward Michell | |

FISHERMEN

| | |
|---|---|
| Hopton Avery | |
| Martyn Avery | |
| Richard Avery sen. | |
| Richard Avery jun. | |
| Robert Gaye | |
| Abraham Martyn | |
| Thomas Martyn | |
| John Reed, | |
| fisherman servant | |
| Edward Tomkin | |

## Lostwithiel
### [Lostwithiell]

BARGEMEN

| | |
|---|---|
| Maurice Barne | 48 |
| Richard Beale | 50 |
| William Bersey | 52 |
| Stephen Talven | 60 |

## St Ewe
### [St Eva]

SEINERS

| | |
|---|---|
| William Allen | 40 |
| Michael Beele, | |
| alias Jorden | 34 |
| Thomas Beel:[e], | |
| alias Jordan | 20 |
| Richard Champyn | 36 |
| Richard Dorkinge | 30 |
| John Dyer | 50 |
| Richard Geene | 26 |
| John Giles | 44 |
| Richard Hambly | 14 |
| Michael Hamlye | 45 |
| Edward Harrys | 25 |
| Sandry Laneye | 50 |

| | |
|---|---|
| William Marke, | |
| alias Stephen | 30 |
| Hughe Morrishe | 50 |
| William Roseveare | 53 |
| John Sintir, | |
| alias Randall | 30 |

## Gerrans
## [*St Gerrans*]

FISHERMEN

| | |
|---|---|
| John Babb | 50 |
| William Babb | 46 |
| Zachary Chinowe | 50 |
| Hugh Hayne | 30 |
| Nicholas Martyn | 55 |
| John Merten | 40 |
| Richard Newey | 25 |
| William Newey | 30 |
| Robert Norman | 30 |
| Solomon Pascowe | 56 |
| John Rosemond | 70 |
| Hugh Sawell | 44 |
| John Thomas | 66 |
| John Thomas jun. | 22 |
| William Thomas | 20 |
| John Tome | 60 |
| Robert Trouser | 50 |
| Edward Williams | 70 |

## Veryan

FISHERMEN

| | |
|---|---|
| William Davies | 60 |
| William Dennis | 40 |
| John Josephe | 40 |
| William Leave | 55 |
| Henry Quicke | 30 |
| Thomas Rawe | 30 |
| Edward Thomas | 30 |
| James Williams | 50 |

## Gorran
## [*Goran*]

SAILORS

| | |
|---|---|
| John Carthen | 35 |
| Nathaniel Cocke | 20 |
| Charles Devonshire | 21 |
| William Devonshire | 33 |

| | |
|---|---|
| William Hennon | 27 |
| William James | 40 |
| Richard Jenkin | 50 |
| Richard Nankarewe | 20 |
| Richard Richards | 25 |
| William Tongkin | 25 |
| John Husband Trevisand | 34 |
| Zachary Tuckar | 40 |

SEINERS

| | |
|---|---|
| John Baker | 50 |
| William Beary | 30 |
| Edward Bowden | 30 |
| John Carewe | 35 |
| Alexander Cetto | 30 |
| Stephen Collyver | 50 |
| Edward Devonshere | 60 |
| Thomas Dingell | 30 |
| Henry Goally | 45 |
| Edward Hennon | 40 |
| Nicholas Lugger | 35 |
| Richard Luke | 55 |
| Roger Medres | 50 |
| Oliver Nicholls, | |
| alias Nanolls | 45 |
| Richard Nicolls | 23 |
| Thomas Pascon | 40 |
| Peter Pereill | 40 |
| Charles Phelipps | 26 |
| Nicholas Robins | 50 |
| William Sanders | 40 |
| Richard Siamond | 40 |
| John Thomas | 40 |
| William Tongkin sen. | 57 |
| William Tremer | 40 |
| John Williams | 34 |
| George Williams | 30 |

FISHERMEN

| | |
|---|---|
| Hugh Bonffill | 40 |
| Richard Cocke | 20 |
| William Dorracke | 50 |
| Richard Golly | 20 |
| John Gorelly | 50 |
| Robert Harnowe | 54 |
| Thomas Harnowe | 20 |
| John Hennon | 35 |
| John Husband | 55 |
| John Husband | 55 |
| John Jenkin | 35 |
| George Jenkins | 40 |

## Gorran cont'd

| | |
|---|---|
| John Longe | 40 |
| Ambrose Luke | 55 |
| Digory Luke | 40 |
| Edward Luke | 30 |
| Daniel Olyver | 37 |
| Edward Olyver | 25 |
| William Pereill | 44 |
| Jeffry Phelips | 20 |
| Thomas Phelips | 30 |
| David Randill | 30 |
| John Richards | 40 |
| George Robin | 20 |
| Stephen Tonkin | 45 |
| Richard Trehaan | 20 |
| William Watts | 30 |
| William Wills | 35 |
| John Wymet | 18 |

## St Anthony-in-Roseland
### [St Anthony]

FISHERMEN

| | |
|---|---|
| Peter Christopher | 46 |
| John Hocken | 40 |
| Richard Peers | 30 |
| John Peters sen. | 63 |
| John Peters jun. | 50 |

## St Just-in-Roseland
### [St Just]

MARINER

Stephen Hore

SAILORS

John Castelton
Stephen Cooke
William Cooke
Thomas Hendy
Jacob Hewgoe
Stephen James
William Leane
Richard Matta
Thomas Matta
Inigo Potter,
  apprentice

GUNNER

Nicholas Tracy

FISHERMEN

Stephen Christopher
George Davy
Hugh Denshere
John Jacke
John Jane
Richard Pyll
Christopher Rawe
Henry Rawe
Jacob Rawe
John Rawe
Martin Rawe
Thomas Rawe
John Vincent
Humphrey Vivian

## St Sampson
### [St Sampsons]

FISHERMEN

| | |
|---|---|
| John Barratt | 56 |
| Richard Beale | 34 |
| Thomas Davy | 43 |
| William Davye | 35 |
| Edward Hoskynge | 23 |
| John Martyn | 56 |
| Thomas Michell | 30 |
| John Tredake | 50 |

SAILORS

| | |
|---|---|
| William Barrat | 30 |
| John Highene | 28 |
| John Lakes | 40 |
| James Palmer | 24 |
| Robert Rollynge | 40 |

## St Blazey
### [Blasie]

FISHERMEN

| | |
|---|---|
| John Carlyan | 28 |
| John Hinckson,<br>  fisherman and servant | 18 |
| John Pryor | 40 |
| Luke Rawatt | 45 |
| William Rawatt | 23 |
| Michael White | 15 |

## St Austell

FISHERMEN

| | |
|---|---|
| Robert Bennet | 40 |
| Moses Chely | 40 |
| Luke Clemence | 40 |
| Richard Daddowe | 40 |
| William Daddowe | 30 |
| Michael Davye | 40 |
| Mathew Evans | 40 |
| John Jagoe | 30 |
| John Jagoe | 40 |
| Richard Lellicke | 40 |
| Nicholas Nancollis | 40 |
| Richard Nancollis | 50 |
| Lewis Parson | 40 |
| Luke Pierce | 50 |
| John Rawatt | 40 |
| Richard Trivethicke | 30 |

## Tywardreath

[*Tywerdreth, Tywerderth*]

SAILORS

| | |
|---|---|
| Paul Kitto | 50 |
| Walter Marke | 23 |
| John Penquite | 44 |
| John Pomery | 44 |
| Manuel Tressise | 45 |
| John Wey | 40 |

FISHERMEN

| | |
|---|---|
| Nicholas Cole | 36 |
| John Colofor | 32 |
| Pascho Colofor | 35 |
| William Colofor | 20 |
| Walter Coren | 56 |
| William Coren | 26 |
| Clement Marke | 60 |
| William Marke | 30 |
| John Nowell | 28 |
| Richard Pockie | 42 |
| John Smyth | 40 |
| John Sorwest | 20 |
| Walter Stephens | 20 |

SHIPWRIGHT

| | |
|---|---|
| Walter Cocke | 22 |

## St Clement

[*Clemens*]

MARINERS

| | |
|---|---|
| John Hill | 50 |
| William Symons | 56 |

## Kenwyn

BARGEMEN

Christopher Geffry
William Ralinge
Thomas Rawlynige

## St Michael Penkivel

[*Penkevell*]

BARGEMAN

John Baly

## Kea

BARGEMAN

| | |
|---|---|
| William Giddie | 50 |

FISHERMEN

| | |
|---|---|
| Teage Burly | 26 |
| Alexander Condon | 30 |
| Gawen Martyn | 40 |
| John Martyn | 33 |
| William Saunder | 30 |
| Andrew Stephens | 50 |
| Thomas Weekes | 25 |
| Frances Weepe | 30 |

## [damaged] port

SAILOR

| | |
|---|---|
| Henry Glanfeild | 50 |

## Feock

[*Feake*]

BARGEMEN

| | |
|---|---|
| Hibbs Campeche | 35 |
| John Clyfe | 26 |
| Gearaine Cocke | 50 |
| John Cocke | 25 |
| George Conggan | 32 |
| Nicholas Cooth | 26 |

**Feock cont'd**

| | |
|---|---|
| Stephen Couggan | 64 |
| Henry Davye | 34 |
| Reynanld Dockett | 40 |
| Roman Drewe | 34 |
| Hercules Fillipp | 30 |
| John Harvye | 23 |
| Timothy Harvye | 24 |
| Richard Hendill | 36 |
| Robert Hobbs | 32 |
| John Kneeboone | 40 |
| Edward Lawrence | 40 |
| Hercules Martyn | 46 |
| John Olyver | 32 |
| Gearence Otes | 22 |
| Robert Otes | 35 |
| Thomas Otts | 20 |
| Roman Richards | 40 |
| Richard Rowter | 26 |
| Richard Service | 30 |
| William Tregonawhan | 30 |
| Richard Tregonawhim | 32 |

FISHERMEN

| | |
|---|---|
| Francis Bennet | 34 |
| Edward Clemore | 24 |
| Michael Cocke, ['bargeman' crossed out] | 35 |
| John Davye | 26 |
| Walter Halvoso | 40 |
| Nicholas John, ['bargeman' crossed out] | 30 |
| Peter Smyth, ['bargeman' crossed out] | 32 |

[signed] James Bagg

| The names of the ships | Burthen | Ordnance | Capable to carry | The owners' names |
|---|---|---|---|---|
| | | | **The Port Fowey** | |
| *Barnard* | 50 tons | 4 | [blank] | William Byrd |
| *Grace* | 40 | 0 | do | Thomas Phillipps[and] William Vyen |
| *Michaell* | 20 | 0 | do | Peter Holman, Richard Spry, and Valentine Band |
| *Success* | 23 | 0 | do | Lewis Spry & Edward Mugford |
| *Nightingall* | 20 | 0 | do | William Bird, Digory Gorge, and Ciprian Goodale |
| *Indeavor* | 14 | 0 | do | Peter Holman |
| *Henry* | 22 | 0 | do | William Byrd & Philip Goodale |
| *Hopewell* | 20 | 0 | do | Digory Gorge |
| | | | **Mevagissey [*Mevagesa*]** | |
| *Mary* | 18 | 0 | do | Richard Butland |
| | | | **Truro** | |
| *Hope* | 30 | 0 | do | Francis Nosworthy |
| | | | **Falmouth** | |
| [a] bark | 20 | 0 | do | Richard Penhallowe |

[signed] James Bagg

# KERRIER HUNDRED

PRO, SP16/34/107

**Place of Abode**

## St Keverne

| Qualitie and Men's Names | Age |
|---|---|
| SAILORS | |
| Nicholas Beimot | 40 |
| Anthony Bowisie | 30 |
| Haniball Drewe | 40 |
| William Mitchell | 30 |
| John Nicholls | 50 |
| John Stewes | 40 |
| John Tregallos | 50 |
| John Willes | 40 |
| FISHERMEN | |
| John Anthony | 30 |
| Nicholas Anthony | 30 |
| John Bonvill | 40 |
| Ranald Bonvill | 40 |
| Walter Bosvine | 50 |
| Richard Bounsie | 50 |
| Thomas Bugg | 40 |
| John Chefer | 54 |
| Richard Chefer | 20 |
| Robert Chefer | 30 |
| Thomas Cotha | 40 |
| William Danderie | 40 |
| Thomas Donnell | 40 |
| John Harrie | 30 |
| Robert Harrie | 30 |
| John James | 40 |
| Richard John | 50 |
| Thomas Martyn | 40 |
| Peter Nessevin | 20 |
| John Nicholas | 30 |
| John Nicholas | 40 |
| Thomas Nicholas | 40 |
| George Nicoll | 30 |
| John Olyver | 40 |
| Richard Owen | 20 |
| Nicholas Paskowe | 20 |
| Sampson Paskowe | 45 |
| Thomas Pearce | 30 |
| George Pole | 40 |
| Thomas Richard | 20 |
| John Richards | 40 |
| William Robart | 30 |
| Michael Robert | 20 |
| Richard Sandes | 30 |
| Harry Thomas | 50 |
| James Thomas | 40 |
| John Thomas | 40 |
| Richard Treglohan | 30 |
| Thomas Treglohan | 40 |
| Richard William | 50 |

## Ruan Major

| FISHERMAN | |
|---|---|
| Michael Kindgie | 35 |

## Mullion
### [*Mullian*]

| FISHERMEN | |
|---|---|
| Richard Hockin | 46 |
| Thomas Huchins | 28 |
| Peter Kellwaie | 40 |
| Bennet Nicholas | 34 |
| William Nicholas | 60 |
| Richard Noble | 34 |
| Francis Sanderie | 40 |

## Landewednack
### [*Landewnacke, Landewnake*]

| FISHERMEN | |
|---|---|
| William Edward | 50 |
| Thomas Harvie | 27 |
| Henry Nicholas | 32 |
| Peter Odger | 50 |
| Thomas Penticost | 32 |
| Barnard Pierce | 26 |
| Constantine Pierce | 36 |
| Sampson Pierce | 44 |
| Thomas Robert | 52 |
| Thomas Rodger | 40 |
| Roger Stephen | 36 |
| William Thomas | 30 |
| Walter Trenarth | 34 |
| Sampson Walter | 30 |

## Budock
### [*Budocke*]

SAILORS

| | |
|---|---|
| Christopher Gwyn | 24 |
| Nicholas Michell | 40 |
| Anthony Richard | 22 |
| John Rootes | 40 |
| Thomas Williams | 25 |

FISHERMEN

| | |
|---|---|
| Stephen Camore | 35 |
| William Lande | 50 |
| Thomas Lanhaderne | 40 |
| Richard Noolacke | 40 |

## Mylor
### [*Myler*]

BARGEMEN

| | |
|---|---|
| Edward Allen | 38 |
| Thomas Allen | 35 |
| William Allen | 36 |
| Thomas Berry | 40 |
| Richard Davie | 36 |
| James Deacon | 28 |
| John Deacon | 30 |
| Henry Edwards | 27 |
| Thomas Hornebrooke | 36 |
| Thomas Micholl | 50 |
| William Robins | 40 |
| Hugh Rodgger | 38 |
| John Rowe sen. | 38 |
| John Rowe jun. | 28 |
| John Welsman | 38 |

## Ruan Minor
### [*Ruan Mynor*]

BARGEMEN FISHERMEN

| | |
|---|---|
| George Carnather | 30 |
| Peter John | 46 |

FISHERMEN

| | |
|---|---|
| John Jacka | 32 |
| William Paule | 30 |
| John Steven | 34 |
| Baldwin Syncocke | 36 |

## Grade

FISHERMEN

| | |
|---|---|
| Andrew Martyn | 23 |
| William Trenarth | 40 |

## Cury
### [*Curye*]

FISHERMAN

| | |
|---|---|
| Thomas Edwards | 23 |

## Manaccan
### [*Manacka*]

MARINERS

| | |
|---|---|
| John Leavy | 65 |
| Francis Templaro | 50 |

MARINER FISHERMAN

| | |
|---|---|
| George Restallacke | 55 |

FISHERMEN

| | |
|---|---|
| John Coman | 21 |
| Harkenval Nealene | 28 |
| Francis Restallacke | 30 |
| James Thomas | 20 |

SAILORS

| | |
|---|---|
| Sampson Coman | 34 |
| John Christover | 25 |
| Richard Thomas | 23 |
| William Thomas | 20 |

## Breage

FISHERMEN

| | |
|---|---|
| William Cappall | 50 |
| Simon Gilare | 80 |
| Thomas Leddia | 26 |
| Richard Paskowe | 36 |
| Barnard Prothe | 60 |
| Thomas Prowes | 35 |
| John Stephen | 90 |
| John Stephen jun. | 50 |
| Thomas Stephen | 44 |
| Thomas Trenara | 50 |

## Gunwalloe
### [*Gunwallowe*]

FISHERMEN

| | |
|---|---|
| John Mashall | 44 |
| Thomas Rafe | 64 |
| Nicholas Robert | 51 |
| Ralph Rowe | 49 |
| Robert Senet | 51 |
| James Wiles | 51 |
| John Wiles | 54 |
| Thomas Wiles | 48 |

## St Anthony-in-Meneage
### [*Anthony in Menege*]

MARINERS

| | |
|---|---|
| John Christover | 70 |
| Richard Michell | 70 |
| Theophilus Pendewe | 40 |

SAILORS

| | |
|---|---|
| Richard Anthony | 50 |
| William Bennet | 40 |
| Walter Bolythou | 40 |
| Robert Bolythowe | 20 |
| Anthony Genken | 70 |
| Peter Genkin | 20 |
| John Jenkin | 50 |
| John Pears | 40 |
| John Pendewe | 50 |
| Walter Staies | 20 |

SAILOR FISHERMAN

| | |
|---|---|
| John Thomas | 40 |

## Constantine
### [*Constenton*]

SAILORS

| | |
|---|---|
| William Anbrose | 50 |
| Stephen Hunt | 60 |
| Michael Noye | 30 |

FISHERMEN

| | |
|---|---|
| Arthur Angone | 20 |
| Sebastian Christopher | 25 |
| Richard Eles | 60 |
| Thomas Hunt | 18 |
| William Laprye | 60 |
| Henry Michell | 30 |
| John Treseder | 50 |
| John Treseder | 20 |

## Mawnan

FISHERMEN

| | |
|---|---|
| John Clise | 18 |
| Martin Edwards | 24 |
| Constantine Huchens | 60 |
| Edward Lalean | 40 |
| Thomas Lowry | 20 |
| Thomas Lucke | 60 |
| Richard Sowle | 30 |

## Penryn

['Samuel Grose' crossed out]

MARINERS

John Pendewe
Richard Smythe
Francis Templaro

[signed] James Bagg

### The Port
### Penryn

| The ship's names | Burthen | Ordnance | Capable to carry | Owner's names |
|---|---|---|---|---|
| *Marchant Bonavent*[ure] | 180 tons | 8 | [blank] | Samuel Grose |
| *Fortune* | 140 | 10 | | Thomas Milhewse |
| *Jane* | 30 | 0 | | Samuel Grose, Sup[erio]r |

[signed] James Bagg

# PENWITH HUNDRED

PRO, SP16/34/106
[dorse] Penwith Hundred

### Place of Abode

## Gulval
### [Gulvall]

**Qualitie and Men's Names**

SAILOR                [ages not given]
Francis Gwennapp

FISHERMEN
Mathew Lawrey
Reginald Lawrey
Hugh Martyn

## Newlyn in Paul
### [Newlin in Pawle]

|  | Age |
|---|---|
| SAILORS | |
| John Rowe | 26 |
| John Teage | 50 |
| FISHERMEN | |
| John Asticke | 30 |
| Ralph Avery | 20 |
| John Barnard | 30 |
| William Bossocowe | 35 |
| John Christover | 40 |
| John Cotten | 25 |
| John George | 30 |
| Mathew Harvye | 30 |
| John Hoskins | 20 |
| Philip Jacke | 30 |
| Nicholas James | 30 |
| Henry Jenken | 30 |
| Phillip Kelynacke | 30 |
| William Lodye | 30 |
| Richard Michell | 26 |
| Nicholas Newhall | 35 |
| John Nowell | 25 |
| John Oaire | 30 |
| Martin Rentfree | 30 |
| Thomas Richard | 35 |
| William Richard | 40 |
| John Rowe | 20 |
| John Rowe | 20 |

| William Symon | 30 |
|---|---|
| John Teage | 20 |
| John Thomas | 20 |
| John Thomas | 40 |
| John Thomas | 40 |
| Richard Thomas | 20 |
| Robert Thomas | 35 |
| Thomas Thomas | 20 |
| John Tocken | 50 |
| John Tockenveane | 35 |
| his servant Edward | 25 |
| John Tocker | 30 |
| John Tonken | 45 |
| Nowell Tonken | 23 |
| Pearce Tonken | 50 |
| Robert Tonken | 23 |
| William Tonken | 20 |
| Richard Williams | 30 |
| William Williams | 30 |
| Michael Yeoman | 40 |

## Mousehole
### [Mowshole, Moushole]

| SHIPWRIGHTS | |
|---|---|
| Peter Rocat | 45 |
| William Rocat | 23 |
| Thomas Wills | 40 |
| SAILORS | |
| Thomas Cooke | 30 |
| John Jenken | 40 |
| Michael Pentreth | 40 |
| William Pentueth, | |
| ['shipwright' crossed out] | 23 |
| John Peres | 50 |
| William Stanldby | 50 |
| John Symon | 50 |
| William Tremayne | 40 |
| FISHERMEN | |
| John Breage | 45 |
| John Crankan | 30 |
| William Crankan | 25 |
| Nicholas Edegrnne | 26 |
| Edward Hanyford | 35 |
| Jenkin Kegwyne | 25 |
| John Kegwyne jun. | 25 |
| Amos Newhall | 40 |
| Martyn Nowell | 30 |

| | | | | |
|---|---|---|---|---|
| Julyard Olyver | 40 | John Thomas | 40 |
| Henry Pascho | 40 | John Trenhaile | 50 |
| Richard Pascowe | 50 | | |
| Henry Pentreth | 26 | **FISHERMEN** | |
| John Rawe | 30 | Robert Carne | 35 |
| John Richard sen. | 38 | John Fennye | 35 |
| John Richards jun. | 26 | Richard Giles | 56 |
| William Roberts | 56 | William Giles | 18 |
| Martyn Rogger | 40 | William Harry | 45 |
| Bennet Rowe | 30 | William Hocken | 30 |
| Richard Sampson | 30 | John James | 20 |
| William Sampson | 40 | John Michell | 60 |
| Richard Trabb | 30 | Nicholas Michell | 35 |
| William Treloan | 40 | John Mitchell | 20 |
| Richard Will | 40 | Syer Odger | 30 |
| Richard William | 30 | William Oliver | 18 |
| John Williams alias Elam | 30 | John Olyver | 40 |
| John Wills | 20 | John Rawe | 40 |
| John Yeoman | 50 | William Rowland | 22 |
| | | William Symons | 56 |
| | | Edward Syse | 30 |

## St Levan
### [Levan]

**FISHERMEN**

| | | |
|---|---|
| William Carowe | 35 |
| John Eles | 25 |
| Robert George | 45 |
| Thomas James | 30 |
| James Jenkin | 40 |
| Henry Jenkine | 20 |
| Clement John | 60 |
| Nowell Laperan | 60 |
| William Mitchell | 30 |
| Robert Wever | 50 |
| Edward William | 60 |
| James William | 35 |

## Penzance
### [Pensance, Pensannce]

**MARINER**

| | | |
|---|---|
| William Maddren | 58 |

**SAILORS**

| | | |
|---|---|
| Alexander Bennet | 32 |
| Henry Clies | 60 |
| Nicholas Gover | 50 |
| Thomas Mitchell | 55 |
| Richard Stephens | 60 |

| | |
|---|---|
| John Tomkin | 40 |

**FISHERMEN SAILORS**

| | |
|---|---|
| William Brocker | 25 |
| Henry Foster | 50 |

**FISHERMAN SERVANT**

| | |
|---|---|
| George Richards | 18 |

## St Hilary
### [Illarie]

**SAILOR**

| | |
|---|---|
| Peter Bossowe | 40 |

**FISHERMEN**

| | |
|---|---|
| Thomas Bossowe | 16 |
| William Bossowe | 17 |
| Henry Manly | 20 |
| William Trewhela | 50 |

## Ludgvan

**SHIPWRIGHT**

| | |
|---|---|
| Stephen Tremenhere | 30 |

**SAILOR**

| | |
|---|---|
| James Mabb | 50 |

## Perranuthnoe
### [*Peranuthuo*]

SAILORS

| | |
|---|---|
| Thomas Francis | 55 |
| Thomas Humphry | 40 |
| Henry John | 50 |
| Richard Laytie | 30 |
| Richard Pore | 30 |
| Pierce Wattie | 20 |

## Marazion
### [*Marchaiowe, Marcahiowe, Marrcahiowe, Marchiowe*[1]]

MARINERS

| | |
|---|---|
| Thomas Boteson | |
| John Eva | 50 |
| William Garland | |
| Henry Mabb | |
| Henry Mabb | 26 |
| John Mabb sen. | 52 |
| John Mabb | 50 |
| John Tremellowe | |

SAILORS

| | |
|---|---|
| James Bowden | 30 |
| Bennet Garland | |

| | |
|---|---|
| Edward Mabb | 24 |
| John Pascowe | 50 |
| John Williams | 33 |

FISHERMEN

| | |
|---|---|
| John Chindower | 20 |
| George Christoper | 30 |
| John Cole | 30 |
| John Gasken | 40 |
| Roger Heyman | 22 |
| John Jeffry | 20 |
| Thomas Jeffry | 40 |
| Jonas Mabb | 40 |
| Oliver Nymis | 30 |
| John Peddie | 50 |
| William Peddie | 20 |
| John Robbins | 23 |
| John Rowsline | 20 |
| Thomas Slade | 30 |
| John Stabb | 58 |
| John Stabb jun. | 22 |
| John Steres | 40 |
| John Trubbe | 40 |
| Tristram Waes | 36 |
| Robert Werie | 20 |
| William Williams | 30 |

[signed] James Bagg

[1] Presumably Marketjew.

# SOUTH WEST DEVON, *c*.1626

SIR JAMES BAGG'S SURVEY

# ⌐OBOROUGH HUNDRED

PRO, SP16/34/98
[dorse] A list of ships and seamen in the
Hundred of Roborough in Devon

### Place of Abode

### Plymouth

| Qualitie and Men's Names | Age |
|---|---|
| MARINERS | |
| Henry Aller | 50 |
| Herbert Ashley | 35 |
| James Baker | 36 |
| Robert Baker | 40 |
| Richard Barker | 36 |
| Robert Bennet | 35 |
| Edward Braye | 40 |
| Henry Burges | 40 |
| Richard Burly | 55 |
| George Burrage | 40 |
| John Carkett | 40 |
| Andrew Collinge | 35 |
| John Corbyn | 50 |
| Robert Cornishe | 58 |
| George Dennys | 50 |
| John Evans | 30 |
| Edward Fishcocke | 30 |
| Henry Flicke | 50 |
| Ingram Furse | 26 |
| Thomas Gill | 35 |
| Walter Hele | 50 |
| Henry Jeffry | 42 |
| George Jennens | 28 |
| William Kitchen | 36 |
| Thomas Luscombe | 44 |
| Thomas Polstagg | 45 |
| Henry Raddon | 28 |

| | |
|---|---|
| Richard Randall | 50 |
| Tristram Reed | 36 |
| Roger Roe | 35 |
| James Seaman | 50 |
| Robert Sharpe | 50 |
| Nicholas Shortt | 40 |
| John Smart jun. | 38 |
| Henry Stache | 40 |
| Nathaniel Walters | 27 |
| William Williams | 60 |
| Edward Wycott | 40 |
| John Wynter | 36 |
| SHIPWRIGHTS | |
| William Braye | 32 |
| Ambrose Diggins | 40 |
| Robert Driver | 50 |
| John Eden | 40 |
| Richard Ellis | 60 |
| John Ford | 30 |
| William Ford | 52 |
| Sampson Jope | 32 |
| Peter Joslyn | 50 |
| Walter Joslyn | 40 |
| Mathew Joslynge | 60 |
| Arthur Kearne | 32 |
| Nathaniel Kinge | 45 |
| Richard Lawrence | 50 |
| Walter Slooman | 55 |
| SAILORS | |
| William Addams | 50 |
| Thomas Beake | 26 |
| William Bestha | 45 |
| Ambrose Blythinge | 35 |
| John Bowden | 22 |
| William Brasie | 30 |
| Allen Browne | 45 |
| Gerrad Burleighe | 60 |
| Richard Burleighe | 42 |
| Thomas Butler | 30 |
| Richard Carpenter | 30 |
| William Cawker | 25 |

**Plymouth cont'd**

| | |
|---|---|
| Nicholas Clarke | 20 |
| Simon Clarke | 27 |
| Mathew Clement | 35 |
| Nicholas Cole | 40 |
| Thomas Collinge | 40 |
| George Corber | 24 |
| John Corber | 33 |
| Philip Corber | 20 |
| William Deane | 56 |
| Stephen Ellacombe | 40 |
| Edward Flemyng | 24 |
| Christopher Flicke | 20 |
| William Frethie | 35 |
| Thomas Goodinge | 40 |
| Thomas Greene | 35 |
| Thomas Growden | 30 |
| Nicholas Harwood | 24 |
| Edward Howe | 36 |
| Richard Knight | 25 |
| Thomas Lavers | 30 |
| Christopher Lawrye | 26 |
| Arthur Laye | 40 |
| Arthur Love | 24 |
| William Love | 28 |
| Andrew Lustie | 30 |
| John Lychington | 35 |
| Thomas Mahowe | 18 |
| John Maye | 38 |
| John Myngo | 35 |
| Richard Pell | 50 |
| William Richards | 35 |
| Thomas Riddecliffe | 26 |
| William Rogers | 31 |
| William Sheere | 30 |
| Charles Somers | 30 |
| Arthur Stevens | 35 |
| James Trate | 30 |
| Robert Wadking | 46 |
| Richard White | 38 |
| Thomas White | 24 |

GUNNERS

| | |
|---|---|
| Geffry Cornishe | 26 |
| John Hills | 30 |
| Edward Parkens | 30 |

FISHERMEN

| | |
|---|---|
| Robert Collander | 34 |

| | |
|---|---|
| John Pennybridge | 35 |
| James Steataver | 50 |
| John Thorne | 32 |
| Gilbert Tratt | 30 |

PILOT

| | |
|---|---|
| John Smart sen. | 60 |

BOATSWAINES

| | |
|---|---|
| Robert Dyer | 35 |
| John Dymond | 43 |
| William Rogers | 35 |

# East Stonehouse

FISHERMEN

| | |
|---|---|
| Peter Adams | 45 |
| John Breye | 30 |
| Benjamin Brooke | 26 |
| Thomas Carne | 14 |
| John Clowter | 20 |
| John Coller | 16 |
| Daniel Corde | 20 |
| James Creese | 36 |
| Thomas Croseman | 30 |
| Arthur Davyes | 22 |
| Richard Dowe | 35 |
| John Fayreweather | 35 |
| Henry Ferris | 33 |
| Daniel Fishe | 20 |
| James Frynche | 25 |
| Nicholas Hocke | 24 |
| Daniel Honycombe | 16 |
| Daniel Ivey | 23 |
| Emanuel Kent | 16 |
| John Lang | 16 |
| John Lawrey | 32 |
| Oliver Martyn | 20 |
| James Merryfeild | 35 |
| Henry Older | 16 |
| Thomas Parnell | 14 |
| Gregory Pentier | 40 |
| Peter Rogers | 50 |
| Stephen Sparke | 16 |
| James Sparroe | 20 |
| John Symons | 28 |
| Thomas Symons | 40 |
| Richard Walcome | 55 |
| John Willomes | 16 |

SAILORS
John Hussey 34
Nicholas Light 22
Gregory Maunder 50
Thomas Michells 45
Edward Rushe 35
Christopher Russell 25
Andrew Toser 25

## Stoke Damerel
### [*Stoke damerell*]
SAILORS
Thomas Cobham 24
John Dyer 30
Francis Mathew 38
John Rexford 60
John Skene 35

## St Budeaux
### [*St Budioxe*]
MARINER
George Euscies 24

SAILORS
John Arnall 26
Tippet Colcott 30
Richard Euscies 24
Stephen Hayman 34
Richard Scobble 35
Nathaniel Wellinge 27

BOATSWAINE
James Kemp 32

## Egg Buckland
SAILOR
Mathew Cleve 30

## Tamerton Foliot
### [*Tamerton folliet*]
SAILORS
Thomas Cawes 28

Peter Jesopp 30
John Sisley 34
Ellis Skynner 28

## Bere Ferrers
### [*Beereferris*]
MARINER
George Stidson 45

SAILORS
John Caninge 23
John Chocke 30
Oliver Clarke 20
John Hutchins 26
William Knight 20
Richard Norley 50
John Rider 24
Thomas Splynte 24
Lawrence Steven 40

## Bickleigh
### [*Bickleighe*]
SAILORS
William Cloake 40
Thomas Nott 42

## Buckland Monachorum
MARINER
Ellis Lawrey 30

SAILORS
Edgcomb Law:[rey],
 servant 22
John Scobble 24

## Meavy
SAILOR
Mathew Jeels 20

[signed] James Bagg

| The Ships' names | Burthen | Ordnance | Capable to carry | The Owners' names |
|---|---|---|---|---|
| | | **Plymouth** | | |
| *Arke* | 120 tons | 8 | 12 | Sir James Bagg, knight |
| *George* | 90 | 0 | 8 | do |
| *Amye* | 80 | 2 | 6 | do |
| *Catt* | 160 | 10 | 16 | Mr Abraham Jennens |
| *William* | 80 | 4 | 8 | do |
| *Prosperous* | 100 | 4 | 8 | do |
| *Grace* | 50 | 2 | 4 | do |
| *Ambrose* | 35 | 2 | 3 | do |
| *Dolphin* | 120 | 12 | 16 | Nicholas Sherwill, John Jope, Robert Gubbes, John Cawes, Walter Helle & others |
| *Clawe* | 50 | 2 | 4 | Robert Rawlins & John Cawes |
| *Pellican* | 40 | 0 | 4 | Mathew [blank and] John Cawes |
| *The Frenchman* | 35 | 0 | 2 | John Cawes |
| *Truelove* | 30 | 0 | 2 | do |
| *Adventure* | 30 | 0 | 2 | do |
| *Eagle* | 100 | 6 | 8 | Mr Thomas Fownes, Abraham Rowe, Walter Hele [and] Thomas Pomeroy |
| *Dove* | 35 | 0 | 2 | Mr Thomas Fownes |
| *Jonathan* | 100 | 8 | 16 | Mr Nicholas Sherwill [and] Mr Abraham Colmer |
| *Returne* | 50 | 2 | 4 | Mr Abraham Colmer |
| *Providence* | 80 | 6 | 12 | Leonard Pomery |
| *Grayehonnd* | 30 | 0 | 2 | do |
| *Consent* | 80 | 6 | 12 | Richard Brendon, John Jope, Thomas Crampporne [and] Jerome Roche |
| *Harts ease* | 40 | 0 | 4 | Mr Abraham Colmer, Richard Brendon [and] Moses Goodyeare |
| *Handmayde* | 30 | 0 | 0 | Richard Brendon [and] William Byrche |
| *Robin* | 50 | 0 | 0 | Robert Rawlins |
| *Exchange* | 40 | 0 | 4 | Robert Trelawney sen. |
| *James* | 40 | 0 | 4 | Robert Trelawney jun. |
| *Susan* | 60 | 0 | 4 | John Martyn jun. & others |
| *Speedwell* | 50 | 0 | 4 | John Martyn sen., Edward Cocke [and] Reynold Streamer |
| *Adam and Eve* | 55 | 0 | 0 | John Martyn jun., Peter Johnson & others |
| *John* | 30 | 0 | 0 | John Martyn jun. [and] Edward Cocke |
| *Hector* | 35 | 0 | 0 | Thomas Ceely [and] John Jope |
| *Swanne* | 60 | 2 | 6 | Nicholas Blake |
| *Phenix* | 45 | 0 | 4 | Nicholas Sherwill [and] John Jope |

| John | 80 | 6 | 8 | John Waddon [and] John White *et alii* |
|---|---|---|---|---|
| *Sunne* | 60 | 4 | 6 | John Paige |
| [a] flyboat | 60 | 0 | 0 | John Gaye [and] George Christian |
| *Blessinge* | 35 | 0 | 2 | Richard Morehouse |
| [a] flyboat | 120 | 6 | 12 | Nicholas Harris *et alii* |
| [a] carvel | 50 | 0 | 4 | do |
| *Bonaventure* | 40 | 4 | 4 | Edward Ameredith, esq. [and] John Smart jun. |
| *Parragon* | 20 | 0 | 0 | Edward Ameredith, esq. |
| [a] flyboat | 70 | 4 | 8 | John Gey [and] William Jenkin |
| *Prymrose* | 40 | 0 | 4 | William Blighe, John Gey [and] William Jenkin |
| *Wren* | 55 | 0 | 4 | Francis Trelawney gent. |
| a french ship | 55 | 4 | 8 | Edward Cocke and William Carkett |
| *Jane* | 30 | 0 | 0 | Thomas Reynardson [and] William Carkett |
| *Globe* | 40 | 2 | 4 | Thomas Crampporne, Nicholas Benet [and] William Alsope |
| *Marygold* | 45 | 0 | 4 | Richard Roddon [and] William Harris |
| *Truedealinge* | 30 | 0 | 0 | Richard Rodden |
| *Hopewell* | 60 | 0 | 6 | David Browne |
| *Sea Ryder* | 25 | 0 | 0 | John Andrewes [and] Michael Holman |
| *Anne* | 40 | 0 | 4 | John White, Humphrey Gayre [and] Stephen Pears |
| *Swalloe* | 40 | 0 | 4 | Richard Gayre [and] Hugh Gayre |
| *Thomas* | 35 | 0 | 0 | Jerome Roche [and] Richard Gayre |
| *Phenix* | 30 | 0 | 0 | Richard Lawrence |
| [blank] | 30 | 0 | 2 | Mr Thomas Fownes [and] Thomas Crampporne |

## East Stonehouse

| *Unicorne* | 80 | 4 | William Rowe |
|---|---|---|---|
| *William & Margaret* | 60 | | William Rowe, William Eliott [and] Edward Deacon |
| *Truelove* | 80 | 2 | William Rowe, Simon Rowe [and] John Rowe |
| *Blessinge* | 50 | | Richard Spurwell |
| *John* | 50 | | do |
| *John* | 20 | | John Ambrouse |
| *Swallowe* | 20 | | Edward Jeffry |
| *Anne* | 20 | | Anne Jeffry |
| [a] flyboat | 120 | | William Tapson |

[signed] James Bagg

# PLYMPTON HUNDRED

PRO, SP16/34/100
[dorse] Part of Plympton Hundred, the
rest not brought in.

### Place of Abode
## Plympton St Maurice
## [*Plympton Earle*]

| Qualitie and Men's Names | Age |
|---|---|
| CAPTAIN & A MARINER | |
| William Prynn | 50 |
| | |
| MARINERS | |
| William Wats | 40 |
| Christopher Webber, | |
| ['sailor' crossed out] | 36 |
| | |
| TRUMPETER | |
| James Cocke | 33 |
| | |
| FISHERMEN AT NEW[FOUND]LAND | |
| Thomas Boaste | 33 |
| Edward Silvester | 26 |
| | |
| SAILORS | |
| Richard Balle | 43 |
| Robert Boyer | 33 |
| Thomas Hessett | 42 |
| John Pomeroye | 24 |
| Michael Prynn | 24 |
| John Wats | 40 |
| Stephen Willinge | 40 |
| Gregory Wotten | 33 |
| | |
| SAILOR APPRENTICES | |
| William Bickford | 20 |
| Arthur Came | 20 |

## Shaugh Prior
## [*Shaugh*]

| MARINER | |
|---|---|
| Jerome Awton, | |
| ['Plympton Earle' crossed out] | 50 |
| | |
| SAILOR | |
| Thomas Boyes | 25 |

## Yealmpton

| FISHERMEN | |
|---|---|
| Andrew Algar | 40 |
| William Arthures | 40 |
| Walter Lowde | 24 |
| Rowland Oker | 40 |
| | |
| SAILOR | |
| Francis Dawton | 34 |

## Plympton St Mary
## [*Plympton Mary*]

| COOPER | |
|---|---|
| John Sheapherd | 44 |
| | |
| FISHERMEN | |
| Josias Cooke | 38 |
| Daniel Lyde | 27 |
| Richard Lyde | 30 |
| Nicholas Lyle | 32 |
| Robert Shepheard | 37 |
| Thomas Talle | 45 |
| John Treas | 25 |
| | |
| SAILORS | |
| John Elize | 40 |
| John Foster | 46 |
| William Hardy | 22 |
| Thomas Rawlinge | 32 |

[signed] James Bagg

# STANBOROUGH HUNDRED

PRO, SP16/34/102

### Place of Abode
## Thurlestone
## [*Thurlston*]

| Qualitie and Men's Names | Age |
|---|---|
| FISHERMEN | |
| John Bridgman | 40 |
| Robert Campe | 33 |
| William Cornishe | 24 |
| John Drew | 25 |
| Thomas Farr | 23 |

| | |
|---|---|
| Nicholas Harvey | 50 |
| Richard Hill | 26 |
| John Lidstow | 56 |
| Philip Lidstow | 28 |
| Thomas Lidstow | 50 |
| John Light | 25 |
| Thomas Mathew | 30 |
| John Pilditche | 40 |
| Samuel Randle | 32 |
| Richard Steere | 26 |
| Henry Torring | 23 |
| John Torringe | 30 |
| Thomas Torringe | 50 |
| William Torringe | 24 |
| Thomas Welche | 36 |

## Holne

MARINERS

| | |
|---|---|
| Abel Cater | 40 |
| Sydrach Windeate | 40 |

## Buckfastleigh
### [*Buckfastleighe*]

SAILORS

| | |
|---|---|
| Andrew Alyoode | 26 |
| John Bovie | 30 |
| George Foxe | 22 |
| John Mudge | 24 |
| Edward Wreathie | 18 |

## South Brent
### [*Brent*]

SAILORS

| | |
|---|---|
| John Didlake | 20 |
| John Ferris | 35 |
| Peter Ferris | 30 |
| Richard Ferris | 20 |
| Simon Mitchell | 20 |
| Walter Pulford | 40 |
| Edward Sowton | 30 |

## Moreleigh
### [*Morleigh*]

SAILOR

| | |
|---|---|
| Thomas Oldriffe | 25 |

FISHERMAN

| | |
|---|---|
| Michael Sugar | 40 |

## Diptford
### [*Dipford*]

MARINER

| | |
|---|---|
| Thomas Dniche | 36 |

FISHERMEN

| | |
|---|---|
| Andrew Cawsie | 26 |
| William Heard | 24 |

SAILORS

| | |
|---|---|
| John Blackaller | 30 |
| Jesse Hingston | 44 |

## Rattery
### [*Ratterie*]

SAILORS

| | |
|---|---|
| John Cozens | 30 |
| John Mitchell | 40 |

## Loddiswell
### [*Loddeswill*]

FISHERMEN

| | |
|---|---|
| William Gervise | 43 |
| Oades Wyott | 23 |

## Kingsbridge

SAILORS

| | |
|---|---|
| James Hill | 55 |
| John Hill | |
| Thomas Hill | 40 |
| Peter Jane | 28 |
| John Joate | 63 |
| William Robins | 18 |

## South Milton

MARINER

| | |
|---|---|
| Henry Braddon | 40 |

FISHERMEN

| | |
|---|---|
| John Addamour | 40 |
| William Blackaller | 50 |
| Walter Sear | 22 |
| John Weatheridge | 23 |
| William Weatheridge | 50 |

## East Allington
### [Eastallington]
SAILORS

| | |
|---|---|
| John Bowden | 48 |
| Richard Putt | 42 |

## West Alvington
### [Westallington]
put not down their age[s]
SAILOR IN HIS MAJESTY'S SERVICE
William Chadder

SAILORS
Edward Lovell
Peter Ward
Richard Whiller

## South Huish
### [South Huishe]
SAILORS
These fourteen are between twenty and forty years of age
Edward Coolle
William Cranche
Richard Evnes
Richard Hardwood
William Hine
Roger Kewe
John Luckiam
John Luckiam
William Luckiam
Richard Lukard
John Madocke
Josias Yabslie
Richard Yabslie
Stephen Yabslie
These five are between forty and sixty years of age
James Chadder
John Cookeworthie
William Crispyn
Richard Lidston
Richard Randell

## Salcombe
MARINERS

| | |
|---|---|
| Peter Brocke | 34 |

| | |
|---|---|
| Richard Cookeworthy | 32 |
| James Dapsey | 30 |
| John Deanell | 30 |
| Thomas Everye | 52 |
| Jaspar Hardy | 40 |
| John Luccombe | 40 |
| Gabriel Martyn | 36 |
| Thomas Martyn | 40 |
| John Maye | 45 |
| Roger Peeter | 30 |
| John Quarme | 30 |
| Hugh Randall | 57 |
| William Reede | 44 |
| Andrew Soullocke | 42 |
| Richard Soullocke | 29 |
| William Soullocke | 42 |
| John Tawley | 56 |
| Mathew White | 52 |
| John Yabsley | 40 |

SAILORS

| | |
|---|---|
| Dionisa [sic] Chope | 30 |
| Thomas Chope | 28 |
| John Chubb | 26 |
| Richard Chubb | 20 |
| Leonard Cookeworthie | 21 |
| John Cookeworthy | 18 |
| James Cranche | 33 |
| Owen Cranche | 25 |
| Owen Cranche | 50 |
| William Evens | 28 |
| Roger Farewether | 26 |
| William Farewether | 35 |
| John Farwether | 50 |
| Robert Fincent | 23 |
| John Francis | 26 |
| Richard Francis | 20 |
| Roger Gill | 38 |
| John Harward | 56 |
| Roger Horswill | 50 |
| Thomas Lainball | 30 |
| George Leonard | 31 |
| Peter Locke | 28 |
| Richard Lovell | 30 |
| Gilbert Luccomb | 34 |
| Richard Luccomb | 27 |
| William Martyn | 40 |
| Nicholas Parker | 32 |
| John Peatell | 29 |
| Thomas Peeters | 57 |

| Andrew Perret | 30 |
| George Perret | 28 |
| George Perret | 40 |
| John Perret | 34 |
| Peter Perret | 30 |
| Thomas Perret | 25 |
| William Perret | 24 |
| William Perret | 41 |
| John Pollard | 46 |
| William Poolinge | 40 |
| Thomas Quarme | 33 |
| William Quinte | 30 |
| Thomas Randall | 25 |
| Richard Satterley | 42 |
| John Swingesburne | 28 |
| John Torring | 26 |
| Robert Townesend | 28 |
| Richard Watts | 30 |
| Thomas White | 27 |
| Henry Williams | 56 |
| Gabriel Woodemesson | 32 |
| William Woodmesson | 42 |
| both servants to William Yabsley | |
| William Millerd | 30 |
| Roger Yabsley | 19 |
| Sailor and servant to William | |
| Soullicke | |
| Richard Weekes | 20 |
| both servants to John Soullocke | |
| Nicholas Phillipps | 19 |
| Peter Pinhaye | 33 |

## Malborough
### [Malboroughe]

MARINERS
| William Cranche | 40 |
| Thomas Edwards | 37 |
| John Gibbes | 43 |

SAILORS
| Hugh Chope | 24 |
| Owen Cranche | 40 |
| Stephen Cranche | 30 |
| Francis Drewe | 23 |
| Owen Gosse | 35 |
| Phillip Gosse | 23 |
| Richard Hayes | 20 |
| Roger Hyne | 23 |
| Robert Luckam | 21 |
| Thomas Randall | 42 |
| John Randell jun. | 23 |
| John Randell sen. | 61 |
| Richard Thomas jun. | 25 |
| Richard Thomas sen. | 60 |
| John Tolke | 30 |
| Andrew Tooker | 22 |
| Roger Woolcomb | 47 |
| Robert Yabsley | 19 |
| John Yeabsley | 40 |

[signed] James Bagg

## The Porte Salcombe

| The Ships' names | Burthen | Ordnance | Capable to carry | The Owners' names |
|---|---|---|---|---|
| Phillipp & Janne | 40 | [blank] | [blank] | Gabriel Martyn [and] John Gibb |
| Prosperous | 50 | | | John Soulloucke |
| Speedwell | 25 | | | do |
| Desperacon | 50 | | | do |
| Charles | 30 | | | John Soullocke & Hugh Randall |
| Elizabeth | 50 | | | William Yablsey & John Yabsley |
| James | 20 | | | William Yablsey |
| Regard | 30 | | | Thomas Every & Richard Every |
| George | 45 | | | John Roope & George Kingston |
| Rebecca | 45 | | | William Soullocke & Roger Perret |
| William | 30 | | | William Soullocke |
| Jonas | 25 | | | do |
| Susan | 30 | | | Andrew Soullocke & John Hareward |

| The Ships' names | Burthen | Ordnance | Capable to carry | The Owners' names |
|---|---|---|---|---|
| **Salcombe cont'd** | | | | |
| *Prymrose* | 30 | | | John Yablsey |
| *Patience* | 40 | | | John Yabsley & William Hine |
| *Mayflower* | 20 | | | do      do |
| *Joahne* | 45 | | | ['Hugh Randall' crossed out] Richard Cookworthie |
| *Abigaile* | 45 | | | Hugh Randall |
| *Elianor* | 45 | | | Hugh Randall and John Luttons |
| *Nicholas* | 45 | | | Andrew Cranche |
| *Prosperous* | 16 | | | John Harwood |
| *Pearle* | 14 | | | John Chubb & James Biccombe |
| *Providence* | 35 | | | Jaspar Hardy & Roger Perrett |
| *Unitie* | 20 | | | Alice Perrett |
| *Mary* | 20 | | | John Gibb & Gabriel Martyn |
| *Margarett* | 30 | | | Thomas Edwards |
| *Susan* | 14 | | | John Deanell |

All insufficient to carry Ordnance.

[signed] James Bagg

# NORTH EAST DEVON, *c.*1626

SIR JAMES BAGG'S SURVEY

## BRAUNTON HUNDRED

PRO, SP16/34/103
[dorse] Braunton Hundred. Devon

### Place of Abode
### Braunton
### [*Brannton*]

| Qualitie and Men's Names | Age |
|---|---|
| GUNNER | |
| Robert Paull | 30 |
| | |
| MARINERS | |
| Thomas Baker | 40 |
| William Brooke | 26 |
| Michael Chewner | 46 |
| Humphrey Halls | 40 |
| Adam Horden | 30 |
| Richard Jenson | 46 |
| Philip Kent | 38 |
| George Tooker | 30 |
| | |
| SAILORS | |
| Robert Avery | 24 |
| William Bennet | 25 |
| Edward Boddin | 28 |
| Philip Brooke | 30 |
| John Bustinge | 23 |
| Philip Bustinge | 23 |
| Silvester Dynnys | 32 |
| Boddin Edward | 28 |
| Robert Griffin | 33 |
| William Harris | 34 |
| Richard Hartnoll | 28 |
| James Kent | 20 |
| John Necke | 27 |
| Arthur Somer | 36 |
| John Symon | 28 |
| Richard Tooker | 20 |

| | |
|---|---|
| Thomas Walter | 26 |
| John Webber | 38 |

### Heanton Punchardon
### [*Heannton Punchardon*]

| FISHERMEN | |
|---|---|
| Tobias Baker | 50 |
| John Barnhouse | 35 |
| John Crocker | 30 |
| Nicholas Herdinge | 26 |
| Nicholas Hooper | 20 |
| Robert Sander | 24 |
| Thomas Sander | 20 |
| Arthur Wilkey | 26 |
| | |
| SAILORS FOR COAL | |
| Philip Sander | 56 |
| Geffery Stoke | 18 |
| Robert Stoke | 48 |
| | |
| SHIPWRIGHTS | |
| James Barnhouse | 30 |
| Thomas Heaward | 34 |

### Pilton

| FISHERMEN | |
|---|---|
| Henry Downe | 20 |
| John Hodge | 22 |
| Philip Huckmore | 32 |
| | |
| MARINERS | |
| George Downe | 40 |
| Oliver Fare | 72 |
| John Nicholl | 52 |
| Philip Peters | 70 |
| Thomas Smyth | 56 |
| Walter Vellacat | 28 |

### Goodleigh

| MARINER | |
|---|---|
| John Downe | 60 |

## Barnstaple
### [*Barnestaple*]

MARINERS

| | |
|---|---|
| William Brooke | 28 |
| James Crosecombe | 34 |
| George Frost | 32 |
| William Gibbers | 30 |
| William Hodge | 54 |
| Richard Jenson | 46 |
| Richard Luggard | 42 |
| William Nicholes | 38 |
| William Norman | 64 |
| William Peters | 44 |
| Peter Predire | 30 |
| John Rowe | 40 |
| George Skampe | 28 |
| Hugh Sloley | 40 |
| John Smyth | 40 |
| Robert Thorne | 34 |
| Roger Wilson | 22 |

SURGEON

| | |
|---|---|
| Andrew Luggard | 35 |

FISHERMAN

| | |
|---|---|
| Nicholas Pugsley | 36 |

GUNNER

| | |
|---|---|
| Thomas Combe | 32 |

SAILORS

| | |
|---|---|
| Lawrence Aley | 40 |
| James Beavell | 34 |
| William Clotman | 24 |
| Edward Colscott | 30 |
| Edmond Hanger | 26 |
| Richard Juell | 24 |
| Charles Maye | 18 |
| John Rowe | 26 |
| John Stephen | 18 |
| John Weetheradge | 23 |
| Richard Wilson | 18 |
| William Witheridge | 18 |
| John Wood | 17 |

## Ilfracombe
### [*Ilfardcombe*]

MARINERS

| | |
|---|---|
| Humphrey Incledon | 52 |
| Hugh Jones | 60 |

PILOT

| | |
|---|---|
| Walter Dyer | 42 |

SAILORS

| | |
|---|---|
| John Basset | 18 |
| Thomas Bradford | 42 |
| Henry Cornishe | 36 |
| William Cornishe | 22 |
| John Davies | 52 |
| George Dennys | 18 |
| Philip Dunn | 38 |
| William Emott | 22 |
| Henry Fraze | 30 |
| Robert Gibbes | 18 |
| William Hartnoll | 56 |
| George Hodge | 34 |
| Edward Keede | 18 |
| Ralph Lyghton | 40 |
| Thomas Norwood | 18 |
| Walter Poope | 22 |
| Roger Rue | 20 |
| John Scoare | 38 |
| John Singe | 30 |
| John Vie | 53 |
| Roger Vie | 22 |

## Combe Martin
### [*Combmartyn*]

FISHERMEN

| | |
|---|---|
| William Dartlett | 40 |
| Richard Edwarde | 50 |
| William Herdinge | 26 |
| Richard Ilwill | 30 |
| William Palmer | 30 |
| Richard Whithay | 20 |

SAILORS

| | |
|---|---|
| David Hill | 50 |
| Richard Latham | 50 |
| William Smyth | 30 |

## Berrynarbor
### [*Berinarber*]

FISHERMEN

| | |
|---|---|
| John Bowen | 26 |
| Nicholas Somer | 30 |
| Nicholas Somer | 26 |
| Humphrey Somer | 20 |

SAILOR
George Somer     46

## Mortehoe
### [*Morthoo*]

FISHERMEN
William Gowdon     25
Edward Olyver     30

MARINERS
Philip Aley     30
Gabriel Britton     50
Thomas Britton     30
Walter Nicholl     40
Walter Skynner     20

SAILORS
Tristram Incledon     25
Hugh Tooker servant to Aley

## Ashford
### [*Aishford*]

SAILORS
Ralph Berry     30
Ciprian Marshe     22
John Marshe     24

## Marwood

COOPER
Peter Chanterell     24

MARINER
John Heyward     40

SAILOR
Richard Stotte     40

## Georgeham
### [*Georgham*]

FISHERMEN
John Dallen     35
George Hoane     23
John Parker     25
James Peryman     26
John Peryn     23
Richard Peryn     21
Richard Phillipp     21

GUNNER
Thomas Bustin     53

MARINERS
William Crascombe     53
William Eliott     36
Hugh Incledon     40
James Sweet sen.     55
Thomas Whiddon     34

SAILORS
Thomas Bowhay     52
Bartholomew Clerike     32
Thomas Fuienheld, sailor
    servant to Crasscombe     24
George Perryman     32
Tobias Rogers     50
James Sweet jun.     29
Edmond Whiddon     38

SHIPWRIGHT
Christopher Rashley     47

[signed] James Bagg

| The names of the ships | Burthen | Ordnance | Capable to carry | The Owners' names |
|---|---|---|---|---|
| | | | | |

### Ilfracombe [*Ilfardcombe*]

| The names of the ships | Burthen | Ordnance | Capable to carry | The Owners' names |
|---|---|---|---|---|
| *Marygold* | 24 tons | 0 | 0 | Richard Wintard & Robert Browne |
| *John* | 18 | 0 | 0 | John Greene & John Hill |
| *Prymrose* | 18 | 0 | 0 | John Vie |

### Watermouth[1]

| | | | | |
|---|---|---|---|---|
| *Elizabeth* | 20 | 0 | 0 | George Somer |

### Pilton

| | | | | |
|---|---|---|---|---|
| *Mary Francis* | 20 | 0 | 0 | Sir Robert Chicester knt |
| *Blessinge* | 23 | 0 | 0 | George Downe |

### Barnstaple [*Barnestaple*]

| | | | | |
|---|---|---|---|---|
| *Delight* | 70 | 3 | 5 | Edward Eastman |
| *Golden Lyon* | 180 | 6 | 12 | Penticost Dotherige, William Palmer, William Gaymon, Richard Medford & Henry Mason |
| *Providence* | 180 | 6 | 12 | Penticost Dotheridge, William Palmer, Richard Medford, Henry Mason & John Witheridge |
| *Pellican* | 150 | 0 | 8 | Richard Beaple, Gilbert Paige, Richard Ferris, George Ferris, William Legh & Roger Hunt |
| *Lytle Concord* | 40 | 0 | 0 | Gilbert Paige, Thomas Harris, William Downe & John Hartnolls |
| *George* | 35 | 0 | 0 | ['William' crossed out] Lewis Downe |
| *Antilope* | 30 | | | William Palmer & Nicholas Garland |
| *Success* | 30 | 0 | 0 | Alexander Horwood, William Hodge, William Nicholes & John Clarke |
| *Blessinge* | 24 | 0 | 0 | William Peters & George Downe |
| *Phenix* | 50 | 0 | 6 | Nicholas Delbridge, Francis Facy & Mary Jenings |

### Braunton [*Brannton*]

| | | | | |
|---|---|---|---|---|
| *Mary* | 15 | 0 | 0 | Walter Bustinge |
| *Samuell* | 15 | 0 | 0 | Euzebius Upcott |

[signed] James Bagg

---

[1] In Berrynarbor parish.

## SOUTH MOLTON [*Southe Molten*] HUNDRED

PRO, SP16/34/101
[dorse] South Molton, Sherewell and Blacktorrington Hundreds in Devon

### Place of Abode
### Bishop's Tawton
[*Bishopps Tawton*]

Qualitie and Men's Names — Age
MARINER
Edward Miller    40

### Swimbridge
SAILOR SERVANT
Robert Smaldon    26
There are no more sailors nor any ships in this hundred

## SHIRWELL [*Sherwill*] HUNDRED

PRO, SP16/34/101

### Shirwell
[*Sherwill*]
MARINER
Robert Pugsley    21

### Charles
[*Charells*]
FISHERMAN
Thomas Fosse    34

### Lynton
FISHERMEN
Anthony Hill    53
Thomas Ingaram    36
Richard Skore    60
Robert Skore    58

Ships or barks not any in this hundred.

## BLACK TORRINGTON [*Blacktorrington*] HUNDRED

PRO, SP16/34/101
This hundred doth not extend to the sea, neither are there any seamen within this hundred as is certified.

[signed] James Bagg

# DARTMOUTH SHIPS, *c.* 1626

SIR JAMES BAGG' S SURVEY
Ships belonging to Dartmouth and Torbay
PRO, SP16/34/99
[dorse] Devon. Dartmouth ships

| Owners | Ship's names | Tons | Ordnance |
|---|---|---|---|
| Nicholas Roope | *Rose* | 140 | 8 |
| do | *Content* | 120 | 6 |
| do | *Swipstake* | 70 | 6 |
| do | *Lawrell* | 20 | |
| do | *Bable* | 20 | |
| John Streite | *Hopewell* | 120 | 4 |
| do | *Handmaide* | 80 | |
| do | *Vallentine* | 60 | |
| do | *Maieflower* | 60 | |
| do | *Faulcon* | 50 | |
| do | *Barke Idle* | 30 | ['60' crossed out] |
| do | *Comfort* | 70 | |
| Robert Phillpott | *Unity* | 60 | |
| William Plumleigh | *Edward* | 80 | 6 |
| do | *Henry* | 30 | |
| do | *William* | 60 | |
| do | *Dolphin* | 150 | 8 |
| Adrian Staplehill | *Fortune* | 120 | 6 |
| do | *John* | 30 | |
| Andrew Walkham | *Mary* | 30 | |
| do | *Mynikin* | 60 | |
| Nicholas Skinner | *Batcheller* | 60 | |
| do | hath another of | 20 | |
| John Rownsevall | *Guift* | 30 | |
| Thomas Hart | *Mary* | 20 | |
| John Newman | *Luke* | 150 | 8 |
| do | *Peter* | 60 | |
| Alexander Coffen | *Pantaple* | 20 | |
| George Plumleigh | *George* | 30 | |
| William Spurway | *Barbara* | 30 | |
| William Kempe | *Trulove* | 40 | |
| Robert Follett | *Medusa* | 40 | |
| Henry Oldinge | *Rebecca* | 30 | |
| do | *Virgin Mary* | 40 | |
| Roger Mathew | *Prosperous* | 80 | 6 |
| John Richards | *Viniard* | 50 | |

| | | | |
|---|---|---|---|
| do | John | 40 | |
| | ['*Love*' crossed out] | | |
| John Holligrove | Lampe | 80 | |
| do | Holligrove | 60 | |
| Robert Mortaine | Guift | 60 | |
| do | Blessinge | 80 | |
| John Lapray | a bark of | 20 | |
| Nicholas Sanders | John | 30 | |
| Alexander Staplehill | An gallant | 80 | 6 |
| do | Bitch | 40 | |
| John Martaine | Mary | 40 | |
| Peter Terrye | Peter | 40 | |
| Andrew Voysey | John | 40 | |
| do | Ede | 30 | |
| John Olliver | John | 20 | |
| Thomas Wardroppe | Sollamonder | 40 | |
| do | Frendshipp | 60 | |
| do | Nutte | 100 | |
| Richard Smyth | Primrose | 40 | |
| William Baggan | Frauncis | 150 | 10 |
| John Shapley | Marchant Royall | 100 | |
| Bartholomew Laskye | Consent | 70 | |
| do | Returne | 70 | |
| Lawrence Addams | Robert | 30 | |
| Philip Laye | Providence | 150 | 10 |
| Arthur Champnoune esq. | Chudleigh | 140 | 8 |
| do | Hope | 70 | |
| Rawleigh Gilbert esq. | Phenix | 80 | |
| William Lane | Samuell | 80 | |
| do | John Baptist | 60 | |
| do | Christopher | 80 | |
| do | Mermaide | 70 | |
| John Lane | Swallowe | 40 | |
| do | Nicholas | 70 | |
| George Roope | Phenix | 80 | |
| do | George | 40 | |
| Humphrey Sheeres | Bitehorse | 80 | |
| do | Faulcon | 30 | |
| John Marten | Handmaide | 80 | |
| do | Cassandra | 60 | |
| Alexander Hamett | Jonas | 80 | 4 |
| do | Stephen | 60 | |
| John ['Geo' crossed out, '*George*' crossed out] | | | |
| Littlejohn | Grace | 80 | 4 |
| do | Desire | 30 | |
| John Berry | Grace | 60 | |
| John Hollawaye | Nicholas | 30 | |
| Nicholas Warryner | Mynion | 30 | |
| Alexander Shapley | Gift of God | 100 | |

**Dartmouth Ships cont'd**

| Owners | Ship's names | Tons | Ordnance |
|---|---|---|---|
| Alexander Shapley | *God's blessing* | 50 | |
| do | *Benediction* | 140 | |
| William Harris | *William and John* | 140 | |
| Sir Edward Seamour | *Samaritan* | 200 | |

Mathew Barons hath 3 ships of 30, 50 & 60 tons.
John Coade hath 2 ships of 30 & 50 tons.

[signed] James Bagg

# NORTH CORNWALL, 1629

FRANCIS BASSET'S SURVEY OF NORTH CORNWALL, 1629
PRO, SP16/135/5
[dorse] R[eceived] March 1629. An Account of what Ships and Mariners are in the
Vice-Admiralty of the north of Cornwall
*Tertio* February 1628 [1629]

A List of the names of all the Mariners, Sailors and Fishermen within the north part of
Cornwall.

Their names      of what parish      their profession      their age

## St Ives

| | Age |
|---|---|
| **MARINERS** | |
| George Diggins | 29 |
| Richard Nance | 50 |
| William Pitts | 55 |
| | |
| **PILOTS** | |
| Geils Hawke | 60 |
| John Lawnder sen. | 55 |
| | |
| **SHIPWRIGHTS** | |
| William Bayly | 19 |
| Robert Bolithoe | 32 |
| Robert Hickes | 19 |
| Stephen Tremenheer | 26 |
| | |
| **SAILORS** | |
| James Barber | 36 |
| John Barber | 22 |
| Nicholas Barber jun. | 16 |
| Richard Barber sen. | 54 |
| William Bastine | 28 |
| Henry Baylie jun. | 40 |
| John Cocke | 28 |
| John Cooke | 36 |
| Ralph Couch | 38 |
| William Couch | 22 |
| Thomas Dyow | 42 |
| George Gregar | 40 |
| George Hichinge | 46 |
| George Hicks | 34 |

| | |
|---|---|
| John Hicks Sr | 41 |
| Richard Hicks | 30 |
| Richard Hicks jun. | 26 |
| William Jacke | 48 |
| John Kittowe | 30 |
| John Lantorne | 30 |
| John Lawnder jun. | 24 |
| Thomas Lawry | 25 |
| Thomas Lylly | 36 |
| John Mareough | 35 |
| Thomas Marshfeild | 32 |
| William Parrenton | 30 |
| William Purchase | 40 |
| Peter Quait | 18 |
| Henry Richard | 24 |
| William Roberte | 30 |
| Robert Roberts | 21 |
| Peter Rosmanewas | 28 |
| John Roswall | 28 |
| Henry Shappplinge | 36 |
| Ephraem Sise | 18 |
| Thomas Sise | 40 |
| Henry Stephen | 30 |
| John Stephen jun. | 35 |
| Richard Stephen | 34 |
| Thomas Stephen sen. | 45 |
| Thomas Tackabord | 26 |
| Hector Tayler | 30 |
| John Tendgan | 32 |
| John Tonkinge | 40 |
| Henry Tregarthen | [blank] |

## St Ives cont'd

| | |
|---|---|
| John Tremymar | 26 |
| James Walkey | 29 |
| John Wattye | 30 |

FISHERMEN

| | |
|---|---|
| Phillip Allen | 46 |
| Richard Allen | 20 |
| Reginald Blasy | 28 |
| John Bosithio | 42 |
| Mathew Browne | 20 |
| John Callaway | 19 |
| Lewis Capell | 24 |
| John Carnyng | 56 |
| William Coggar | 26 |
| John Cozen | 54 |
| William Davye | 32 |
| Henry Hayne | 22 |
| Thomas Hickes | 35 |
| Alexander Hockinge | 24 |
| Lewis Hockinge | 30 |
| Thomas Hooper | 34 |
| Gregory Jenkine | 42 |
| John Jory | 20 |
| John Keaste | 50 |
| John Luke | 56 |
| Leonard Luke | 30 |
| William Michell | 40 |
| Michael Nettel | 50 |
| John Oppy | 56 |
| George Paynter | 27 |
| Richard Pearse | 45 |
| Thomas Penhillicke | 30 |
| Thomas Poulteer | 29 |
| Henry Randall | 34 |
| John Richard | 23 |
| John Rowe | 40 |
| Thomas Sterry | 30 |
| Christopher Tregarthen | 37 |
| Phillip Treglowne | 38 |
| John Trembethowe | 34 |
| John Vallatt | 27 |
| James Wattye | 50 |
| John Wattye | 40 |
| Richard White | 24 |
| William Wolkocke | 27 |

Sum 97

There are belonging to St Ives 3 barques one of them being 45 ['B' crossed out] tons whereof Mr Thomas Puretoy being sole owner, the other being 20 tons whereof Thomas Sise is sole owner, the last being 25 tons whereof Mr James Prade and Stephen Barber ['is so' crossed out] are owners.

## Boscastle
### [*Botreauxcastell*]

1 barque 30 tons Edward Josling, owner.
1 barque 12 tons William Stephens, owner.
1 barque 26 tons John Tubb, owner
and 1 barque 25 tons Roger Tubb, owner.

## Padstow
### [*Padstowe*]

1 barque 16 tons Mr John Prideaux owner
1 barque 16 tons John Norman owner
1 barque 26 tons William Rommoe of Penryn [*Perine*] owner.

## Crantock
### [*Crantocke*]

SAILOR

| | |
|---|---|
| Philip Harrise | 40 |

FISHERMEN

| | |
|---|---|
| John Michell jun. | 30 |
| John Skovern sen. | 48 |
| John Skovern | 36 |
| Thomas Skovern | 28 |
| William Skovern | 27 |
| William Tippett | 54 |
| Bennet Wills | 67 |

## St Columb Minor
### [*Lower St Collumb*]

SAILORS

| | |
|---|---|
| Charles Beard | 55 |
| Christopher Castell | 50 |
| Christopher Davye | 32 |
| John Emmett | 34 |
| Thomas Emmett | 16 |
| William Emmett | 23 |
| John Hendra | 50 |

| | |
|---|---|
| Thomas House | 22 |
| James James | 17 |
| John James | 30 |
| Humphrey Ould | 27 |
| John Richard | 50 |
| Richard Roberts | 30 |
| Francis Sare | 17 |
| Nicholas Warren | 50 |

## Endellion
### [*Endellian*]

MARINER

| | |
|---|---|
| Roger Davys | 50 |

SAILORS

| | |
|---|---|
| John Anger | 40 |
| Ralph Billing | 54 |
| Richard Billing | 20 |
| Thomas Billing | 16 |
| Christopher Brea | 20 |
| William Browne | 30 |
| Ferdinand Collen | 30 |
| Thomas Colline | 27 |
| Joseph Collins | 34 |
| Robert Davye | 40 |
| Thomas Denman | 45 |
| Thomas Emmett | 30 |
| William Emmett | 20 |
| Christopher Grigge | 50 |
| William Grigge | 40 |
| Thomas Guy | 30 |
| John Hickes | 52 |
| Humphrey Jackett | 32 |
| John James | 40 |
| Thomas James | 40 |
| George Jeffery | 47 |
| Gilbart Jeffery | 15 |
| Christopher Olliver | 30 |
| John Olliver | 26 |
| Richard Olliver | 20 |
| Nicholas Parson | 19 |
| Edward Poulstagg | 30 |
| Thomas Renoden | 20 |
| Anthony Stone | 60 |
| John Tom | 25 |
| ['Anthony Trebell' crossed out] | 60 |
| William Trefry | 30 |
| Arthur Triplett | 25 |
| John Tripplett | 35 |

| | |
|---|---|
| John Waye | 50 |

FISHERMEN

| | |
|---|---|
| William Browne | 50 |
| John Browninge | 25 |
| Richard Carveth | 38 |
| John Colline | 20 |
| Richard Couch | 18 |
| John Dea | 18 |
| John Grigge | 22 |
| Ralph Guy | 40 |
| George Hickes | 43 |
| William Hickes | 40 |
| Thomas Oliver | 16 |
| John Parker | 18 |
| John Rawe | 50 |
| William Trefry | 21 |

## St Minver
### [*St Mynver*]

SAILORS

| | |
|---|---|
| William Hickes | 56 |
| Mathew Morishe | 50 |
| John Style | 55 |

FISHERMEN

| | |
|---|---|
| Oliver Ball | 34 |
| John Hicks | 31 |
| Richard Ivye | 40 |
| John James | 60 |
| Walter Jeffery | 40 |
| Ambrose Marke | 50 |
| Anthony Myllard | 55 |
| Nicholas Olliver | 33 |
| Oatts Pope | 24 |
| George Shoale | 60 |
| Humphrey Style | 30 |
| Nicholas Style | 27 |

## Boscastle
### [*Botreauxcastell*]

MARINERS

| | |
|---|---|
| Edward Joslinge | 55 |
| William Stephens | 46 |
| John Tubb | 46 |
| Roger Tubb | 30 |

SAILORS

| | |
|---|---|
| John Avery | 25 |

| Boscastle cont'd | | John Edward | 40 |
|---|---|---|---|
| Thomas Avery | 30 | Edward Harrise | 60 |
| John Brure | 26 | Gregory Hodge | 40 |
| Humphrey French: | 23 | Richard Morishe | 23 |
| Richard James | 40 | John Norman | 30 |
| William James | 25 | Michael Parken | 25 |
| Erasmus Quinte | 18 | Henry Peeter | 22 |
| John Quinte | 20 | William Peeter | 18 |
| John Salter | 32 | John Peter | 20 |
| | | Henry Quinte | 22 |
| | | Robert Riffell | 20 |

## Padstow

### [Padstowe]

| | | Henry Rissell | 50 |
|---|---|---|---|
| | | Henry Roch | 24 |
| MARINERS | | John Sandry | 55 |
| Thomas Barrett | 40 | John Swymmner | 21 |
| Walter Kittowe | 40 | John Tippett | 50 |
| Peter Quinte | 36 | Nicholas Tippett | 20 |
| William Wilson | 40 | John Welch | 32 |
| | | William Weste | 40 |
| SAILORS | | | |
| Nicholas Androw | 26 | FISHERMEN | |
| John Beale | 34 | John Bordwood | 34 |
| James Bennett | 40 | William Jelbert | 20 |
| John Bond | 25 | Richard Jeles | 48 |
| Nicholas Bone | 60 | William Jels | 40 |
| Nathaniel Bullock | 30 | John Richard | 36 |
| John Cornishe | 30 | William Sandry | 20 |
| Robert Cornishe | 23 | John Sard | 50 |
| John Denn | 20 | Erasmus Speare | 50 |
| Philip Dyer | 25 | John Speare | 20 |
| Roger Edmund | 22 | Richard Trelathde | 55 |

# APPENDIX A

DARTMOUTH CORPORATION SURVEY OF SHIPS, c.1619
Devon Record Office, DD61940

[dorse] The contributions for the ships. A rate for the contribution money.
[In 1619 several ports, including Plymouth, Exeter, Barnstaple and Dartmouth, were asked to contribute toward the costs of a naval expedition against the 'Turks' of North Africa. This document is an account of a rate of three shillings per share that Dartmouth imposed on shipowners.]

The names of the ships belonging to the port of Dartmouth [*Dartmouthe*] and the members thereof besides those that belong to Torbay [*Torbaye*].

|  | shares | [£ | s | d] |
|---|---|---|---|---|
| Mr Paidge for the *Friendship* | 18 | 2 | 14 | 0 |
| Robert Follet for the *Pellican* | 13 | 1 | 19 | 0 |
| John Richards & John Budley the *Joane* | 22 | 3 | 6 | 0 |
| Mr Robert Martin for the *Blessing* | 31 | 4 | 13 | 0 |
| and the *Gyfte* | 19 | 2 | 17 | 0 |
| Mr William Plumleighe & Henry Mills | | | | |
| for the *Edward* & for the bark | 30 | 4 | 10 | 0 |
| Mr John Winchester for the *John* | 22 | 3 | 6 | 0 |
| & for the *Ede* | 10 | 1 | 10 | 0 |
| Mr Robert Gilles for the *Gyfte* | 13 | 1 | 19 | 0 |
| and for the *Jonas* | 14 | 2 | 2 | 0 |
| Mr Gias ['Nicholas Sanders for the *Richard*' crossed out] | 13 | 1 | 19 | 0 |
| The *Hopewill* | 35 | 5 | 5 | 0 |
| The *Handmaid* | 28 | 4 | 4 | 0 |
| The *Fawlcon* | 22 | 3 | 6 | 0 |
| The *Comfortt* | 16 | 2 | 8 | 0 |
| Mr John Streate The *Mayflower* | 24 | 3 | 12 | 0 |
| The *Primrose* | 16 | 2 | 8 | 0 |
| The *Gabriell* | 13 | 1 | 19 | 0 |
| The *Valentine* | 13 | 1 | 19 | 0 |
| Robert Hallet for the *Eagle* | 0 | 1 | 6 | 0 |
| Robert Follett for the *William* | 22 | 3 | 6 | 0 |
| & for the *Medusa* | 0 | 0 | 12 | 0 |
| John Plumleigh & partners for the *Grace* | 22 | 3 | 6 | 0 |
| Roger Mathews for the *Prosperous* | 30 | 4 | 10 | 0 |
| Mr Gourney & partners for the *Anne* | 24 | 3 | 12 | 0 |
| the *Silphine* | 16 | 2 | 8 | 0 |
| Alred Staplehill the *Samuell* | 13 | 1 | 19 | 0 |
| the *Phenix* | 8 | 1 | 4 | 0 |
| William Kempe & partners for the *Swiftsure* | 16 | 2 | 8 | 0 |

## The ships of Dartmouth and Torbay cont'd

|  | shares | [£ | s | d] |
|---|---|---|---|---|
| Edward Follet & partners for the *John Bonaventure* | 15 | 2 | 5 | 0 |
| Andrew Voysie for the *Revenge* & | 43 | 6 | 9 | 0 |
| for his bark | 0 | [blank] | | |
| Robert Phillpott for the *Unytie* | 24 | 3 | 12 | 0 |
| Christopher Wellworthe | 16 | 2 | 8 | 0 |
| Edward Winchester for the *Rebecca* | 19 | 2 | 17 | 0 |
| John Holligrov for the *Grace* & the | 34 | 5 | 2 | 0 |
| [illegible] *Holligrove* | 22 | 3 | 6 | 0 |
| Andrew Wakham for the *Mynikin* | 22 | 3 | 6 | 0 |
| Edward Follett for the *Little Contentt* | 9 | 1 | 7 | 0 |
| John Francis for the *John Baptist* | 18 | 2 | 14 | 0 |
| Nicholas Flutte for the *Hopewell* | 24 | 3 | 12 | 0 |
| John Lepreye for the *Primrose* | 13 | 1 | 19 | 0 |
| George Plumleig for the *George* | 13 | 1 | 19 | 0 |
| John Newman for the *Diana* | 10 | 1 | 10 | 0 |
| the *Content* | 54 | 8 | 2 | 0 |
| Nr Nicholas Roape the *Rose* | 58 | 8 | 14 | 0 |
| the *Sweepstake* | 26 | 3 | 18 | 0 |
| the *Nicholas* | 16 | 2 | 8 | 0 |
| Mr Thomas Gourneye for the *Christofer* | 30 | 4 | 10 | 0 |
| Christopher Wood for the *Mary* | 0 | 0 | 15 | 0 |
| George Cade for the *Dove* | 0 | 1 | 8 | 0 |

### Townstall

|  | shares | [£ | s | d] |
|---|---|---|---|---|
| George Roape for the *George* | 22 | 3 | 6 | 8 |
| & for the *Phillip* | 16 | 2 | 8 | 0 |

### Brixham

|  | shares | [£ | s | d] |
|---|---|---|---|---|
| Humphrey Sheers the *Prosperous* | 22 | 3 | 6 | 0 |
| the *John* | 16 | 0 | 0 | 0 |
| the *Fawlcon* | 13 | 1 | 19 | 0 |

### Dittisham [*Ditsham*]

|  | shares | [£ | s | d] |
|---|---|---|---|---|
| Nicholas Wariner for the *Mynion* | 13 | 1 | 19 | 0 |
| Richard Lane for the *Samuell* | 30 | 4 | 10 | 10 |
| & the *John Baptist* |  | | | |

### Cornworthy [*Corneworthy*]

|  | shares | [£ | s | d] |
|---|---|---|---|---|
| Robert Perrott for the *Hope* and | 26 | 3 | 18 | 0 |
| for his bark | 8 | 1 | 4 | 0 |

### Kingswear [*Kingswere*]

|  | shares | [£ | s | d] |
|---|---|---|---|---|
| Alexander Hammatt for the *Jonas* | 28 | 4 | 4 | 0 |
| & for the *Little Jonas* | 8 | 1 | 4 | 0 |

| | | | | | |
|---|---|---|---|---|---|
| Alexander Shaplye for the *Blessing* & for his flyboat | | 42 | 6 | 6 | 0 |
| George Littlejohn for the *Blessing* | | 13 | 1 | 19 | 0 |
| Thomas Adams for the *Robert* | | 13 | 1 | 19 | 0 |

### Torbay [*Torbaye*]

| | | | | | |
|---|---|---|---|---|---|
| Mr John Martin | the *Anmaid* | 30 | 4 | 10 | 0 |
| | the *Supply* | 22 | 3 | 6 | 0 |
| | the *John* | 17 | 2 | 14 | 0 |
| Henry Barons & partners for the *Grace* | | 18 | 2 | 14 | 0 |
| & for their new ship the *Providence* | | 28 | 4 | 4 | 0 |
| Thomas Ball for the *Peeter* | | 22 | 3 | 6 | 0 |
| Thomas Paddon for the *Returne* | | 22 | 3 | 6 | 0 |
| Robert Gorde for the *Trew Love* | | 10 | 1 | 10 | 0 |
| Henry Zeveye for the *Tallentt* | | 0 | 0 | 10 | 0 |

| | | | | |
|---|---|---|---|---|
| Peter Tyrry for the *Grace* | [blank] | | | |
| John Watkn and Gilbert Roape | 0 | 0 | 12 | 0 |
| Peter Elleit | 0 | 0 | 3 | 0 |
| Nicholas Skinner for the *Katherine* | 0 | 0 | 12 | 0 |

### Salcombe [*Salcome*]

| | | |
|---|---|---|
| | the *Tryall* | 40 |
| | the *Nicholas* | 17 |
| | the *Pascow* | 17 |
| George Loy | the *George* | 17 |
| John Roap | the *William* | 17 |
| John Luckom | the *El[ea]nor* | 17 |
| William Yoesbley | the *Elizabethe* | 14 |
| Mr Cokewrthy | the *Releif* | 13 |
| John Sullock's bark | 18 tons | |
| William Yeasblei's bark | 16 do | |
| William Sullock's bark | 16 do | |
| Andrew Sullock's bark | 16 do | |
| John Yeabslie's bark | 16 do | |
| John Luccom's bark | 14 do | |
| John Roap's bark | 16 do | |
| Alice Perret's bark | 16 do | |
| Roger Vincent's bark | 14 do | |
| John Davy's bark | 12 do | |
| Thomas Edwards'[bark] | 17 do | |
| John Snelling's bark | 12 do | |
| John Gibb's bark | 16 do | |

Mr Andrew Cranche & James Cokworthe their note of rate [sic] for the Rate of their shipping according to the Council's order.

# APPENDIX B

SHIPS DOCKED AT DARTMOUTH, 1618-1619
Devon Record Office, DD61947

[Extract]
[p. 1] A note of all such receipts & payments received & paid by me Pascho Jago for several things being Receiver for this year 1618 as followeth.

| [pp. 25-6] Doct | tons | £ | s | d |
|---|---|---|---|---|
| Mr Robert Martyn 2 ships in dock 4s 7d for | 110 | | | |
| Mr Roger Mathewe & Mr Voysye 2 ships in dock 6s for | 145 | | | |
| Mr John Street for 2 ships | - | 0 | 4 | 0 |
| Mr Holland for the *Johanne* | 44 | 0 | 1 | 10 |
| John Frannch for his ship docte | 30 | 0 | 1 | 0 |
| John Shapliet for his ship docke | 140 | - | 11 | 8 |
| Not doct | | | | |
| Mr Paige for his ship not docte | 30 | - | 0 | 7 |
| Mr John Follet for the *Pellicant* | 25 | - | 0 | 6 |
| Mrs Holligrove for her 2 ships 2s 1d | 99 | - | | |
| Mr Gills for the *Jonas* | 24 | - | 1 | 0 |
| Thomas Ball for his 2 ships 1s 8d | 80 | - | | |
| George Plumleigh for his barke | 24 | | | |
| Mr Cooke for his ship | 45 | - | 1 | 0 |
| George Rowpe for his 2 ships | 70 | - | 3 | 0 |
| Mr William Plumleigh for his ship | 60 | | 1 | 3 |
| Mr Laskye for his ship | 55 | | 1 | 2 |
| Mr Sheres for the *P*[ro]*sperus* | 50 | | 2 | 0 |
| Mr John Winchester for the *John* | 44 | | 0 | 11 |
| Mr Gorny for his 2 ships | 120 | | 2 | 5 |
| Edward Winchester for the *Rebecka* | 40 | 0 | 0 | 10 |
| Andrew Wackham for his ship | 45 | 0 | 0 | 11 |
| | [Total] | 1 | 14 | 1 |
| Robert Philpoot for the *Unitye* | 48 | 0 | 1 | 0 |
| for the *Plymerose* | 80 | 0 | 5 | 0 |
| Sir Richard Hawkings for his ship with Mr Lewes Forteschue | 60 | - | | |
| promised to pay it rated [sic] | | 0 | 6 | 0 |

# APPENDIX C

SHIPS AT PLYMOUTH, 28 AUGUST 1627
Letter from Sir James Bagg to Edward Nicholas
Public Record Office, SP16/75/43

[dorse] To my noble friend Edward Nicholas esq. secretary to the Duke of Buckingham his Grace. The sea.
[dorse] 28 August 1627. Rec[eived]. James Bagg sends a list of ships at Plymouth; desires Lord Holland to be his guest. to send a certificate about the tenths.
[dorse] 28 August 1627. Sir James Bagg Vice-Admiralty
My beloved friend,

I am myself enforced to see the boarding of the horses, and not willing to stay these from you, wanting time. I have made my lines to you the shorter but have caused my servant to copy out that I write to Mr Secretary Coke which will declare to you what I have done for the ships, what my other desires and questions are, which I pray you well to consider of and to hasten them to me, for time slips away and it will make me mourn to have the Duke live in expectation.

The *Jonathan* will be provided in ten days, she is a ship of defence and fit for the service.

I have received your packet to Mr Mason sent to me the 20th as also that of yours to his Grace under yours of the 21th. Both with Secretary Coke's shall go I hope this night or in the morning (if the wind favour) in the *Fortune* where the horses and oxen are. The best man there of trust is the groom Mr Gryme sent that shall have them.

I give you thanks for your care to procure me the two thousand pounds. I beseech you to persevere in it, and to get me if I be employed as much money more as may be for both I and the service will want it. I refer you for these particulars of the press Commission for billeting, victualing of the soldiers and all other circumstances to that of mine to Mr Secretary.

I pray have an eye to the Lord of Warwick's envy against me. It is said the Earl of Holland will to the Duke, I am his servant, my house is his, I pray present it, and I doubt not but I am full in his favour I being my Lords's true servant.

I wish with my soul the Dutchman's news had been true of the fort's surrender, but the affirmation that he was going to Rochelle is contradicted for his lading assuredly was salt and men use not to carry coals to Newcastle, but assuredly he came thence.

For Sir Francis Steward, I yet hear no news of him or any of his acts when I do you shall know it and I will never but let you have that I will present to any, for my obligations are great unto you in so much as in faith I will be apt to adventure my life in any good office I may be happy to do you.

When I have gained a little time I will write unto you of what concerns my Lord as Admiral and me his servant, we must fall upon some course to punish the fugitive seamen or sink all service, let me truly be remembered to your sweetest wife, to your brother and sister Jik [sic]. And good Mr Edward think of the business for the tenths, send such a certificate from the Commissioners as you shall think fit, that I may convey by Mr Buxton my desires to his Grace, whom God ever prosper and you and me

Your true friend and servant
[signed] James Bagg

Plymouth the 28th of August 1627



Letter from Sir James Bagg to Sir John Coke.
PRO, SP16/75/43 (i)

[dorse] 28 August 1627. Sir James Bagg to me. Admiralty.
Copy.
Right honourable,

I received yours of the 21th the 27th although it was sent by post, the enclosed to Sir Ferdinando Gorges he hath; for your honours to his grace, it goes in the *Fortune* that carries the five horses and twelve oxen which is ready for the first wind.

I have made a survey of what ships are here to be found fit for transportation of the soldiers. I have enclosed a list of them, of their burthens, ordnance, masters' and owners' names. They are to be made ready in six days or less for the sea, being new returned from New[found]land from whence daily more are expected, but I must put your Honour's knowledge in memory that neither will the master, owner nor mariners without command entertain this journey. And therefore if you intend they shall serve his majesty you must be pleased to send me warrants to take up the ships and their provisions to require the owners to prepare and make them ready and to press the masters and mariners, and besides as you give directions for victuals so to supply me with money, so will the service be the better done. If it be also his Majesty's will that I provide victuals for the soldiers transportation I desire to understand it as soon as may be, as also the allowance both for time and condition that so I may not err.

If the soldiers be to be billeted in these parts before they be put aboard I desire to be named in that Commission that I may either spur those on to do service that are unwilling or oppose them, if they be willfully backwards.

By my next I shall be bold to send unto your Honour an account of my disbursements for the oxen, mariners, and the press, with my humble petition to your honour to be the means to procure me my money which I will receive to no other use than to use in his Majesty's service which now requires all dutiful assistance from all his honest servants and true subjects.

And it will cheer the hearts of them to see exemplary punishment inflicted upon those that out of their ill affections willfully refuse to aid his Majesty in their loans, amongst which there are two that are now out of Cornwall sent for, one Mr Trefusus, a justice of peace, and Mr Coriton's nephew, an absolute refuser and not guided so much by any particular reason to himself but by example of others for when he was demanded by Sir Bernard Greenfeild and Sir William Wrey whether he would lend or not, he made answer that he would do as Mr Bevill Greenfeild and Mr Nicholls did, who do not lend, so as some combination seems to be in him.

But Mr Nicholls is likewise sent for and did (being a Commissioner) never declare himself and as Mr William Rowse a Commissioner enformed Mr John Mahun and myself, refuseth to lend: these ill examples in them hath made others backward, and their punishment will draw them on at last to pay in their money, here, and in that

Commission I could not but appear a true servant to his Majesty and shall be ready (if your honour's said cause) to send you certificates of those men's carriages but if there be no cause I shall pray that I appear not their accuser.

I have been informed that the Earl of Warwick stands displeased with me and will by the power of some of his friends intend me harm. Let me receive your countenance and any of his accusations I will answer and justify myself truly to obey and serve his Majesty and honour the Duke of Buckingham, for whose sake it shall not grieve me to suffer.

I am too long, yet cannot but pray your honour to remember my humble duty to the Lord Viscount Conaway and still to continue in your service and favour.

Plymouth [*Plimouth*] 28th August 1627

Your honour's humble servant
[signed] J[ames] B[agg]

Postscript

Sir I must add to my former the information of one Mayne of Oreston, which I have now enclosed, by which I conceive those preparations of the French at St Malo [*Malloes*], were most to continue their trade with Spain [*Spayne*], where in a merchant course I believe they are gone. And by a man of Jersey (who is now here) I am informed those ships put twice forth of St Malo [*Mallo*] and twice put in again, out of fear that some English attended their courses.

Your honours',
[signed] J[ames] B[agg]

List

| The Ship's name | Of what place | Bur-then | Decks | Ord-nance | Owners' names | Masters' names | Where bound |
|---|---|---|---|---|---|---|---|
| The *Jonathan* | of London | 350 | 3 | 28 | Mr Geere and others of London | Capt. Hooper | stays for to expect a freight |
| The *Catte* | of Dartmouth | 240 | 2 | 8 | Mr Shapley of Dartmouth [*Darmouth*] and others | | to Dartmouth ready for the sea |
| The *Eagle* | of Plymouth | 140 | 2 | 6[1] | Mr Abraham Row & others of Plymouth | | nowhere bound |
| The *Providence* | of Plymouth | 100 | 2 | 6 | Mr Leonard Pomery of Plymouth | | nowhere bound |
| The *Retorne* | of Plymouth | 160 | 2 | 4 | Mr William Row of Millbrook | | came from Newfound-land no-where bound |
| The *Wrenne* | of Plymouth | 100 | 2 | | Mr Francis Trelewney | | nowhere bound |
| The *Grayhound* | of Plymouth | 50 | 2 | | Mr Leonard Pomery | | nowhere bound |
| The *Charles* | of Dover | 40 | 1 | | Henry Serjeant | | to Dover empty |
| The *Tyger* | of London | 40 | 1 | | William Ellis | | to London empty |

[1] and 4 murderers [small cannon or mortars].

# APPENDIX D

## PLYMOUTH AND DARTMOUTH SHIPS, 9 OCTOBER 1627
Letter from Sir James Bagg to Edward Nicholas
Public Record Office, SP16/80/77

[dorse] To my worthy friend Edward Nicholas esq. Secretary to the Duke of Buckingham his Grace. Plymouth 9th of October, 8 at night.
[dorse] 9 October 1627 Sir James Bagg sendeth list of ships at Plymouth & Dartmouth
Noble friend,

I received you and yours by Mr Bold the one enclosed in the other, In them you discovered your ['yo' crossed out] true respect of me your friend but in vain you give recommendation of the bearer whose welcome is not yours but his own. And although I delight in his brave and grave company yet I should have been glad he had a wind, as he had a ship the first hour of his arrival so had he now been at St Martins, who is yet here, & hath received from my hands that your letter sent me in yours of the 5th of this present and by him will with all possible speed be conveyed the first wind that bloweth.

I have formerly sent you a list of the ships made ready for the thousand men now to go under the Earl of Holland and I now send you the list of such ships' names as are both in this port and Dartmouth. You may not be carried away with the opinion that the owners of these ships will willingly contract and so employ themselves but it is nothing else but warrant and command that must draw them to it. Yet nevertheless that being sent, I will treat and if I find it any way to save charges to his Majesty I will that way endeavour to agree with them for provisions be assured I will fit a proportion for them, so as money be presently given me. For you know my wants and until I receive I cannot either to the preservation of my credit or the doing of the service go on without it. Therefore consider to find a way to give me money, directions and warrant. And know, as the wants require speedy supply to be sent I will double my diligence, abate my sleep, and not willingly rest ere I perform my service.

It is somewhat hard to persuade any of our merchants to go to Rochelle or Rhè upon their own adventure, for they are so hard of belief, as they will not give credit that any money will there be paid them, but rest assured they shall have their goods taken away and bills given them, which I otherwise promise them.

To this same purpose Sir Sackfeild Crowe wrote unto me. I have sent him the list of ships, the proportion of victuals these parts will afford, the rates and the time, but nothing can be done without ready money, then the work will be easy to me.

For the *Jonathan* she is near laden with pilchards and fish bound to the straits, and will be ready for that voyage three weeks or a month hence. For the *Hector* I wrote to you in my last, so hath Sir Henry Manwaring, she is here & will be serviceable if you think it fit to employ her.

If you conceive it convenient I pray confer with Sir Sackfeild Crowe and let me with speed receive your resolutions for the advantage of this service.

I resolve to do what I can in preparing all I may before I receive your answer, and will according to that guide myself after I have received it.

With my business at the Isle of Rhè I will interest our friend Mr Bold who now drinks your health to ['you' crossed out].

your most affectionate friend & servant
[signed] James Bagg

Plymouth 9th October 1627


PRO, SP16/80/77(ii)

| ships' names | burthen | ordnance | owners | decks | mariners |
|---|---|---|---|---|---|

A list of ships belonging to the port of Plymouth.

## Plymouth

| ships' names | burthen | ordnance | owners | decks | mariners |
|---|---|---|---|---|---|
| The *Jonathan* | 150 | 10 | Nicholas Sherwill | 2 | [blank] |
| *Prosperous* | 140 | 6 | Abraham Jennens | 2 | |
| *Adam & Eve* | 120 | 0 | John Martyn | 2 | |
| *Marygold* | 90 | 0 | Richard Rodden | 2 | |
| *Speedwell* | 70 | 3 | Edward Cocke | 2 | |
| *Phenix* | 50 | 2 | Nicholas Sherwill | 2 | |
| *Margarett* | 140 | 3 | Thomas Bespich | 2 | |
| *Gloabe* | 60 | 3 | Thomas Cramporne | 2 | |
| *Heartsease* | 60 | 2 | Abraham Colmer | 2 | |
| *Christian* | 50 | 0 | Robert Gubbes | 2 | |
| *John* | 100 | 8 | John White | 2 | |
| *Anne* | 60 | 0 | Humphrey Gaire | 2 | |
| *Swallow* | 50 | 0 | do | 2 | |
| *Sunne* | 70 | 2 | John Paige | 2 | |
| *Dolphin* | 240 | 16 | Walter Vele | 2 | |
| *Returne* | 80 | 4 | Abraham Colmer | 2 | |
| *John* | 50 | 0 | ['John Cawse' crossed out] Edward Cocke | 2 | |
| *Lions Clawe* | 70 | 0 | John Cawse | 2 | |
| *William* | 140 | 8 | Abraham Jennens | 2 | |
| [blank] | 70 | 6 | John Scoble | 2 | |

## Stonehouse

| ships' names | burthen | ordnance | owners | decks |
|---|---|---|---|---|
| *William & Margarett* | 60 | 0 | William Rowe | 2 |
| *Blessinge* | 60 | 0 | Richard Spurwell | 2 |
| *John* | 70 | 0 | do | 2 |

## Millbrook [*Milbrooke*]

| ships' names | burthen | ordnance | owners | decks |
|---|---|---|---|---|
| *Tryall* | 160 | 8 | William Rowe | 2 |
| *Concord* | 120 | 1 | do | 2 |
| *George* | 100 | 0 | Richard Bealye | 2 |
| *Portion* | 100 | 6 | Richard Rowe | 2 |
| *Abraham* | 100 | [blank] | John Evans | 2 |
| *Unytie* | 90 | 6 | do | 2 |

| ships' names | burthen | ordnance | owners | decks | mariners |
|---|---|---|---|---|---|
| | | **Saltash** | | | |
| The *Isaac* | 80 | [blank] | Edward Herring | 2 | [blank] |

A list of ships belonging to the port of Dartmouth

### Dartmouth

| ships' names | burthen | ordnance | owners | decks |
|---|---|---|---|---|
| The *Providence* | 200 | 10 | Philip Ley | 3 |
| *Dolphin* | 180 | 10 | [blank] | 2 |
| *Blessinge* | 140 | 8 | Andrew Voysey | 2$^1$/$_2$ |
| *Arke* | 220 | 10 | Lord Baltamore | 2 |
| *George* | 180 | 0 | do | 1$^1$/$_2$ |
| *Francis* | 200 | 10 | William Bogan | 3 |
| *Hopewell* | 150 | 6 | [blank] Streets | 2$^1$/$_2$ |
| *Fortune* | 200 | 5 | [blank] Staplehille | 2 |
| *Anne gallant* | 100 | 5 | Alexander Staplehill | 2 |
| *Whitehorse* | 120 | [blank] | [blank] Sheeres | 2 |
| *Flower* | 160 | 6 | Andrew Voysey & Mr Newman | [blank] |
| *An Advisor* | 10 | 8 murderers | Gilbert Staplehill | 1 |
| [blank] | 150 | 0 | John Holligrove | 2 |
| *Burnt Cowe* | 150 | 8 | William Plumley | 2 |
| *Handmayde* | 120 | 6 | John Martyn | 2 |
| *Blessinge* | 150 | 6 | Alexander Shapley | 2 |
| *Gift of God* | 220 | 6 | Mr [blank] Shapley | 3 |
| *Chidley* | 140 | 8 | Mr [blank] Champnoone | 2$^1$/$_2$ |
| *Jonas* | 120 | 5 | Mr [blank] Hamett | 2$^1$/$_2$ |
| *Adventure* | 150 | 8 | Mr [blank] Harris | 2 |
| [blank] | 300 | 14 | Baronet Seymour | 2 |
| [blank] | 200 | [blank] | do | 2 |
| *Rose* | 240 | 11 | Mr Nicholas Roope | 2 |
| *Content* | 150 | 7 | Mr [blank] Roope | 2 |
| ['Co' crossed out] a flyboat | 200 | 4 | Mr Champernone | 2 |
| *Hope* | 100 | 0 | Mr Champernoone | 2 |

# APPENDIX E

VICE-ADMIRALTY OF NORTH CORNWALL, 17 JANUARY 1629
Letter from Francis Basset to Edward Nicholas
Public Record Office, SP16/132/31

[dorse] R[eceived]. 4 February 1628 Mr Bassett to me.
[dorse] For Edward Nicholas esq. my Honourable friend at his house in Chancelry in Westminster
Worthy Sir,
 I once more ask leave to complain to you of the injury done to me by some one most injurious who intercepts and keeps what ever letters you direct to me. I am confident you have at some time or other vouchsafed an answer unto some of mine always importing business. I have not received one to your last 7 or 8 I have sent you. Besides not long since there was a command for the stay of all ships before the[y] go forth of our fleet. I received that command and therein prove distasteful and a wrong deed unto divers within those ports of my Vice-Admiralty for not receiving orders for the opening of them. I kept at least 20 sail almost 20 days after others were discharged in all the ports of this kingdom and at last ventured to permit them to pass without warrant so to do. Once before in the like occasion I was so served and then dispatched a messenger to London of purpose for orders which had been formerly sent me, but [they] never came to my hands. Lately as I hear there were commands greeted unto me as to other Vice-Admirals for my personal attendance on the Commissioners. How to God I [have] never received any and therefore cannot but doubt but that those letters are intercepted and ['ted' crossed out] detained unjustly to abuse me. There is now a command but five days since come to my hands for taking a muster of all mariners & fishermen. It bears date the 23th of December and came to me but the 12th of this present by one of my neighbours why [who] had it from he knows not whom. I will speed that service all I can and will be hearty & honest to all other commands. And humbly pray you as heretofore to protect my innocency which will be your glory and you shall ever have a faithful servant in yours.

[signed] Francis Bassett
Tehidy [*Tehidie*] this 17 January 1628 [1629]

# APPENDIX F

FIRE SHIPS PREPARED AT PLYMOUTH, 8 SEPTEMBER 1628
Public Record Office, SP16/116/69(a)

[Extract]
For his Majesties service and by his Command.
A list of ships prepared at Plymouth by Sir James Bagg knight bound for Rochelle for fire ships.

A particular note of the wants of the fire ships which could not be bought at Plymouth for ready money wherefor your Lordship is prayed to give command that their wants be furnished them.

| Ships' names | Captains' names | Burthen | Men | Price without some charge of neccesary and fitting |
|---|---|---|---|---|
| *St Peter* Rochelle | Peter Renald ['James Caddott' crossed out] | 150 | 10 | [blank] |
| *Robert* Plymouth | Nicholas Lauereno | 134 | 12 | 195 0 0 |
| *Marye Anne* | Andrew Bryne | 120 | 12 | 190 0 0 |
| *George* | James Jamen | 65 | 8 | 180 0 0 |
| *Christian* | John Blankett | 8 | 12 | 246 0 0 |
| *Flame* | Vincent Renald | 60 | 8 | 90 0 0 |
| *Swanne* | Daniel Fallourd | 150 | 12 | 315 0 0 |
| *Pearle* | Stephen Cadott | 180 | 13 | 190 0 0 |
| *William Margarett* | Henry Gallope | 87 | 10 | 230 0 0 |
| *Sparke* | John Sparke | 105 | 12 | 215 0 0 |
| *Speedewell* | Richard Bonithon | 60 | 9 | 180 0 0 |
| *John* of Lyme | George Dennis | 60 | 9 | 120 0 0 |
| *Allteration* | Richard Meade | 75 | 10 | 195 0 0 |
| *Jonas* Nicholas | Wadham | 62 | 8 | 82 0 0 |
| *Edward* | Dartmouth James Randall | 150 | 11 | 160 0 0 |
| *Gosehauke* | Henry Allworth | 180 | 10 | 215 0 0 |
| *Lightning* | William Jarvyes | 150 | 11 | 215 0 0 |
| *Golden Catt* | John Aitking | 293 | 13 | 300 |
| *Rose* | Dartmouth John Corbin | 240 | 13 | 350 0 0 |

[signed] James Bagg

114

| From whome bought | Shallops | Oares | Mus-kets | Ban-dol-iers | Swords | Match | Powder | Pikes | Mus-ket shot |
|---|---|---|---|---|---|---|---|---|---|
| Capt. Bragneau | Plymouth shallop | 16 | 6 | 6 | [blank] | 9 | [blank] | 4 | 12 |
| | 2 barrels of powder which could not be provided at Plymouth. | | | | | | | | |
| Peter Taylor | Plymouth shallop | 8 | 8 | 8 | [blank] | 12 | 2 | 6 | 16 |
| | ['2 barrels' crossed out] | | | | | | | | |
| John Gay | Rochelle shallop | 8 | 8 | 9 | [blank] | 12 | 0 | 6 | 16 |
| Bartholomew Nicholls | Plymouth shallop | 8 | 6 | 6 | [blank] | 9 | 2 | 4 | 12 |
| Robert Gubbs | Dartmouth shallop | 8 | 8 | 8 | [blank] | 12 | 2 | 6 | 16 |
| Nicholas Roope | Dartmouth shallop | 8 | 5 | 5 | [blank] | 8 | 2 | 4 | 10 |
| Nicholas ['Roope' crossed out] Blake | Plymouth shallop | 8 | 8 | 8 | [blank] | 12 | 2 | 6 | 16 |
| Alexander Cousens | Dartmouth shallop | 8 | 9 | 9 | [blank] | 40 | 2 | 6 | 18 |
| William Rowe | [blank] | 6 | 7? | 6 | 6 | 12 | [blank] | 5 | 14 |
| | 2 barrels of powder, 7 banderoles and a shallop | | | | | | | | |
| John Sparke | Plymouth shallop | 8 | 9 | 9 | 6 | 14 | 2 | 8 | 18 |
| Nicholas Sherwill | Plymouth shallop | 8 | 5 | 5 | 6 | 8 | [blank] | 4 | 10 |
| | 2 barrels of powder | | | | | | | | |
| John Harvye | [blank] | 8 | 5 | [blank] | 6 | 8 | [blank] | 4 | 10 |
| | 2 barrels of powder, 5 banderoles and a shallop | | | | | | | | |
| Mathew Brooks | Plymouth shallop | 12 | 6 | [blank] | 6 | 9 | 2 | 4 | 12 |
| | 6 banderoles | | | | | | | | |
| Mr Lumleigh | Dartmouth shallop | 5 | 5 | 5 | 6 | 9 | [blank] | 4 | 12 |
| | 2 barrels of powder | | | | | | | | |
| Mr Plumleigh | Dartmouth shallop | 8 | 8 | 8 | 6 | 12 | [blank] | 6 | 16 |
| | 2 barrels of powder | | | | | | | | |
| Captain Hockeridge | Dartmouth shallop | 10 | [?6] | [?6] | 6 | 14 | 2 | 6 | 18 |
| | 9 banderoles | | | | | | | | |
| Moyses Slanye | Dartmouth shallop | 12 | 9 | 8 | 6 | 14 | 2 | 8 | 18 |
| Mr Shapleigh | Dartmouth shallop | 9 | 12 | [blank] | 6 | 18 | [blank] | 10 | 24 |
| | 2 barrels of powder and 12 banderoles | | | | | | | | |
| Nicholas Roope | Dartmouth shallop | 8 | 12 | [blank] | 6 | 18 | [blank] | 8 | 24 |
| | 2 barrels of powder and 12 banderoles | | | | | | | | |

# APPENDIX G

BOOK OF NAVAL MUSTER RETURNS, 1628/9
Public Record Office, SP16/155/31

[dorse] A Collection of all the ships, barques and other vessels with their several burthens & also of all seamen, sailors and mariners within the Vice Admiralty of the county of Devon.
A brief ['account' crossed out] Collection of all Ships & Vessels together [...torn] [' of Mar' crossed out] Seamen, Marin[...torn] ['Watermen &' crossed out] fishermen and watermen belonging to the several ports & places hereafter named according to several ['certificates sent' crossed out] taken and certified musters ['taken A' crossed out] in the 4 [or] 5 year of his Majesties Reign *Anno Dom.* 1628 by direction of the Right Honourable the Lords Council for the execution of the office of Lord Admiral of England.

Sir James Bagg    Vice-Admirals
Sir John Drake

## Roborough Hundred
### Plymouth

Ships & pinnaces 56 whereof  1 of 160 tons
3 of 120 tons
3 of 100 tons
6 of 80 tons
1 of 70 tons
5 of 60 tons
3 of 55 tons
6 of ['6' crossed out] 50 tons
2 of 45 tons
9 of 40 tons
6 of 35 tons
9 of 30 tons
2 of 20 tons

### Stonehouse

Ships & Pinnaces 9 whereof  1 of 120 tons
2 of 80 tons
1 of 60 tons
2 of 50 tons
3 of ['30' crossed out] 20 tons

## Plymouth

Seamen 113 whereof          Sailors 91
Shipwrights 15
Gunners 3
Boatswains 3
Pilots 1
Fishermen 5

## Stonehouse & other places within Roborough hundred

Seamen 41 whereof          Sailors 40
Boatswain 1
Fishermen 33

['Plimouth Portsmouth & Torbay' crossed out]

## Dartmouth

Ships & pinnaces 92 whereof          1 of 200 tons
4 of 150 tons
4 of 140 tons
3 of 120 tons
3 of 100 tons
14 of 80 tons
7 of 70 tons
15 of 60 tons
5 of 50 tons
12 of 40 tons
18 of 30 tons
6 of 20 tons

## Part of Plympton [*Plimpton*] hundred

Seamen 22 whereof          Captain 1
Sailors 19
Trumpeter 1
Cooper 1
Fishermen 13

## South Molton hundred

Sailors 2

## Sherwill hundred

Sailors 1
Fishermen 5

# Stanborough hundred

| Salcombe barques 27 whereof | 3 of 50 tons |
|---|---|
| | 6 of 45 tons |
| | 2 of 40 tons |
| | 1 of 35 tons |
| | 6 of 30 tons |
| | 2 of 25 tons |
| | 4 of 20 tons |
| | 3 of 15 tons |

## Salcombe & alibi within Stanborough [*Stanborow*] hundred
Sailors 150
Fishermen 30

# Braunton hundred

## Braunton, Ilfracombe [*Ilfarcombe*] & other places within the hundred of Braunton

| Ships & pinnaces 18 whereof | 2 of 180 tons |
|---|---|
| | 1 of 150 tons |
| | 1 of 70 tons |
| | 1 of 50 tons |
| | 1 of 40 tons |
| | ['2' crossed out] 1 of 35 tons |
| | 2 of 30 tons |
| | 3 of 24 tons |
| | 2 of 20 tons |
| | 2 of 18 tons |
| | 2 of 15 tons |
| Seamen 125 whereof | Sailors 116 |
| | Gunners 3 |
| | Shipwrights 3 |
| | Pilot 1 |
| | Surgeon 1 |
| | Cooper 1 |

# CORNWALL: SOUTH

A Collection of all the ships, barques & other vessels with their several burthens, & also of all seamen, sailors & mariners within the Vice-Admiralty of the South ['countie' crossed out] of Cornwall.

Sir James Bagg Vice-Admiral

## Hundred of East

### Several villages

| Ships & pinnaces 29 whereof | 1 of 200 tons |
|---|---|
| | 1 of 130 tons |

|                      |                  |
|----------------------|------------------|
|                      | 2 of 120 tons    |
|                      | 2 of 90 tons     |
|                      | 3 of 80 tons     |
|                      | 4 of 60 tons     |
|                      | 4 of 50 tons     |
|                      | 7 of 40 tons     |
|                      | 2 of 30 tons     |
|                      | 1 of 15 tons     |
| Seamen 424 whereof   | Sailors 386      |
|                      | Gunners 14       |
|                      | Shipwrights 13   |
|                      | Pilots 8         |
|                      | Trumpeter 1      |
|                      | Cooper 1         |
|                      | Fishermen 30     |

## Several places within the hundred of West

Barques 10 ['whereof' inserted 'barques' crossed out]

|                           |                  |
|---------------------------|------------------|
|                           | 1 of [blank] tons |
|                           | 1 of [blank] tons |
|                           | 4 of 40 tons     |
|                           | 1 of 30 tons     |
|                           | 1 of 20 tons     |
|                           | 1 of 18 tons     |
|                           | 1 of 16 tons     |
| Boats 25 of 8 or 10 tons  |                  |
| Seamen 120 whereof        | Masters 11       |
|                           | Sailors 108      |
|                           | Carpenter 1      |
|                           | Fishermen 25     |

## Hundred of Powder

### Several places within hundred of Powder

|                      |                  |
|----------------------|------------------|
| Barques 11 whereof   | 1 of 50 tons     |
|                      | 1 of 40 tons     |
|                      | 1 of 30 tons     |
|                      | 4 of 20 tons     |
|                      | 2 of 22 tons     |
|                      | 1 of 18 tons     |
|                      | 1 of 14 tons     |
| Seamen 175 whereof   | Sailors 137      |
|                      | Gunners 1        |
|                      | Bargemen 36      |
|                      | Shipwright 1     |
|                      | Fishermen 167    |

# Hundred of Penwith [*Penwth*]
## Several places within hundred of Penwith

Seamen 46 whereof      Sailors 42
                              Shipwrights 4
                              Fishermen 128

# Hundred of Kerrier [*Kirriar*]
## Several places within the hundred of Kerrier [*Kirriar*]

['Sailors 42' crossed out]

Barques 3 whereof             1 of 180 tons
                              1 of 140 tons
                              1 of 30 tons
Seamen 56 whereof          Sailors 39
                              Bargemen 17
                              Fishermen 43

North Cornwall Francis Basset esq. Vice-Admiral
Vice-Admiralty of North Cornwall taken 3 February 1628 [1629]
Francis Bassett

A Collection of the barques, mariners, sailors & fishermen within the Vice-Admiralty of the north of Cornwall taken 3 February 1628 [1629].

## St Ives

Seamen 53 whereof          Mariners 3
                              Pilots 2
                              ['saisors' crossed out] Sailors    44
                              Shipwrights 4
                              Fishermen 44
Barques 3 whereof           1 of 45 tons
                              1 of 20 tons
                              1 of 25 tons

## Boscastle [*Botreaux Castle*]

Barques 4 whereof           1 of 30 tons
                              1 of 12 tons
                              1 of 26 tons
                              1 of 25 tons
Seamen 13 whereof           Mariners 4
                              Sailors 9

## Padstow [*Padstowe*]

Barques 3 whereof          2 of 16 tons
                           1 of 26 tons
Seamen 33 whereof          Mariners 4
                           Sailors 29
                           Fishermen 11

## Crantock [*Crantocke*]

Seamen                     Sailor 1
                           Fishermen 7

## St Columb Minor [*Low St Columb*]

Seamen                     Sailors 15

## Endellion [*Endellian*]

Seamen 36 whereof          Mariner 1
                           Sailors 35
                           Fishermen 14

## St Minver [*St Mynver*]

Seamen                     Sailors 3
                           Fishermen 12

# APPENDIX H

THE NAVAL TALLY OF 1635
Public Record Office, SP16/283/120

[Extract]
[January 1635, see PRO, SP16/270/64, 282/135]
A Brief collection of all ships of 100 tons & upwards together with the seamen, fishermen & watermen belonging to the several port & places hereafter named. According to several musters taken and certified ['in the 4th year' crossed out] *Anno* ['163' crossed out] 1628 By directions of the right honourable the Lord Commissioners for the Admiralty of England.

**Vice-Admiralty of Devon**            ships
Plymouth from 100 to 160 tons            8
Dartmouth from 100 to 200 tons            15
In several other ports from 150 to 180    3    [Total] 26
Seamen {453} whereof            Pilots        2
                        Boatwains    4
                        Gunners        6
                        Shipwrights  18
                        Trumpeters    1
                        Surgeons      1
                        Coopers        2
                        Mariners    419
                        Fishermen    86

**Vice-Admiralty of the south of Cornwall**
Ships from 120 to 200 tons                6
Seamen {731} whereof            Pilots ['6' crossed out] 8
                        Masters      11
                        Gunners      15
                        Shipwrights  19
                        Trumpeters    1
                        Cooper        1
                        Mariners    676
                        Fishermen    393
                        Bargemen      53

**Vice-Admiralty of the north of Cornwall**
Seamen {154} whereof            Pilots        2
                        Shipwrights    4
                        Mariners    148
                        Fishermen    88

123

A['tota' crossed out]ll ['of' crossed out] the ships mentioned in this account ['332, 30 ' crossed out] 362

Besides the ships aforesaid there have been built & repaired since this survey was taken diverse other ships of 100 tons & upwards. vizt ['th' crossed out]

|              |     |     |
|--------------|-----|-----|
| New built    | 88  |     |
| repaired     | 49  | 137 |
|              | 137 |     |

['new built 88 prize ships and others repaired 49' crossed out] 137
which added to the former number certified, maketh in ['all ' crossed out] total ships 499

['Besides the ships' crossed out] total of all seamen ['mentioned' crossed out] of every sort mentioned in this account are as follows ['vizt' crossed out] 10,238

|                               |         |                          |
|-------------------------------|---------|--------------------------|
| The Trinity House men         | 285     | ['Seamen' crossed out]   |
| Masters 943                   | 943     | ['948' crossed out]      |
| Masters mates                 | 157     |                          |
| Quarter Masters               | 54      |                          |
| Pilots 76                     | 7['4' crossed out]6 |              |
| Pursers                       | 1       |                          |
| Boatswains                    | 63      |                          |
| Gunners 183                   | ['187' crossed out] 183 |          |
| Armorer['s' crossed out]      | 1       |                          |
| Trumpeters 6                  | 6       |                          |
| Drummer['s' crossed out]      | 2       |                          |
| Shipwrights 117               | ['114' crossed out] |              |
| Surgeons 14                   | 14      |                          |
| Coopers 7                     | 7       |                          |
| Mariners 8,329                | ['858' crossed out] 8,329 |        |
| Besides   fishermen           | 3,080   |                          |
| bargemen & ferrymen           | 67 5,667 |                         |
| watermen                      | 2,520   |                          |
|                               | ['5,667' crossed out] |            |

In this account there is not mention of the ships or seamen that belong to ['Bristol' crossed out] Falmouth Newcastle.

Nor what are in the counties of   Somerset
York
Chester
Sussex
North Wales

And but part of South Wales

This survey was taken about February ['January' crossed out] 1628 towards the end of the wars when shipping was at lowest & the seamen were most abroad at sea seeking for prizes.

# INDEX OF PLACE-NAMES

# INDEX OF PERSONAL-NAMES

Surnames have been indexed as they appear in the text with the most modern form normally appearing first.

ABBOTT, John, 52, 67
Abraham, Henry, 1, 19; John, 26
Abram, George, 30; John, 30
Adam, John, 64; Richard, 5, 11, 46; Robert, 46; Teige, 12
Adams (Addams), Edmund, 44; Edward, 29; George, 7, 30; James, 44; John, 62; Lawrence, 97; Morrice, 46; Nicholas, 22; Peter, 4, 82; Robert, 1, 47; Thomas, 105; Walter, 7, 33, 62; William, 29(3), 40, 81
Addamour, John, 87
Adgar (Adger), Christopher, 44; John, jun., 44
Adgeney, George, 19
Adler, Henry, 1
Adrescott, Thomas, 19
Agarye, Nicholas, 33
Aitking, John, 114
Aleword (Allward), John, 30, jun., 30; William, 30
Aley, Lawrence, 92; Philip, 93(2)
Alford (Alforde, Allford), John, 36; Robert, 39; Thomas, 19, 38
Alger (Algar), Andrew, 8, 86
Alkens, William, 19
Allen, Edward, 76; George, 1; Philip, 54, 100; Richard, 54, 100; Thomas, 76; William, 19, 68, 70, 76
Aller, Henry, 81
Alley, Stephen, 60
Allnworth (Allworth), Henry, 114; Robert, 40
Allwill, John, 36
Alsopp (Alsope), William, 3, 85
Alyoode, Andrew, 87
Ambrouse (Anbrose), John, 85; William, 77

Amell, John, jun., 19, sen., 19
Ameredith, Edward, esq., 85(2)
Amye, Thomas, 44, 47
Anderson, William, 3
Andrew, Ambrose, 16; Christopher, 40; Ellis, 40; Henry, 1, 40; John, 40, jun., 8; Thomas, 40
Andrewes, John, 85
Androw, John, 16; Nicholas, 55, 102
Andye, John, 48
Anger, Ezechia, 27, 64; John, 101; Richard, 68; William,
Angone, Arthur, 77
Anthony, Adrian, 3; John, 74; Nicholas, 75; Richard, 77
Appleton, Peter, 3
Apter, John, 13
Archer, Christopher, 34; Richard, 34; Robert, 19; Thomas, 13
Arnall, John, 83
Arnold, John, 40
Arthur (Arthures), Richard, 3; William, 86
Ascott, Henry, 1
Ash (Ashe), William, 19, 34
Ashfoord, William, 19
Ashley (Ashly, Ashlye), Edward, 50; Herbert, 81; John, 50(2); Mathew, 50; Richard, 50; Robert, 49; William, 7, 50
Asticke, John, 78
Atkins, Henry, 62; John, 3; Steven, 64
Augar (Auger), John, 26, jun., 44
Aunger, John, 56
Austen (Austinn), David, 1; John, 17, 22, 29; Richard, 22; Robert, 16; Thomas, 18(2)
Auton (Awton), Jerome, 7, 86; William, 3
Avenn, John, 15
Avent, Arthur, 36; William, 60
Avery (Averye), Christopher, 29; Edith, 43; Hopton, 70; John, 46, 101; Martyn,

70; Ralph, 78; Richard, 43, sen., 70, jun., 70; Robert, 35, 91; Thomas, 42, 43, 60, 102; William, 8
Axford, George, 19
Aydie, Henry, 33

BABB, Barnard, 51; Gawyn 38; George, 39; Gregory, 36; Hugh, 34; Jeffery, 39; John, 71, 38, jun., 38, sen., 39; Juell, 42; Richard, 38; Robert, 36; Thomas, 36; Vincent, 51; Walter, 51; William, 38, 71
Babbage (Babbedg, Babidge), Arthur, 62; Michael, 19; William, 27
Backeare, George, 41
Badcocke, John, 70
Baddock, Thomas, 66
Badford, Gregory, 17
Badge, Edward, 9
Badiford, Roger, 17; Thomas, 17
Badston, Timothy, 50
Bagg, James, ix, xi, xii, xiii, xiv, xv, xvii, xviii, xix, xx, xxii, xxxiv, 65(2), 67, 69, 74(2), 77, 80, 83, 84, 85, 86, 89, 90, 93, 94, 95, 98, 107(3), 108(3), 109 (2), 110(2), 111, 114(2), 117, 119, sen., xii; Thomas, 19
Baker (Bacher), Andrew, 9; Gawyn, 39; Hugh, 29; James, 3, 81; John, 3, 9, 17, 30, 52, 71; Nicholas, 8, 9; Peter, 39; Philip, 15; Robert, 1, 81; Thomas, 91; Tobias, 91; William, 33, 34, 46
Bale, Jerman, 66; Richard, 1; Robert, 17
Balhatchet, Philip, 59
Ball (Balle), Edward, 38; John, 12, 32, 33; Nicholas, 40; Oliver, 56, 101; Richard, 32, 35, 86; Robert, 11; Roger, 70; Thomas, 33, 105, 106; Will, 33; William, 11
Ballamye, Edward, 3
Baltimore, Lord, *see* Calvert
Bambury, John, 62
Bamfeild (Bamfeilde), Henry, 45; John, 44; Thomas, 44
Band (Bande), Christopher, 19; James, 22(2); Robert, 28; Valentine, 74
Banes, Engram, 19
Bannell, John, 27
Barber, James, 54, 99; John, 1, 54, 99;

Nicholas, jun., 99, sen., 99; Richard, 54; Stephen, 54, 100
Barden, William, 63
Bardens, Mathew, 30
Barefoot, William, 3
Barker, Edward, 68; Richard, 1, 81; Robert, 66
Barkwell, Andrew, 35
Barlett, Joseph
Barlye, William, 50
Barnacott (Barnecot), Henry, 7, John, 60
Barnard, John, 78
Barne, Elias, 61; John, 61; Maurice, 70
Barnhouse, James, 91; John, 91
Barns (Barnes), Bonadventur, 33; Humphrey, 33; John, 49
Baron, Edward, 40, 50; George, 30; Henry, 41
Barons, Henry, 105; John, 1, 33; Mathew, 98; Richard, 29; William, 3, 29
Barrat (Barratt), John, 72; William, 72
Barren, Steven, 30
Barret, Nicholas, 66; Richard, 63; Thomas, 102
Barrows, John, 3
Barry (Barrey, Barrye), Gawyne, 38; John, 60, 66; Philip, 34; Thomas, 38
Barter (Bardar, Bartar, Bartor), Andrew, 19; Bartholomew, 32; James, 32; Jeffery, 35; John, 30(3), 41, 43; Michael, 30(2); Nicholas, 35; Thomas, 30, 32; Walter, 32; William, 30(3), 32
Bartlett, Edward, 51; Francis, 49; John, 61; Joseph, 62; Peter, 62; Richard, 51
Bartley, Peter, 29
Bartone, John, 33
Baskyn, Walter, 7
Bass (Basse), Edward, 48; John, 30, 45; Thomas, 46
Bassell (Basill), William, 19, 42, 46
Bassett, Francis, x, xv, xvi, 53, 54, 55, 113(3), 121; John, 92
Bastard, John, 14, 19; Peter, 19
Bastine, William, 99
Baston, Henry, 19
Batch, Arthur, 13
Batchelour, Oliver, 1
Batchfell, George, 3
Bater, John, 59

34; John, 42; Richard, 42

Bockaram, Thomas, 26

Boddin, Edward, 91

Bodinge, Richard, 41

Bodwaye, Walter, 69

Body (Boddye), Cutbert, 62; John, 36(2), 60; Mathew, 60; Thomas, 60

Bogan (Baggan), William, 97, 112

Bogar, Richard, 4

Bohey, Emanuel, 61

Bold, Mr, 110, 111

Boles, John, 34

Bolt, Nicholas, 46, 47

Bolithoe (Bolythowe, Bolythou), Robert, 54, 77, 99; Walter, 77

Bomery (Bomerye, Bomry), Robert, 32; Thomas, 32; Valentine, 32

Bond (Bonde, Boond), Abel, 64; John, 102; Richard, 63; Sampson, 65; William, 38, 49, 64, 70

Bondage, John, 64

Bone, John, 55; Nicholas, 102

Bonfeild (Bonfeid, Bonfell, Bonfild, Bonffill), Edward, 51; Hugh, 71; John, 36, 51, jun., 36; Robert, 51, *see* Bonvill

Bonithon, Richard, 114

Bonner, John, 19

Bonsoll, Richard, 60; William, 61

Bonvill, John, 75; Ranald, 75, *see* Bonfeild

Bonyface, John, 59; Robert, 59

Boone, John, 59, 68

Boorde (Boord), John, 34; Richard, 16;

Bordwood, John, 102

Boringe, Benjamin, 41

Borrond, John, 63

Bortemm, John, 27

Bortynn, Thomas, 27

Bosithio, John, 100

Bosvine, Walter, 75

Boswhiddon, Martin, 36

Bossocowe, William, 78

Bossowe, Peter, 79; Thomas, 79; William, 79

Boteson, Thomas, 80

Bound (Bownd), Edward, 61; Robert, 33; Thomas, 41; William, 61

Bounsie, Richard, 75

Bourchier, Edward, earl of Bath, xii

Bovie, John, 87

Bowden (Bawden), Ambrose, 10; Edward, 71; Elias, 39; Henry, 3; James, 80; John, 13, 16, 34, 39, 81, 88; Joseph, 19; Nathaniel, 46; Robert, 41; William, 64

Bowen, John, 92

Bowhay (Bowhey), Richard, 27; Peter, 19; Thomas, 93

Bowisie, Anthony, 75

Bowlen, George, 1

Bowmann, John, 19

Bowringe, Richard, 69

Boyen, John, 28

Boyer, Robert, 86

Boylman, Richard, 41

Boyne, John, 69

Boys (Boyes), Daniel, 19; Philip, 19; Thomas, 86; William, 13

Boysye, Nicholas, 43

Braddon, Anthony, 36, 37; Gabriel, 31; Henry, 40, 87; Peter, 13; Thomas, 38(2)

Bradford, John, 22; Oliver, 36; Thomas, 92; William, 22

Bragneau, Captain, 115

Brande, John, 62

Branscomb (Branscombe, Bronscombe), George, 7; Thomas, 38; Edward, 38

Brasye (Brasie, Brese), Thomas, 34; Richard, 1; William, 81

Braunde, Thomas, 32

Bray (Braye, Brea, Breye), Christopher, 101; Edward, 81; Henry, 1; John, 3, 4, 56, 82; Robert, 5; Stephen, 3; William, 81

Breage, John, 78

Bremblecomb, John, 19

Bremcomb (Bremcombe), Henry, 3; Richard, 1

Brend, Edmond, 59

Brendon, Richard, 84(3)

Brett, Leonard, 60

Brickham, Thomas, 7

Brickills, Thomas, 36

Bricknoll, Christopher, 38; John, 38; Lawrence, 42; Robert, 38(2); Thomas, 38

Briddick, Andrew, 9

Bridgman, John, 12, 86

Briget, Thomas, 61

Briggs, John, 28

William, 51
Came, Arthur, 86; John, 11; Peter, 26; Robert, 12; Thomas, 7
Camore, Stephen, 76
Campe, James, 8; John, 8, 16; Robert, 86, *see* Kemp
Campeche, Hibbs, 73
Candish, Mathew, 7
Caninge, John, 83
Candrowe, Thomas, 54
Candy, Thomas, 62
Cane, Thomas, 19
Canter, William, 19
Capell (Cappall), Lewis, 100; William, 76
Card, Thomas, 31
Carder, Richard, 46
Cardew, Talland, 66
Cardy (Cardye), Henry, 28; John, 28; Richard, 28; William, 28
Carell (Carrell), Christopher, 31; John, 31; Richard, 34; Stephen, 31; William, 31
Carew (Carewe, Carowe, Carrow, Carrowe, Caruo), Ambrose, 60; Andrew, 66; John, 71; Richard, xxii, xxiv; Thomas, 66; William, 68, 79
Carey (Carye), Christopher, 19; Robert, 47; William, 47, 48
Carkeele, Baldwyn, 2; John, 1; William, 1
Carkett, George, 61; John, 81; William, 85(2)
Carlyan, John, 72
Carlyne, Pascho, 66
Carnather, George, 76
Carne, John, 69; Mathew, 68; Robert, 79; Thomas, 82; William, 62
Carneney (Carnying), John, 54, 100
Carpenter, Richard, 81; William, 66, 81
Carter, George, 50; James, 1; John, 22, 50, 51; Walter, 50
Carthen, John, 71
Carvell, Gregory, 45
Carveth, Richard, 56, 101
Carvile, Thomas, 1
Casell (Castell), Christopher, 100; Osmound, 10
Caselye, Peter, 22

Casewell, Christopher, 23; Richard, 52
Cassier, Melchisadek, 40
Castelton, John, 72
Cater, Abel, 13, 87; Nicholas, 23; William, 31, 37
Cattlefoord, John, 31
Catton, John, 28
Cawkeer (Cawker, Cawkyer), Bartholomew, 10; John, 10; Mark, 14; Robert, 10; Thomas, 10; William, 14, 81
Cawlinge, John, 56, *see* Callinge
Cawly (Cawlye), Andrew, 49; Charles, 50; James, 50; John, 50; William, 50(3)
Cawse (Cause, Cawes, Cawsie), Andrew, 87; Henry, 9; John, 62, 84(4), 111(2); Robert, 9; Thomas, 83
Cawson, Edward, 40
Cawsye, George, 23
Champernowne (Champernone, Champernoone, Champnoone, Champnoune), Mr, 112; Sir Arthur, xx, esq., 97
Ceely, Thomas, 84
Cetto, Alexander, 71
Chadd, William, 88
Chadder, James, 88
Champyn, Richard, 70
Channon (Chanon), Charles, 50; Edward, 50; John, 49
Chanterell, Peter, 93
Chaplinn, Nathaniel, 34
Chappell, Oliver, 40
Chappen, Stephen, 8
Chappleman, William, 62
Chapter, John, 31, 34
Chard, William, 28
Charke, John, 61; Penticost, 62
Chaslyn, Tristram, 63
Cheblye, John, 27
Cheese, Richard, 42
Chefer, John, 75; Richard, 75; Robert, 75
Chely, Moses, 73
Cherswill, Michael, 14
Cheswell, Ambrose, 15
Chevalle, John, 56
Chewner, Michael, 91
Cheyny (Cheynye), Lewis, 44; Richard, 48

# INDEX OF SUBJECTS

# INDEX OF SHIPS

tions by foreign Governments. These include the award of a gold watch to Coxswain T. Cocking and money awards to the crew for the rescue of 33 lives from the s.s. *Bessemer City*, of New York, in November, 1936. A letter of thanks was received from the Italian Government for the saving of 15 lives from the s.s. *Aida Lauro*, of Naples, in July, 1936. The Hungarian Government presented a Gold Cross of Merit to Coxswain T. Cocking for the rescue in January, 1938 of 18 lives from the s.s. *Alba*, of Panama, manned by Hungarians, whilst the Mayor, Mr. C. W. Curnow, received the Order of Merit, in recognition of the gallantry and courage displayed by the people of St. Ives. In 1951 the French Government awarded the Chevalier du Merite Maritime to ex-Coxswain Henry Peters for his services to the French Merchant Navy. Nearly 500 lives have been rescued by St. Ives lifeboats since full records were kept.

The present lifeboat—the *Edgar George Orlando and Eva Child*—is a motor Liverpool type, twin screw, 35' 6" x 10' 8", built in 1948. Launching is effected with the aid of a powerful motor tractor, towing a carriage, on which the lifeboat is mounted.

*Present Coxswain*, Daniel Roach, Full Time, appointed October 1st, 1956.

The officials of the St. Ives Lifeboat are : president, Mr. G. G. Warren ; hon. secretary, Captain W. H. H. Treloar ; hon. treasurer, Mr. W. R. Rowe.

---

A number of interesting relics and photographs relating to the St. Ives Lifeboat Station are preserved in the excellent little museum of the St. Ives Old Cornwall Society, in Gabriel Street (over the Public Library).

Printed & Published by W. & J. Jacobs Ltd., Fore Street, St. Ives.

It was evident that another great disaster at sea had occurred on that same dreadful night ; but for some days uncertainty continued to reign, as the tremendous waves made it impossible to undertake a thorough examination of the coastline at Tregerthen Point, where it was believed a ship had gone ashore.

Eventually, however, suspicion became certainty. The wrecked ship proved to be the s.s. *Wilston*, from Glasgow, bound with a cargo of coal for the Mediterranean, and having a crew of 32 on board. There were no survivors ; and the vessel herself was pounded into an unrecognisable mass of scrap iron by the mountainous waves that hurled themselves, day after day, upon this savage and exposed coastline. To the little village of Zennor came a pathetic group of enquirers, hoping—and fearing—to identify their kinsfolk amongst the shattered human remains which had been brought on shore.

But at St. Ives itself, this news passed almost unheeded. The townsfolk were too preoccupied with their own sorrow at that time to be able to spare much thought for this greater tragedy. There were the inquests on the lifeboat victims to be held, the relief fund for dependents to be organised, the funerals to be attended in the wind-swept cemetery overlooking the actual scene of the late disaster. In those dark days, the silent, empty lifeboat house seemed pathetically symbolic of the grief which had stricken the little town.

But a new boat was soon forthcoming, and a new crew was at once ready to man her. The sea had taken much that was precious and irreplaceable ; but it could never destroy the courage of the St. Ives fishermen, nor their quiet determination to uphold an ancient tradition of unflinching loyalty and service to a great and noble cause.

(I must express my thanks to Mr. Patrick Howarth, Publicity Secretary of the R.N.L.I., for the help and encouragement he has given me during the preparation of this pamphlet).

## FACTS AND FIGURES

31 Medals—15 silver and 16 bronze—have been awarded by the R.N.L.I. There have also been several presenta-

Godrevy Point, having drifted right across the entrance to St. Ives Bay.

It began to look as if these men might all reach the doubtful safety of the shore ; but then the lifeboat overturned for the third time, and when she righted herself, William Freeman found he was the only man still holding on.

A few minutes later the boat was hurled up high and dry on the rocks at Gwithian. Mr. Freeman clambered out, and began to ascend the cliff. At the top he found a farmhouse ; and arousing the inhabitants, poured into their astounded ears the tragic story of that night of death and disaster at sea.

The lifeboat crew included several men who had been involved in the previous disaster the year before. The full list of names is as follows : Thomas Cocking, Coxswain, who had been associated with the lifeboat for forty three years, having held his leading position for eleven of these; Messrs. M. Barber and W. Barber ; Mr. R. Q. Stevens, 1st Mechanic ; Mr. J. B. Cocking, 2nd Mechanic ; Mr. J. Thomas, Signalman ; and Messrs E. Bassett and W. Freeman, both volunteers. All were fishermen by trade.

What added to the poignancy of the tragedy was the fact that some members of the crew were closely related to each other. The two Barbers were brothers, and had worked the boat *Our John* for their widowed mother ; whilst Mr. J. B. Cocking was the son of the Coxswain. Several left widows and small children to mourn their loss. In its long and bitter experience of the sea, St. Ives had never known such a catastrophe as this.

World-wide sympathy was immediately expressed for the relatives. A sum exceeding £10,000 came in by public subscription ; and the R.N.L.I., in accordance with its invariable practice, awarded generous pensions to the widows and dependents of the drowned lifeboatmen.

No one living here at the time will ever forget the nightmare horror of the days which succeeded the tragedy. While the storm continued to rage, men kept watch along the coast for the bodies of the lifeboat crew. These were found ; but other bodies began to wash in, also.

Pendeen. The full fury of the storm was now encountered; and when some distance off Clodgy Point, a tremendous wave, striking the boat on the starboard bow, capsized her, hurling four of the crew into the sea. They were never seen alive again.

The lifeboat herself was now in serious difficulties. The engine was re-started, but it was found that a rope had fouled the propeller. An anchor was dropped, but the rope parted, and the doomed vessel began to drift helplessly

**The "John and Sarah Eliza Stych," wrecked at Gwithian on 23rd January, 1939.** *(Copyright—Studio, St. Ives, Ltd.)*

before the storm. The survivors on board sent up distress flares, which were seen and answered by a rocket from the coastguards on shore. But no help could be given to the lifeboatmen ; they were now utterly at the mercy of the wind and waves.

The vessel capsized a second time, and another man was thrown out and lost. With only three of the crew now remaining on board, the lifeboat began to approach

the Island, of the L.S.A. searchlights, and of innumerable hand torches.

Despite the heroic action of the townsfolk, many of whom risked their lives time and time again to snatch the drowning seamen from the water, two were lost, and three brought ashore dead. The St. Ives people readily opened their hearts and their homes to the survivors. " Never have I witnessed such kindness," said the *Alba's* Captain afterwards. " They are undoubtedly people of the sea, and they knew what to do first, and what we needed most."

Coxswain Cocking received the silver medal of the Royal National Lifeboat Institution and the crew bronze medals for their part in this heroic rescue. In addition, each man received a monetary award and an inscribed vellum.

The crew's names were : William Peters (Second Cox-swain), Matthew Barber (Bowman), J. B. Cocking (Assistant and Acting Mechanic), John Thomas (Signal-man), Thomas Cocking, jun., H. Peters, W. Barber, P. Paynter.

The second lifeboat disaster occurred on January 23rd, 1939 ; and it is by far the most tragic event connected with the history of the station.

In the early hours of that never-to-be-forgotten day, a message was received at St. Ives saying that a vessel was in need of assistance off Cape Cornwall. A tremendous gale was then blowing from the W.N.W., with mountain-ous seas bearing down upon the coast.

To many observers, it seemed impossible that the life-boat could be launched under such appalling conditions ; but the lifeboatmen did not hesitate.

Somewhere, in the blackness of the night, a ship lay in danger ; and it was their duty to go to her assistance. Amongst those who helped to man the lifeboat on that occasion was Mr. William Freeman, a volunteer, who came forward at the last moment to make up the full complement required; he was destined to be the only man to return alive from that ill-starred mission.

With the help of some ninety volunteers, the *John and Sarah Eliza Stych* was launched. Leaving the harbour, she headed west along the coastline in the direction of

and the line paid out, intending to use this on the return journey ; but unfortunately, as it happened, the anchor failed to hold. Getting near the steamer, the Coxswain ordered the *Alba's* crew to get aboard immediately, for the tide was then two hours after the ebb, and every moment's delay increased the danger.

Despite this warning, it was six or seven minutes before the crew appeared—carrying their trunks ! These Coxswain Cocking ordered them to leave behind. Heavily laden with twenty-three shipwrecked seamen and her own crew of nine, the lifeboat moved away from the *Alba*.

" I told the Captain," said Coxswain Cocking, in a subsequent interview, " to order his men to lie down on deck, and this they did. I let go the anchor, intending to haul the lifeboat clear of the wreck, and put her head to sea. A ground swell, however, was stirring up the sand so much that the anchor would not hold, and I came astern on the engine. As we got clear of the bow of the steamer, a tremendous sea struck us broadside on. The lifeboat turned turtle, throwing nearly all of its occupants into the sea." (Mothers, wives and other relatives of the lifeboat crew, standing on shore, were helpless witnesses of this event, and their cry of terror and anguish will never be forgotten by those who heard it). " Fortunately, the lifeboat was of the self-righting type, and was on an even keel again in a few seconds.

" I was thrown some yards from the boat, and said to myself, ' keep a cool head.' By waiting, the sea brought me nearer the lifeboat, and I was able to swim to her, being hauled aboard by my son. Unfortunately, some of the crew of the steamer were unable to regain the lifeboat, and we could do nothing for them, as the lifeboat was unmanageable . . . She was gradually driven ashore until she struck. A line was thrown to us, and we got ashore one after another, being helped over the rocks by hundreds of inhabitants, who braved the rough seas to assist us."

The members of the St. Ives Life Saving Apparatus were responsible for getting the line to the lifeboat ; and their prompt and effective action undoubtedly saved many lives. The whole of these rescue operations was carried out in the eerie glare of the headlamps of cars stationed on

occurred almost exactly within a year of each other, in 1938 and 1939. On each occasion, the lifeboat was wrecked and totally destroyed, the first time with the loss of five rescued seamen, the second with the drowning of all save one of the lifeboat's crew.

Just after seven o'clock on the evening of January 31st, 1938, during a severe storm, the double boom of the lifeboat rockets apprised the town that a wreck had occurred. The ship involved was the *Alba*, a 3,700 ton vessel

**After the 1938 disaster. The shattered Lifeboat straddles the rocks at Porthmeor**.      *(Copyright—Western Morning News)*

registered at Panama, bound from Barry to Civita Vecchia, in Italy, with a cargo of coal. In attempting to run for shelter in St. Ives Bay, she had mistaken her position in the murk and darkness, and run aground on the rocks on the north-west side of the Island.

The lifeboat was promptly launched, and battled her way through the heavy seas until she came in sight of the steamer. Before getting under the lee of the ship, Coxswain Thomas Cocking ordered the anchor to be dropped,

and drowned, and the other, a boy, was taken off by the *Covent Garden*.

"The lifeboat, with a fresh crew, taking a line from the New Pier Head, dropped down on the *Mary Ann*, and one by one the poor, drenched, half-frozen crew were taken off, one of the lifeboat's crew getting on board the vessel to assist the Captain, who had met with a serious injury to his left leg. The crew thus rescued were at once landed, and the lifeboat, with a fresh crew, started to rescue the crew of the brig *Frances*, of Porthcawl.

"She was, however, swept by the strong current almost to Porthminster Point. The boat "—the lifeboat is meant here—" was hauled in clear of the breakers, ropes put on her, and was dragged by hundreds of both sexes across the beach to windward of the brig.

"With a fresh crew of volunteers, Acting Coxswain Murphy went afloat for the fifth time, and after a gallant struggle reached the brig and rescued the crew of six men. And thus ends the story of these gallant deeds ; but for the two poor fellows who were washed overboard from the *Rambler*, all lives would have been saved.

"The Royal National Lifeboat Institution have not been slow to mark their appreciation of the conduct of those connected with the memorable lifeboat services on the 2nd inst. Mr. Martin, of the Coastguard, and Mr. Murphy, who never left the boat during the five attempts, have the silver medal of the Institution, and the crews double pay. It is not generally known that the brave Coxswain of the lifeboat, Paul Curnow, was at this time laid up with severe broken ribs, the result of a fall, to which is now added the pain of not sharing in the glory of his fellows, and of the two, Paul feels this the most."

The wholehearted way in which the people of St. Ives supported the lifeboatmen in effecting these spectacular rescues, and the readiness with which fresh volunteers came forward to replace the exhausted crews are fully typical of the fine spirit which has always been displayed here on such occasions.

The more recent history of the St. Ives Lifeboat Station has been marked by two appalling tragedies, which

tion, re-experience something of the excitement, the terror, and the heroism of that occasion to-day : —

" It is seldom, if ever, that so many wrecks have to be reported from here. A heavy ground sea prevailed on Saturday morning, and by night a furious gale was blowing from E.S.E. There were several vessels in the Bay.

" The Hayle tug had the three-mast schooner *Helena* in tow, when the ropes parted, and the vessel had no alternative but to run for St. Ives Pier. She ran before the gale amongst a number of vessels.

"From the shore nothing could be heard in the darkness but shouting and the crashing of timbers above the roar of the wind and the waves. The *Helena* struck the French lugger *Pierre et Marie*, cutting down her stern and sinking her. She then fouled the *Eclipse*, of St. Ives, making a clean sweep of her stanchions, bulwarks and rails, and doing herself serious damage.

" While this was going on in the Pier, a vessel ran ashore on Porthgwidden Cove, the French schooner, *Euphemie*, with coals from Swansea for France. The crew landed safely when the tide ebbed, but the vessel went to pieces on Sunday morning. During the night a smack ran in between Smeaton's Pier and the Wood Pier, and sank a small mackerel boat. Every vessel in the Pier received damage of some kind on that memorable night.

" At daylight on Sunday morning two schooners and a brig were discovered moored off the harbour in dangerous positions. At mid-day and at dead low water the wind cast to the N.E., a strong gale, and in a short time those on board the vessels saw only a roaring sea of breakers under their sterns.

" The lifeboat was got afloat, and shortly after the *Mary Ann*, of Plymouth, broke from her anchors and grounded near Pednolver Point. The *Rambler*, of Carnarvon, broke adrift and ran aground near the New Pier in a terrible sea, falling right across the breakers, which made a clean sweep over her. Two men in the rigging were washed overboard. One disappeared after a while, the other, the Captain, supported by a piece of wood, was picked up by the lifeboat. Two men still remained on board the vessel, one was washed overboard

III, Emperor of the French, who sent a gold medal for the Coxswain, and a silver medal for each member of the crew.

Lady St. Aubyn, distributing these medals at a ceremony in the Town Hall, which was "crowded to excess" for the occasion, said : "In presenting to you the honourable distinction which His Majesty the Emperor of the French has been pleased to bestow upon you, I only express the sentiments of pride which all who are here present must feel, that the first reward of this kind that has been given in Great Britain has been granted to the skill and bravery of a Cornish lifeboat crew."

Shortly after this, Mr. Levett was succeeded as Coxswain by Mr. Paul Curnow, perhaps the most celebrated of all the old St. Ives lifeboatmen. Paul was a blacksmith by trade, his little smith's shop being at Chy-an-Chy, on the Wharf, just across from the present life-boat slipway. He died in 1913, at the ripe old age of 94, having taken part in many notable rescues. Perhaps his most memorable achievement was in saving part of the crew of the s.s. *Bessie*, of Hayle, which was beached on Lelant sands in 1866 during a violent storm. The six-oared *Moses* was, by herself, unable to make headway through the terrible sea then running ; but when the ten-oared *Richard Lewis*, of Penzance, arrived on the scene —having been brought overland on her carriage by eight large horses—the two lifeboats, working in concert, suc-ceeded in getting off all nine members of the *Bessie's* crew.

It was on February 2nd, 1873, that the St. Ives lifeboat, *Covent Garden*, carried out one of the most dramatic series of rescues ever undertaken by a lifeboat in the course of a single day's work. On that occasion, a sudden and tremendous storm littered the Bay with wrecks of all descriptions ; and the lifeboat put to sea no less than five times to snatch the crews of the doomed vessels from a watery grave.

A crudely-written but vigorous account of these remarkable happenings appeared at the time in the pages of the old *Cornish Telegraph*, of Penzance. Reading it now, after such a lapse of time, we can still, in imagina-

were under the boat until she righted—a period of at least two minutes.

The remainder of the crew then regained the boat, with the exception of one man who had been driven some distance away ; but he was presently picked up by his comrades. Undaunted by the danger and exhaustion, the crew succeeded in getting the boat into the channel to leeward of the ship, but owing to the strong undertow, the lifeboat could not be placed alongside for a considerable time. After persevering for at least half an hour, they managed to approach within a hundred yards, and brought the boat up, being unable to venture nearer. The crew of the French vessel then prepared a raft, with whose aid three men, including the mate, were able to float very close to the bow of the *Moses*.

Unfortunately, three or four heavy successive seas broke over them, and swept two away to their deaths, including the mate, the third sailor reaching the lifeboat only with considerable difficulty. He was scarcely taken on board when the lifeboat again capsized, but righted in less than a minute. The Captain of the *Providence* and two seamen then put off from the wreck in their small boat, hoping thus to reach the *Moses*, but their little craft was swamped. The lifeboatmen, pulling valiantly to their assistance, succeeded in picking them up, and brought all the rescued men safely to harbour. " The lifeboat's crew," says a contemporary report, " were, as might be expected, greatly exhausted ; the highest praise is due to them for their courage and exertions, and it is to be hoped they will not be forgotten by the proper authorities. Their names are : Nicholas Levett (Coxswain) ; Paul Curnow (Second Coxswain) ; Thomas Veal ; William Veal ; Richard Curnow ; Nathaniel Oliver ; William Perkin Veal ; Ishmael Job ; and John Blewett."

The " proper authorities " did not fail in their duty. The R.N.L.I. voted a silver medal and £2 in money to Coxswain Nicholas Levett, and £16 to the crew, accompanied by a vote of thanks, inscribed on vellum, to each man, in recognition of his outstanding courage and daring. In addition to this, £115 was raised by public subscription, and divided amongst the brave lifeboatmen. But the most notable award of all came from Napoleon

Probably as a result of these difficulties, the *Moses* was not launched until September 18th :—

" On Monday, with the wind strong from the north and in a heavy sea, the new lifeboat was launched for her first trip, under the charge of Mr. Warren, R.N., Chief Officer of Coastguard.

" She was rowed round the Head "—the Island—" to Porthmeor Beach, and brought into the broken surf, where she was kept for some time, with the seas breaking round and over her. After returning to the pier, the crew, part of whom belong to the Coastguard, put on the life-belts, jumped overboard, and remained swimming about for some time." (They certainly took lifeboat practices seriously in those days !) " The boat was then brought to the beach and taken to the new boathouse from which she can be removed to any part of the coast with the greatest ease. During the trial, there were hundreds of persons on the hills and beach looking on, and it is the opinion of the crew and spectators that she will answer every purpose she is intended for."

One of the most famous rescues effected by the *Moses* took place on October 28th, 1865, when the French brig, *Providence*, was wrecked on Hayle Bar during a severe storm. The gallantry, courage, and perseverance of the lifeboat crew on this occasion deserve the highest praise, and set a standard which has been worthily maintained here ever since.

At daybreak that morning — a Saturday — the *Providence* was observed driven ashore on the western spit of Hayle Bar. She was flying a French colour of distress, and appeared in great danger, a severe gale then blowing from the N.W., with a tremendous sea.

The St. Ives lifeboat, with a crew of nine men, left the Pier shortly before 8 a.m. On crossing Hayle Bar a very heavy sea caused the rope, to which the drag-bag, or drogue was attached (for helping her through the surf) to break, and the lifeboat then flew before the storm in an almost perpendicular position, her bow completely sub-merged. She then overturned, throwing out all hands, except the Coxswain (Mr. Levett, Chief Boatman of the Coastguard) and Paul Curnow (Second Coxswain) who

headway before the breakers have time to beat the boat broadside on to the beach. The hauling up of the lifeboat on her carriage is accomplished with equal facility (!) This lifeboat is the noble gift of the same benevolent lady who last year presented the Newquay (Cornwall) and two other boats to the Institution."

A commodious house was built to accommodate this vessel near the Island, on a site given by the Earl of Mornington. The building is still in existence, being now used as a store.

Fowler Tractor with the Lifeboat in tow in St. Ives Harbour.

All visitors to St. Ives are at once charmed by the crooked picturesque streets of the old town. Due allowance was not made for these by the designers of the *Moses*, however, with the result that an amusing little contretemps occurred when an attempt was made to take the new lifeboat, with her carriage, to the boathouse. It was found that one of the streets leading from the Wharf to the Island was too narrow to allow the carriage to pass, so that she had to be temporarily secured on the sand near the Custom House.

resultant nation-wide quickening of interest in life-saving at sea, was the factor which probably led to the decision to establish the first lifeboat at this port.

This was in 1840, when, according to one authority, a Mr. Praed, a local Member of Parliament, approached the Royal National Lifeboat Institution with a view to the provision of a lifeboat here.

This vessel was designed and constructed by Mr. Francis Adams, an ingenious St. Ives shipbuilder. She was clinker-built, and had two bows ; so that, both ends being alike, the boat was always in a position to advance or retreat, the change of direction being effected very simply by the rowers turning round and sitting on opposite sides of the same thwarts, and pulling from a different set of thowels. It was claimed that this change around could be performed in less than a minute. Many of the dangers incident to manoeuvring near a wreck were by this means either eliminated or minimised. The lifeboat was 30-ft. long, and her extreme breadth amid-ships 5-ft. 10-ins. ; she rowed six oars, and, in addition, there were two steersmen, one stationed at either end. In her general fitting up, she closely resembled a gig ; but water-tight compartments were fitted under the decks at the bows, thus making her unsinkable.

In 1848 this lifeboat is said to have been housed in a shed 400 yards above high water mark, being then in charge of a Mr. Hockin· No records exist of the services she rendered, nor have the names of any members of her crew come down to us.

It would almost seem that this station lapsed for a while after this, as the first reference to St. Ives in the Institution's Service Books, which date back to 1850, con-cerns the placing here of the lifeboat *Moses*, in 1860.

Described as being one of the R.N.L.I.'s best single-banked lifeboats, this vessel arrived in mid-July, accom-panied by a transporting tractor. The boat was 30-ft. long, 7-ft. wide, and, like her predecessor, rowed six oars.

"By an ingenious contrivance," says an old report, "she is launched off the carriage with her crew on board. With their oars in their hands they are enabled to obtain

N EARLY 150 years ago, at the time of the Napoleonic Wars, the Rev. Richard Warner, of Bath, undertook a holiday excursion in Cornwall. He subsequently published an account of his travels under the title "A Tour Through Cornwall in the Autumn of 1808," a book which has now become very scarce.

Warner made a detour specially to visit St. Ives, and in the course of his description of the place, says :

"A strong gale blew (from the northward) when we visited it, and threw a terrible sea into the harbour. In general, we were informed, this noble basin was considered as a very safe anchorage, though storms have occurred which covered its surface with wrecks.

"On the 14th day of the preceding November (in 1807, that is) a melancholy scene of this kind had been exhibited to the inhabitants of St. Ives, when three vessels were thrown upon the rocks of the harbour before their eyes, totally destroyed, and the greater part of their crews swallowed up.

"The affecting sight made its proper impression on some of the spectators, who immediately endeavoured to raise a subscription for building and maintaining a *life-boat*, to prevent in future the most dreadful consequences of such shipwrecks, the loss of the unhappy seamen ; but so insensible were the merchants of the place to the dangers and sufferings of the hardy race who fill their coffers, that the philanthropic attempt was frustrated by the impossibility of raising the poor pittance required for the purpose !

"As we had this information from a merchant of St. Ives, I take it for granted that it is correct. Should it not be so, I must crave pardon of its affluent inhabitants for a representation so disgraceful to their feelings."

At that period, it must be remembered, there was no national organisation in existence to assist in the provision of lifeboats around our coasts ; and the "poor pittance," of which Warner speaks, might well have been an impossible sum for the small fishing community —which is all that St. Ives then was—to provide from purely local resources.

The famous "Grace Darling" episode of 1838, with its

# THE STORY OF
# St. IVES LIFEBOAT

# BY CYRIL NOALL